Cultural Evolution

Cultural Evolution argues that people's values and behavior are shaped by the degree to which survival is secure; it was precarious for most of history, which encouraged heavy emphasis on group solidarity, rejection of outsiders and obedience to strong leaders. For under extreme scarcity, xenophobia is realistic: if there is just enough land to support one tribe and another tribe tries to claim it, survival may literally be a choice between Us and Them. Conversely, high levels of existential security encourage openness to change, diversity and new ideas. The unprecedented prosperity and security of the postwar era brought cultural change, the environmentalist movement and the spread of democracy. But in recent decades, diminishing job security and rising inequality have led to an authoritarian reaction. Evidence from more than 100 countries demonstrates that people's motivations and behavior reflect the extent to which they take survival for granted – and that modernization changes them in roughly predictable ways. This book explains the rise of environmentalist parties, gender equality and same-sex marriage – and the current reaction producing Trump, Brexit and France's National Front, through a new, empirically tested version of modernization theory.

Ronald F. Inglehart is the Lowenstein Professor of Political Science at the University of Michigan. He holds honorary doctorates from Uppsala University, Sweden, the Free University of Brussels, Belgium, and the University of Lueneburg, Germany. Inglehart helped found the Euro-Barometer surveys and is founding president of the World Values Survey Association, which has surveyed representative national samples of the publics of 105 countries containing over 90 percent of the world's population. He is a fellow of the American Academy of Arts and Sciences and of the American Academy of Political and Social Science. In 2011, he won the Johan Skytte prize in Political Science, often considered the highest prize awarded in the field.

Cultural Evolution

People's Motivations Are Changing, and Reshaping the World

Ronald F. Inglehart
University of Michigan

CAMBRIDGE
UNIVERSITY PRESS

CAMBRIDGE
UNIVERSITY PRESS

University Printing House, Cambridge CB2 8BS, United Kingdom

One Liberty Plaza, 20th Floor, New York, NY 10006, USA

477 Williamstown Road, Port Melbourne, VIC 3207, Australia

314–321, 3rd Floor, Plot 3, Splendor Forum, Jasola District Centre,
New Delhi – 110025, India

79 Anson Road, #06-04/06, Singapore 079906

Cambridge University Press is part of the University of Cambridge.

It furthers the University's mission by disseminating knowledge in the pursuit of
education, learning, and research at the highest international levels of excellence.

www.cambridge.org
Information on this title: www.cambridge.org/9781108489317
DOI: 10.1017/9781108613880

First published 2018
4th printing 2019

Printed in the United Kingdom by TJ International Ltd. Padstow Cornwall

A catalogue record for this publication is available from the British Library.

ISBN 978-1-108-48931-7 Hardback

This book is dedicated to my wife, Marita, and my children, Sylvia, Elizabeth, Rachel, Ronald and Milo, with love.

CONTENTS

FIGURES

TABLES

ACKNOWLEDGMENTS

This book draws on co-authored work with Paul Abramson, Wayne Baker, Roberto Foa, Ronald Charles Inglehart, Pippa Norris, Christopher Peterson, Eduard Ponarin, Jacques Rabier and Christian Welzel. I am deeply indebted to these friends, colleagues and my son, and express my warmest thanks. They are, in effect, co-authors of this book.

I also express my gratitude to the people who made this book possible by carrying out the World Values Survey (WVS) and the European Values Surveys (EVS) in over one hundred countries, from 1981 to 2014. Thanks to the following WVS and EVS Principal Investigators for creating and sharing this rich and complex dataset: Anthony M. Abela, Suzanne Adams, Q.K. Ahmad, Salvatore Abbruzzese, Abdel-Hamid Abdel-Latif, Marchella Abrasheva, Mohammen Addahri, Alisher Aldashev, Darwish Abdulrahman Al-Emadi, Fathi Ali, Abdulrazaq Ali, Rasa Alishauskene, Helmut Anheier, Jose Arocena, Wil A. Art, Soo Young Auh, Taghi Azadarmaki, Ljiljana Bacevic, Olga Balakireva, Josip Baloban, David Barker, Miguel Basanez, Elena Bashkirova, Abdallah Bedaida, Jorge Benitez, Jaak Billiet, Alan Black, Eduard Bomhoff, Ammar Boukhedir, Rahma Bourquia, Fares al Braizat, Lori Bramwell-Jones, Michael Breen, Ziva Broder, Thawilwadee Bureekul, Karin Bush, Harold Caballeros, Manuel Villaverde, Richard Bachia-Caruana, Claudio Calvaruso, Pavel Campeaunu, Augustin Canzani, Giuseppe Capraro, Marita Carballo, Andres Casas, Henrique Carlos de O. de Castro, Pi-Chao Chen, Pradeep Chhibber, Mark F. Chingono, Hei-yuan Chiu, Vincent Chua, Margit Cleveland, Mircea Comsa, Munqith

Dagher, Andrew P. Davidson, Herman De Dijn, Ruud de Moor, Pierre Delooz, Peter J.D. Derenth, Abdel Nasser Djabi, Karel Dobbelaere, Hermann Duelmer, Javier Elzo, Yilmaz Esmer, Paul Estgen, Tony Fahey, Nadjematul Faizah, Tair Faradov, Roberto Stefan Foa, Michael Fogarty, Georgy Fotev, Juis de Franca, Aikaterini Gari, Ilir Gedeshi, James Georgas, C. Geppaart, Bilai Gilani, Mark Gill, Stjepan Gredlj, Renzo Gubert, Linda Luz Guerrero, Peter Gundelach, David Sulmont Haak, Christian Haerpfer, Abdelwahab Ben Hafaiedh, Jacques Hagenaars, Loek Halman, Mustafa Hamarneh, Tracy Hammond, Sang-Jin Han, Elemer Hankiss, Olafur Haraldsson, Stephen Harding, Mari Harris, Pierre Hausman, Bernadette C. Hayes, Gordon Heald, Camilo Herrera, Felix Heunks, Virginia Hodgkinson, Nadra Muhammed Hosen, Joan Rafel Mico Ibanez, Kenji Iijima, Fr. Joe Inganuez, Ljubov Ishimova, Wolfgang Jagodzinski, Meril James, Aleksandra Jasinska-Kania, Fridrik Jonsson, Dominique Joye, Stanislovas Juknevicius, Salue Kalikova, Tatiana Karabchuk, Kieran Kennedy, Jan Kerkhofs S.J., J.F. Kielty, Johann Kinghorn, Hans-Dieter Kilngemann, Renate Kocher, Joanna Konieczna, Hennie Kotze, Hanspeter Kriesi, Miori Kurimura, Zuzana Kusá, Marta Lagos, Bernard Lategan, Michel Legrand, Carlos Lemoine, Noah Lewin-Epstein, Juan Linz, Ola Listhaug, Jin-yun Liu, Leila Lotti, Ruud Lijkx, Susanne Lundasen, Brina Malnar, Heghine Manasyan, Robert Manchin, Mahar Mangahas, Mario Marinov, Mira Marody, Carlos Matheus, Robert Mattes, Ian McAllister, Rafael Mendizabal, Jon Miller, Felipe Miranda, Mansoor Moaddel, Mustapha Mohammed, Jose Molina, Alejandro Moreno, Gaspar K. Munishi, Naasson Munyandamutsa, Kostas Mylonas, Neil Nevitte, Chun Hung Ng, Simplice Ngampou, Juan Diez Nicolas, Jaime Medrano Nicolas, Elisabeth Noelle-Neumann, Pippa Norris, Elone Nwabuzor, Stephen Olafsson, Francisco.Andres Orizo, Magued Osman, Merab Pachulia, Christina Paez, Alua Pankhurst, Dragomir Pantic, Juhani Pehkonen, Paul Perry, E. Petersen, Antoanela Petkovska, Doru Petruti, Thorleif Pettersson, Pham Minh Hac, Pham Thanh Nghi, Timothy Phillips, Gevork Pogosian, Eduard Ponarin, Lucien Pop, Bi Puranen, Ladislav Rabusic, Andrei Raichev, Alice Ramos, Anu Realo, Jan Rehak, Helene Riffault, Ole Riis, Angel Rivera-Ortiz, Nils Rohme, Catalina Romero, Gergely Rosta, David Rotman, Victor Roudometof, Giancario Rovati, Samir Abu Ruman, Andrus Saar, Rajab Sattarov, Rahmat Seigh, Tan Ern Ser, Sandeep Shastri, Shen Mingming, Musa Shteivi, Renata Siemienska, Maria Silvestre Cabrera, Richard Sinnott, Alan Smith, Jean Stoetzel,

Kancho Stoichev, Marin Stoychev, John Sudarsky, Edward Sullivan, Marc Swyngedouw, Tang Ching-Ping, Farooq Tanwir, Jean-Francois Tchernia, Kareem Tejumola, Noel Timms, Larissa Titarenko, Miklos Tomka, Alfredo Torres, Niko Tos, Istvan Gyorgy Toth, Joseph Troisi, Tu Su-hao, Claudiu Tufis, Jorge Vala, Andrei Vardomatskii, David Voas, Bogdan Voicu, Malina Voicu, Liliane Voye, Richard M. Walker, Alan Webster, Friedrich Welsch, Christian Welzel, Meidam Wester, Chris Whelan, Robert Worcester, Seiko Yamazaki, Birol Yesilada, Ephraim Yuchtman-Yaar, Josefina Zaiter, Catalin Zamfir, Brigita Zepa, Ignacio Zuasnabar and Paul Zulehner.

The WVS and EVS data used in this book consists of 358 surveys carried out in successive waves from 1981 to 2014 in 105 countries containing over 90 percent of the world's population. This book also uses data from the Euro-Barometer surveys launched by Jacques-Rene Rabier in 1970; the Euro-Barometer surveys served as a model for the EVS, the WVS and numerous other cross-national surveys, and were the source of key items used in the Values Surveys. Jan Kerkhofs and Ruud de Moor organized the European Values Study and invited me to organize similar surveys in other parts of the world, which led to founding the World Values Survey. Jaime Diez Medrano archived both the WVS and the EVS datasets and made them available to hundreds of thousands of users, who have analyzed and downloaded the data from the WVS and EVS websites.

I am grateful to Jon Miller, William Zimmerman, Arthur Lupia, Kenneth Kollman and other colleagues at the University of Michigan for comments and suggestions. I am also grateful to Anna Cotter and Yujeong Yang for superb research assistance and gratefully acknowledge support from the US National Science Foundation, and the foreign ministries of Sweden and The Netherlands, each of which supported fieldwork in several countries in various waves of the World Values Survey. I also thank the Russian Ministry of Education and Science for a grant that made it possible to found the Laboratory for Comparative Social Research at the Higher School of Economics in Moscow and St. Petersburg, and to carry out the World Values Survey in Russia and eight other Soviet successor countries in 2011. This study was funded by the Russian Academic Excellence Project "5–100." The University of Michigan's Amy and Alan Loewenstein professorship in Democracy and Human Rights, which I am grateful to hold, provided valuable research assistance for this work.

INTRODUCTION: AN OVERVIEW OF THIS BOOK

People's values and behavior are shaped by the degree to which survival is secure. For most of the time since humans first appeared, survival has been precarious. This dominated people's life strategies. Population rose to meet the food supply, and most people lived just above the starvation level. When survival is insecure, people tend to close ranks behind a strong leader, forming a united front against outsiders – a strategy that can be called the Authoritarian Reflex.

In the decades following World War II, something unprecedented occurred in economically advanced countries: much of the postwar generation grew up taking survival for granted. This reflected (1) the unprecedented economic growth of the postwar era in Western Europe, North America, Japan and Australia; (2) the emergence of welfare state safety nets that guaranteed that almost no one died of starvation; and (3) the absence of war between major powers: since World War II, the world has experienced the longest such period in recorded history.

Unprecedentedly high levels of economic and physical security led to pervasive intergenerational cultural changes that reshaped the values and worldviews of these publics, bringing a shift from Materialist to Postmaterialist values – which was part of an even broader shift from Survival values to Self-expression values. This broad cultural shift moves from giving top priority to economic and physical safety and conformity to group norms, toward increasing emphasis on individual freedom to choose how to live one's life. Self-expression values emphasize gender equality, tolerance of gays, lesbians, foreigners and other outgroups, freedom of expression and participation in decision-making in economic and political life. This cultural shift brought massive social and political changes, from stronger environmental protection policies and anti-war movements, to higher levels of gender equality in government, business and academic life, and the spread of democracy.

Long before this happened, substantial cross-cultural difference already existed that can be traced to geographically shaped differences in vulnerability to disease and hunger. Various analysts, working from different perspectives, have described these cultural differences as Collectivism versus Individualism, Survival versus Self-expression values, or Autonomy versus Embeddedness, but they all tap a common dimension of cross-cultural variation that reflects a society's level of "existential security" – the degree to which survival seems safe or insecure. During the decades since World War II, growing existential security has been propelling most of the world's societies toward greater emphasis on Individualism, Autonomy and Self-expression values.

Countries that rank high on Self-expression values are much likelier to adopt legislation favorable to gays and lesbians than societies that emphasize Survival values. They also tend to rank high on the UN Gender Empowerment Measure, which reflects the extent to which women hold high positions in political, economic and academic life. Survey data demonstrate that the underlying norms have been changing for fifty years, while these societal changes are relatively recent. The cultural changes preceded the institutional changes and seem to have contributed to them.

High levels of existential security are also conducive to secularization – a systematic erosion of religious practices, values and beliefs. Secularization has spread among the publics of virtually all advanced industrial societies during the past fifty years. Nevertheless, the world as a whole now has more people with traditional religious views than ever before, because secularization has a strong negative impact on human fertility rates. Practically all of the countries in which secularization is most advanced now have fertility rates far below the replacement level – while many societies with traditional religious orientations have fertility rates two or three times as high as the replacement level.

Mass attitudes toward both gender equality and homosexuality have been changing in a two-stage process. The first phase was a gradual shift toward greater tolerance of gays and greater support for gender equality, which took place as younger generations replaced older ones. Eventually, this reached a threshold at which the new norms were seen as dominant in high-income societies. Conformist pressures then reversed polarity and began to support changes they had formerly opposed, bringing much more rapid cultural changes than those produced by population replacement. By 2015, a majority of the US Supreme Court supported same-sex marriage: even elderly judges wanted to be on the right side of history.

This "feminization" of cultural norms in developed societies has also contributed to declining rates of violence and declining willingness to fight for one's country. Moreover, countries that have high levels of Self-expression values are much likelier to be genuine democracies than countries that rank low on these values. But do Self-expression values lead to democracy, or does democracy cause Self-expression values to emerge? The causal flow seems to move mainly from Self-expression values to democracy. Democratic institutions do not need to be in place for Self-expression values to emerge. In the years preceding the massive global wave of democratization that occurred around 1990, Self-expression values had emerged through a gradual process of intergenerational value change, not only in Western democracies but also in many authoritarian societies. Accordingly, once the threat of Soviet military intervention was withdrawn, countries with high levels of Self-expression values moved swiftly toward democracy.

Cultural change reflects changing strategies to maximize human happiness. In agrarian societies with little or no economic development or social mobility, religion makes people happier by lowering their aspirations in this life, and promising that they will be rewarded in an afterlife. But modernization brings economic development, democratization and growing social tolerance – which are conducive to happiness because they give people more freedom of choice in how to live their lives. Consequently, although *within* most countries religious people are happier than less-religious people, the people of modernized but secular countries are happier than the people of less-modernized but highly religious countries. Thus, though religion is conducive to happiness under pre-modern conditions, once high levels of economic development become possible, the modern strategy can be even more effective than the traditional strategy as a way to maximize happiness.

But *can* human happiness be maximized? Until recently, it was widely held that happiness fluctuates around fixed set-points (possibly determined by genetic factors) so that neither individuals nor societies can lastingly increase their happiness. That claim is not true, as this book demonstrates. From 1981 to 2011 happiness rose in 52 of the 62 countries for which substantial time-series data were available, and fell in only 10; during the same period, life satisfaction rose in 40 countries and fell in only 19 (3 showed no change). The two most widely used indicators of happiness rose in an overwhelming majority of countries. Why?

The extent to which a society allows free choice has a major impact on happiness. During the three decades after 1981, economic development, democratization and rising social tolerance increased the extent to which people in most countries have free choice in economic, political and social life, bringing higher levels of happiness. The shift from Survival values to Self-expression values seems conducive to greater happiness and life satisfaction.

In recent decades, globalization has transferred massive amounts of capital and technology to other parts of the world, bringing rapid economic growth especially in East Asia, Southeast Asia and India. Half the world's people are escaping from subsistence-level poverty. In the long run, this is likely to produce cultural and political changes similar to those it has already produced in high-income countries. But outsourcing now puts the workers of high-income countries in competition with the workers of low-income countries, exporting jobs and undermining the bargaining power of rich countries' workers. Automation has played an even greater role in reducing the number of industrial workers, who are now a small minority of the workforce in developed countries.

Initially, their jobs were replaced by large numbers of well-paid jobs in the service sector. But high-income societies such as the USA are entering a new phase of development that we refer to as Artificial Intelligence Society. It has the potential to abolish poverty and extend human health and life expectancy, but if left to market forces alone it tends to produce a winner-takes-all society in which the gains go almost entirely to those at the very top. In high-income countries, inequality of both income and wealth have been rising sharply since 1970. In 1965, the CEOs of major corporations in the USA were paid 20 times as much as their average employee. By 2012, they were paid 354 times as much. Unless offset by appropriate government policies, this winner-takes-all tendency undermines long-term economic growth, democracy and the cultural openness that was launched in the postwar era.

Artificial intelligence makes it possible for computer programs to replace not just industrial workers but also highly educated people, including lawyers, doctors, professors, scientists and even computer programmers. In high-income countries such as the USA, the real incomes of industrial workers have declined since 1970 and the real incomes of those with college degrees and post-graduate degrees have declined since 1991.

In Artificial Intelligence Society, the central economic conflict is no longer between the working class and the middle class, but between the 1 percent and the 99 percent, as Nobel prize-winning economist Joseph Stiglitz has put it.[1] Secure, well-paid jobs are disappearing – not just for the working class but even for the highly educated.

High levels of existential security are conducive to a more tolerant, open outlook – but conversely, declining existential security triggers an Authoritarian Reflex that brings support for strong leaders, strong in-group solidarity, rigid conformity to group norms and rejection of outsiders. This reflex is currently bringing growing support for xenophobic populist authoritarian movements in many countries, from France's National Front, to the United Kingdom's exit from the European Union, to the rise of Donald Trump in the USA. But – unlike the xenophobic authoritarianism that emerged during the Great Depression – this does not result from objective scarcity. These societies possess abundant resources. Insecurity today results from growing inequality – which is ultimately a political question. With appropriate political realignment, governments could be elected that restored the high levels of existential security that were conducive to the increasingly confident and tolerant societies that emerged in the postwar era.

Pushing the Envelope

This book presents a new version of modernization theory – Evolutionary Modernization theory – which generates a set of hypotheses that we test against a unique data base: from 1981 to 2014, the World Values Survey and European Values Study carried out hundreds of surveys in more than 100 countries containing over 90 percent of the world's population.[2] Figure I.1 depicts these countries. The data, together with the questionnaires and fieldwork information, can be downloaded from the WVS website at www.worldvaluessurvey.org/

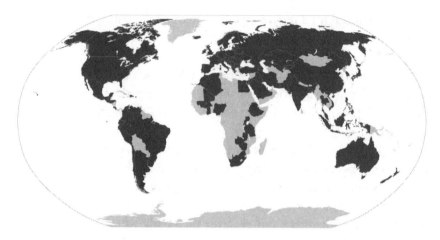

Figure I.1 Countries that have been surveyed at least once in the Values Surveys are darkly shaded. These countries contain over 90 percent of the world's population.

Some cross-national survey projects limit themselves to conducting surveys in countries with long-established survey research organizations. This is intended to ensure that they obtain high-quality fieldwork, but it largely limits them to doing research in high-income societies. From the start, the World Values Survey has endeavored to cover the full range of variation, including low-income countries. Two effects work against each other here: (a) the presumed increase in measurement error that comes from including lower-income societies with less-developed survey research infrastructure – which tends to weaken the correlations between attitudes and predictor variables; and (b) the increased analytical leverage that comes from including the full range of societies – which tends to strengthen these correlations. Which effect is stronger? The results are unequivocal. If the presumably lower quality of the data from lower-income countries outweighed the analytical leverage gained from their inclusion, including them would weaken one's power to predict relevant societal phenomena. Empirical analysis reveals that the predictive power from analyzing all available societies is considerably stronger than that obtained by analyzing only the data from high-income countries:[3] the gains obtained by analyzing the full range of variation more than compensates for any loss of data quality.

Graphs but No Equations

Although I've spent many happy hours poring over detailed statistical tables, it's clear that this is not a universal taste. Unless they're specialists in the field, most readers tune out when they encounter a series of regression equations. I think the ideas discussed here will interest a broad audience if presented in a non-technical way. Consequently, this book contains no regression equations and no complex statistical tables – but it does report the *findings* from many quantitative analyses. And it contains quite a few graphs, which can summarize relationships based on vast amounts of data in simple, vivid patterns –showing, for example, that as countries get richer, their level of gender equality increases.

This book is designed to help the reader understand how people's values and goals are changing, and how this is changing the world. I hope you enjoy it.

1 EVOLUTIONARY MODERNIZATION AND CULTURAL CHANGE

Overview

A society's culture is shaped by the extent to which its people grow up feeling that survival is secure or insecure. This book presents a revised version of modernization theory – Evolutionary Modernization theory – which argues that economic and physical insecurity are conducive to xenophobia, strong in-group solidarity, authoritarian politics and rigid adherence to their group's traditional cultural norms – and conversely that secure conditions lead to greater tolerance of outgroups, openness to new ideas and more egalitarian social norms. It then analyzes survey data from countries containing most of the world's population, showing how, in recent decades, changing levels of economic and physical security have been reshaping human values and motivations, and thereby transforming societies.

For most of history, survival was insecure, with population rising to meet the food supply and then being held constant by starvation, disease and violence. Under these conditions, societies emphasize strong in-group solidarity, conformity to group norms, rejection of outsiders, and obedience to strong leaders. For under extreme scarcity, xenophobia is realistic: if there is just enough land to support one tribe and another tribe tries to claim it, survival becomes a zero-sum struggle between Us and Them. Under these conditions, a successful survival strategy is for the tribe to close ranks behind a strong leader, forming a united front against outsiders – a strategy that can be called the Authoritarian Reflex. Conversely, high levels of existential security open the way for greater individual autonomy and more openness to diversity, change and new ideas.

The concept that deference to authority was linked with xenophobia and other forms of intolerance was first presented in the classic *The Authoritarian Personality*,[1] which viewed authoritarianism as a personality trait caused by harsh child-rearing practices. The Authoritarianism concept was controversial from the start,[2] giving rise to an enormous literature. Its original theoretical basis and the instrument originally used to measure it have been largely superseded, but over the past seven decades, scores of studies have confirmed that there is a strong tendency for deference to authority to be linked with xenophobia, intolerance and conformity to group norms. This seems to reflect a deep-rooted human reaction to insecurity. A review of a massive body of evidence from surveys, experiments and statistical data concludes that a syndrome of authoritarian racism, political and moral intolerance exists and that it is caused by individuals' innate predispositions to intolerance, interacting with changing levels of societal threat.[3] My own research indicates that given generations tend to have relatively high or low levels of authoritarianism, in so far as they have been raised under low or high levels of existential security.

In the twentieth century, industrialization, urbanization and mass literacy enabled the working class to become mobilized in labor unions and Left-oriented political parties, which elected governments that implemented redistributive policies, providing an economic safety net. This was reinforced by the fact that during the decades following World War II, the publics of advanced industrial societies experienced unprecedented levels of existential security as a result of exceptionally rapid economic growth and the absence of war. Their younger members grew up taking survival for granted. This brought an intergenerational value shift from giving top priority to economic and physical security, toward greater emphasis on free choice, environmental protection, gender equality and tolerance of gays. This in turn led to major societal changes such as a surge of democratization around 1990 and the legalization of same-sex marriage.

Classic Modernization Theory and Evolutionary Modernization Theory

Modernization theory has a long history. The idea that economic development brings predictable social and political changes has been controversial ever since it was proposed by Karl Marx. It is intellectually exciting because it not only attempts to explain what happened in the past, but also to predict what will happen in the future. So far, most efforts to predict human behavior have failed, and the key predictions made by Marx's early version of modernization theory were wrong: industrial workers did not become an overwhelming majority of the workforce, bringing a revolution of the proletariat; and the abolition of private property did not bring an end to exploitation and conflict – it led to the rise of a new ruling class, the communist party elite. Human behavior is so complex and influenced by such a wide range of factors that any claim to provide precise, deterministic predictions is unrealistic.

A central feature of modernization is that it makes life more secure, eliminating starvation and increasing life expectancy. At high levels of development, this brings pervasive changes in human motivations, enabling people to shift from life strategies based on the perception that survival is insecure, to strategies that take survival for granted and give top priority to a wide range of other human aspirations.

The feeling that survival is insecure leads to ethnocentric solidarity against outsiders and internal solidarity behind authoritarian leaders. Indeed, under conditions of extreme scarcity, survival may require closing ranks in a battle for survival. Since humanity lived at the brink of starvation throughout most of its existence, an Authoritarian Reflex evolved in which insecurity triggers support for strong leaders, strong in-group solidarity, rejection of outsiders and rigid conformity to group norms. Conversely, high levels of security allow more room for individual free choice and more openness to outsiders and new ideas.

Evolution has shaped all organisms to give top priority to survival. Organisms that did not do so died out, and the vast majority of all species that ever existed are now extinct. Thus, people evolved to give top priority to obtaining whatever is needed for survival when it is in short supply. One can live without oxygen for only a matter of minutes, and when it is scarce people focus all their efforts on getting it. One can live without water for a matter of days but when it is scarce, people struggle desperately to obtain it, killing for it if necessary. When dependable supplies of air and water are available, people take them for granted and give top priority to other goals. One can survive without food for weeks, but when it is scarce it takes top priority. Throughout history food has usually been scarce, reflecting the biological tendency for populations to rise to meet the available food supply.

There is a huge difference between growing up knowing that survival is insecure, and growing up taking survival for granted. For most of history survival has been precarious, and survival is such a basic goal that it dominates people's life strategies, influencing almost every aspect of their lives. But in recent decades an increasing share of the world's population has grown up assuming that they will not starve, and in societies where survival is taken for granted, major changes are occurring in job motivations, religion, politics, sexual behavior and how children are raised.

Social change is not deterministic but some trajectories are more probable than others. In the long run, once economic development gets under way, certain changes are likely to happen. Industrialization, for example, brings urbanization, occupational specialization and rising levels of formal education in any society that undertakes it. Farther down the line, it brings greater prosperity and better nutrition and health care, which lead to rising life expectancy. Still later, changes in the nature of work and improved means of birth control make it possible for increasing numbers of women to take jobs outside the home. This, together with related cultural changes, leads to rising gender equality.

The cultural heritage of some societies resists these changes, because sociocultural change is path dependent and cultural heritages are remarkably enduring. Although classic modernization theorists from Karl Marx to Max Weber thought that religion and ethnic loyalties would die out, religion and nationalism remain major forces. Thus, Protestant societies allowed women to vote decades earlier than Catholic societies; and conversely, Japan incorporated women into the workforce more slowly than other developed countries. But a growing body of evidence indicates that as modernization proceeds, these and other changes become increasingly probable. Even Japan is now moving toward gender equality. Value systems reflect a balance between the driving forces of modernization and the persisting influence of tradition.

The exceptionally rapid economic growth and the welfare states that emerged in advanced industrial societies after World War II brought major cultural changes. For the first time in history, a large share of these countries' populations grew up feeling that survival could be taken for granted. The cohorts born under these conditions began to give high priority to other goals, such as environmental quality and freedom of expression.

This led to a process of intergenerational value change that has been transforming the politics and culture of high-income societies, and is likely to transform China, India and other rapidly developing societies when they reach a stage where a large share of the population grows up taking survival for granted. The best-documented aspect of this process is the shift from "Materialist" values (which give top priority to economic and physical security) to "Postmaterialist" values (which emphasize free choice and self-expression). But this is just one component of a still broader shift from Survival values to Self-expression values[4] that is transforming prevailing norms concerning politics, religion, gender equality, tolerance of outgroups, and bringing growing support for environmental protection and democratic institutions.[5] The rigid cultural norms that characterized agrarian societies are giving way to norms that allow greater individual autonomy and free choice – and are conducive to successful knowledge societies.

Converging Evidence of the Importance of Existential Security

Working independently, anthropologists, psychologists, political scientists, sociologists, evolutionary biologists and historians have recently developed strikingly similar theories of cultural and institutional change: they all emphasize the extent to which security from survival threats, such as starvation, war and disease, shape a society's cultural norms and sociopolitical institutions.

Thus, Inglehart, Norris, Welzel, Abramson, Baker and other political scientists and sociologists argue that a new worldview is gradually replacing one that dominated Western society for centuries.[6] This cultural change is driven by the profound difference between growing up feeling that survival is precarious, and growing up taking survival for granted. Similar conclusions have been reached by researchers in other disciplines. Thus, a team of psychologists and anthropologists led by Michele Gelfand distinguishes between cultures that are "tight" versus "loose," arguing that these qualities are shaped by the ecological and human-made threats that societies historically encountered.[7] These threats increase the need for strong norms and punishment of deviant behavior to maintain order. Tight societies have autocratic governing systems that suppress dissent, provide strong deterrence and control of crime, and tend to be more religious. Testing these predictions against survey data from 33 countries, Gelfand et al. find that nations that encountered severe ecological and historical threats have relatively strong norms and low tolerance of deviant behavior.

Similarly, a group of biologists and psychologists led by Corey Fincher and Randy Thornhill provide convincing evidence that vulnerability to infectious disease is linked with collectivist attitudes, xenophobia and rejection of gender equality – all of which hinder the emergence of democracy.[8] They rated people in 98 societies on a collectivist–individualist scale, finding that a high threat of disease goes with collectivist attitudes, controlling for wealth and urbanization. And similarly, biopsychologist Nigel Barber finds that religion helps people cope with dangerous situations – but religious belief declines as economic development brings greater economic security and health.[9] These findings echo the predictions of evolutionary modernization theory.

Working from still another perspective, classicist and historian Ian Morris, after examining a vast array of historical evidence, concludes that "each age gets the thought it needs" – with foraging, farming and industrial societies developing appropriate value systems through an evolutionary process similar to the one described in evolutionary modernization theory.[10]

I argue that economic development brings increased economic and physical security and reduced vulnerability to disease – which are conducive to cultural openness, democratic institutions and more liberal social legislation.

This is consistent with classic claims by Theodor Adorno et al. that dogmatism, rigidity and intolerance become prevalent when people grow up perceiving threats, and with Milton Rokeach's thesis that existential threats make people paranoid, defensive and intolerant; absence of threats makes them secure, outgoing and tolerant.[11] In keeping with these claims, Self-expression values – which include tolerance of homosexuality – are most widespread in prosperous societies with secure living conditions.[12] Socioeconomic development directly affects people's sense of existential security, determining whether physical survival seems uncertain or can be taken for granted. Consequently, as we will see, the values and beliefs found in developed societies differ pervasively from those found in developing societies.

The Rise of Postmaterialism in the West

The earliest and most extensive evidence that the basic values of developed societies are changing concerns the shift from Materialist values to Postmaterialist values. More than 45 years ago, I argued in *The Silent Revolution* that "A transformation may be taking place in the political culture of advanced industrial societies. This transformation seems to be altering the basic value priorities of given generations as a result of changing conditions influencing their basic socialization."[13]

This theory of intergenerational value change is based on two key hypotheses:[14]

1. *A scarcity hypothesis*. Virtually everyone values freedom and autonomy, but people give top priority to their most pressing needs. Material sustenance and physical security are closely linked with survival, and when they are insecure, people give top priority to these Materialistic goals; but under secure conditions, people place greater emphasis on Postmaterialist goals such as belonging, esteem and free choice.

2. *A socialization hypothesis*. The relationship between material conditions and value priorities involves a long time-lag: one's basic values largely reflect the conditions that prevailed during one's preadult years, and these values change mainly through intergenerational population replacement.

The scarcity hypothesis is similar to the principle of diminishing marginal utility. It reflects the distinction between the material needs for physical survival and safety, and non-material needs such as those for self-expression and esthetic satisfaction.

During the past several decades, advanced industrial societies have diverged strikingly from previous history: a large share of their population has *not* grown up under conditions of hunger and economic insecurity. This has led to a shift in which needs for belonging, esteem and free choice have become more prominent. The scarcity hypothesis implies that prolonged periods of high prosperity encourage the spread of Postmaterialist values, while enduring economic decline has the opposite effect.

But there is no one-to-one relationship between socioeconomic development and the prevalence of Postmaterialist values, for these values reflect one's subjective sense of security, which is partly shaped by a society's income level but also by its social welfare institutions and its security from violence and disease. Per capita income is one of the best readily available indicators of the conditions leading to this value shift, but the theoretically crucial factor is one's sense of existential security.

Moreover, as the socialization hypothesis claims, people's basic value priorities do not change overnight. One of the most pervasive concepts in social science is that one's basic personality structure crystallizes by the time one reaches adulthood. Considerable evidence indicates that people's basic values are largely fixed when they reach adulthood, and change relatively little thereafter.[15] If so, we would expect to find substantial differences between the values of young and old in societies that have experienced rising levels of security. Intergenerational value change occurs when younger generations grow up under different conditions from those that shaped earlier generations.

These two hypotheses generate several predictions concerning value change. First, while the scarcity hypothesis implies that prosperity is conducive to the spread of Postmaterialist values, the socialization hypothesis implies that societal value change will take place gradually, largely through intergenerational population replacement. A sizeable time-lag exists between economic changes and their political effects.

The first empirical evidence of intergenerational value change came from surveys carried out in 1970 in six West European societies, to test the hypothesized shift from Materialist to Postmaterialist values.[16] These surveys revealed large differences between the value priorities of older and younger generations. If, as claimed, these age differences reflected intergenerational value change and not simply a tendency for people to become more Materialist as they grow older, we would expect to see a gradual shift from Materialist to Postmaterialist values as younger birth cohorts replaced older ones in the adult population. If this was happening, the implications were far-reaching, for these values were closely linked with a number of important orientations ranging from emphasis on political participation and freedom of expression, to support for environmental protection, gender equality and democratic political institutions.

The value change thesis was controversial from the start. Critics argued that the large age-difference found in 1970 reflected life-cycle effects rather than intergenerational change: young people naturally prefer Postmaterialist values such as participation and free speech, but as they aged, they would come to have the same Materialist preferences as their elders, so the values of society as a whole would not change.[17]

The value change hypothesis, by contrast, holds that young people are more Postmaterialist than their elders only if they have grown up under substantially more secure living conditions. Consequently, we would not expect to find intergenerational value differences in stagnant societies – and if future generations no longer grew up under more secure conditions than their elders, we would no longer find intergenerational value differences. But the degree of security experienced during one's formative years has a lasting impact. Consequently, as relatively Postmaterialist postwar birth cohorts replaced older, more Materialistic ones in the adult population, we should witness a gradual shift from Materialist to Postmaterialist values.

The differences between the formative experiences of the postwar birth cohorts and all older cohorts produced major differences in their value priorities. But children initially have little political impact. These differences didn't become evident at the societal level until the first postwar birth cohort became politically relevant young adults two decades after World War II – contributing to the era of Student Protest in the late 1960s and 1970s. A widespread slogan among the protesters at that time was "Don't trust anyone over thirty!"

This book analyzes cultural change, using evidence from hundreds of representative national surveys carried out from 1981 to 2014 in more than 100 countries,[18] together with economic, demographic and political data. This massive body of evidence demonstrates that the predicted intergenerational shift from Materialist to Postmaterialist priorities has been occurring. But, as we will see, it is only one aspect of a broader cultural shift from Survival values that give top priority to the survival needs, to Self-expression values that emphasize gender equality, environmental protection, tolerance, interpersonal trust and free choice. It also includes a shift from emphasis on hard work toward emphasis on imagination and tolerance as important values to teach a child. It is bringing new political issues to the center of the stage and encouraging the spread of democracy.

Cultural Change and Societal Change

Changing values can change societies. A culture is a set of norms and skills that are conducive to survival in a given environment, constituting a survival strategy for a society. Like biological evolution, culture evolves through a process analogous to random mutations and natural selection, but since culture is learned, it can change much more rapidly than biological evolution.

In recent decades, the prevailing values of highly developed countries have changed profoundly, transforming cultural norms concerning gender roles, abortion, divorce, birth control and sexual orientation that had persisted for centuries. One of the most dramatic examples is the emergence of new gender roles. Throughout history, women have generally been subordinate to men and limited to a very narrow set of roles, first as daughters and then as wives and mothers. In recent decades, this has changed radically. Increasingly, almost any job that is open to men is also open to women. Two generations ago, women comprised a small minority of those receiving higher education. Today, women comprise a majority of the university students in most industrialized countries and a growing share of the faculty. Less than a century ago, women could not even vote in most countries; today they not only vote, they hold a growing share of the parliamentary seats in many democracies and a growing share of the top political positions. After centuries of subordinate status, women are increasingly taking positions of authority in academic life, business and government.

In another example of recent societal change, openly gay politicians have become mayors of major cities, members of parliament, foreign ministers and heads of government. Since 2000, a growing number of countries have legalized same sex marriage. The rate of change varies enormously, with low-income countries[19] (especially Islamic ones) strongly resisting change. In many countries, homosexuality is still illegal, with some countries imposing the death penalty for homosexual behavior. Thus, in recent Egyptian surveys, 99 percent of the population said that homosexuality is "never" justifiable – which means that even the gays were condemning it. For those adhering to traditional norms, these cultural changes are alarming. They have given rise to some of the hottest political issues in developed countries. And they help explain the current conflict between Islamic fundamentalists and Western societies. The publics of high-income societies have been changing rapidly, while the publics of most Muslim-majority countries have changed very little – and from their perspective, the social norms of today's high-income countries are decadent and shocking. A growing gap has opened up between people holding traditional values in Islamic countries and the developed world. Once, many people in these countries saw Western democracies as a model to emulate. Today, Islamic fundamentalists see Western culture as something to guard against.

Cognition and Emotions as Sources of Value Change

Classic modernization theory needs to be modified in another respect – its one-sided emphasis on cognitive factors in shaping cultural change. Weber attributed the rise of a secular, rational worldview to the spread of scientific knowledge: scientific discoveries had made traditional religious explanations of the world obsolete; as scientific knowledge spread, religion would inexorably give way to rationality, he claimed. Similarly, some modernization theorists argued that education drives the modernization process: within most countries, the more educated tend to have modern worldviews, and as educational levels rise, traditional religious worldviews will inevitably give way to secular-rational ones.

This emphasis on cognitive forces captures only part of the story. Emotional and experiential factors, such as whether people feel that survival is secure or insecure, are at least equally important in shaping people's worldviews. Higher levels of formal education are indeed linked with Secular-rational values and Self-expression values, but higher education is not just an indicator of the extent to which one has absorbed knowledge. It is also an indicator of the extent to which one has experienced relatively secure conditions during one's formative years, since children from economically secure families are much likelier to get higher education.

But each society also has a distinct social climate reflecting the prevailing mass outlook, which helps shape people's outlook. Thus, although higher education generally encourages people to place more emphasis on Self-expression values, there is much more difference in the degree of emphasis on Self-expression values *between* the highly educated people of different nations, than between the highly educated and the general public *within* given nations.[20]

The cognitive component of education is largely irreversible – while one's sense of security and autonomy is not. The feeling that the world is secure or insecure is an early-established and relatively stable aspect of one's outlook. But this outlook can be affected by economic and political events, and massively affected by catastrophic events such as the collapse of the Soviet Union. Such events are rare, but an entire group of countries experienced them in 1989–1991, when communism collapsed throughout Central and Eastern Europe. The people of the Soviet successor states experienced sharp declines in living standards, and lived through the collapse of their social and political systems, and the collapse of a belief system under which they had lived for many decades. Scientific *knowledge* did not disappear – it continued to grow, and educational levels remained high in these societies. But the prevailing sense of existential security and individual control over one's life fell sharply. If the emergence of modern values were solely determined by cognitive factors, then Secular-rational values and Self-expression values would have continued to spread. But if these values are shaped by feelings of existential security, we would expect to find a regression from modern values toward increasing emphasis on Survival values and religion in the ex-Soviet societies. As we will see, this is exactly what happened. Cultural change is not simply determined by cognitive factors. To an even greater extent, it is shaped by people's first-hand experience with existential security or insecurity.

An Alternative Explanation: Rational Choice

This book argues that whether one has grown up perceiving survival as precarious or secure, together with historical cultural differences, has a major impact on people's behavior – but we should consider a major alternative theory: rational choice.

Two contrasting theories are competing to explain how individuals and societies behave: rational choice theories and cultural models. The rational choice school, which dominated economics and political science until recently, is based on the assumption that human behavior reflects conscious choices designed to maximize one's utilities. This approach gives little weight to historical or cultural factors, assuming that – facing the same incentives – everyone will make the same choices. This school has developed elegant and parsimonious models, but a growing body of empirical evidence indicates that these models don't adequately explain how humans actually behave. Accordingly, behavioral economics has become increasingly influential in recent years, incorporating emotional and cultural explanatory factors.

There is no question that conscious choices by political elites can have important and immediate impacts. For example, when the US Supreme Court legalized same-sex marriage in 2015, it was immediately followed by a surge of such marriages. The proximate cause was the Supreme Court decision. But a deeper cause was a long-term shift in mass attitudes. Same-sex marriage had been not merely illegal but unthinkable for centuries. But, as data from the Values Surveys demonstrate, this norm was gradually weakening through a process of intergenerational value change that took place over many decades. Public support for same-sex marriage became increasingly widespread and articulate until the laws themselves were changed.

A large body of psychological research demonstrates that the overwhelming majority of activity in the human brain takes place at an unconscious level. Since we are only aware of conscious processing, we tend to assume that it determines our decision-making. And since humans are adept at rationalizing whatever choices they make, after the fact one can always fit a rational choice explanation to any set of events. But experimental research indicates that human decisions are heavily influenced by unconscious biases or intuitions.[21] Moreover, conscious and unconscious processing occur in different regions of the brain. Brain scanning indicates that when a decision is made, activity occurs first in unconscious areas and is then followed by activity in conscious areas: apparently, the decision is determined by unconscious factors, which are then rationalized into a coherent narrative by the brain's conscious component.[22] Similarly, recent findings in psychology and cognitive neuroscience suggest that moral beliefs and motivations come from intuitions and emotions that evolution has prepared the human mind to develop; and moral judgment is a product of quick and automatic intuitions that then give rise to slower, conscious reasoning that finds reasons to support the individual's intuitions.[23]

Having emotions is ultimately more conducive to survival than being purely rational. The fact that emotions evolved enables people to make lasting commitments to stand by one's friends or one's tribe through thick and thin, in situations where a purely rational person would defect if it were profitable. Emotions make it possible for people to work together in trusting, long-term relationships. In the long run, natural selection behaves as if it were more rational than sheer rationality itself.[24]

Emotions enable people to make quick choices in situations where a rational analysis of the options might be almost endless. Conscious reasoning then develops a coherent narrative – so that rational choice seems to be determining human behavior. But since, in the long run, natural selection is very effective at producing cultural norms that have a good fit with their environment, the end result often resembles what would emerge from a process of rational choice. Accordingly, cultural change often can be modeled pretty accurately using game theory.[25] Rational choice models of cultural change may not reflect how given norms actually evolved historically – but they may capture the underlying logic of why a given arrangement fits its environment, and consequently survives. Such models are like evolutionary biologists' explanation that polar bears evolved white coats "in order to be less conspicuous against the snow." Biologists are perfectly aware that polar bears did not consciously decide to develop white coats, but this is a parsimonious way to describe how random mutations and natural selection led to this result. In contemporary social science, rational choice theorists often describe complex evolutionary processes as if they resulted from rational bargaining and conscious choice – even when they reflect evolutionary processes involving complex events with unforeseen consequences, rather than conscious choices.

Slow and Fast Cultural Change

A culture is a set of learned behavior that constitutes a society's survival strategy. The norms governing this strategy usually change very slowly, often persisting for centuries, but under certain conditions they can change rapidly. Though fashions change quickly, basic values tend to change slowly through intergenerational population replacement, with multi-decade time-lags between the emergence of root causes and the time when cultural change becomes manifest in a society.[26] Empirical analysis of the Materialist/Postmaterialist value shift indicates that basic values change gradually, largely through intergenerational population replacement.[27] Instead of spreading across the entire world evenly, as awareness of the optimal choice might do, this shift occurs only when a society reaches a threshold where a sufficiently high level of economic and physical security enables younger birth cohorts to grow up taking survival for granted. In contrast to this, rational choice theory holds that key institutions are adopted through conscious elite choices – which could change from one day to the next. It also tends to assume that institutions determine culture, in which case basic cultural norms would also change rapidly.

Rational choice explanations do not account for the fact that cultural change tends to occur through intergenerational population replacement or for the persisting influence of religious cleavage and historical events that occurred many centuries ago.

Rising levels of existential security have been reshaping the world in recent decades. Life expectancies, incomes, and school attendance rose from 1970 to 2010 in every region of the world.[28] Poverty, illiteracy and mortality are declining globally.[29] And war, crime rates and violence have been declining for many decades.[30] The world is now experiencing the longest period without war between major powers in recorded history. This, together with the postwar economic miracles and the emergence of the welfare state, produced conditions under which a growing share of the world's population has grown up taking survival for granted, bringing intergenerational shifts toward Postmaterialist values and Self-expression values.[31]

But in addition to the shifts linked with intergenerational population replacement, given birth cohorts can become increasingly tolerant of new social norms due to diffusion of these values through education and exposure to the mass media – which now present these norms in a much more favorable light than they did decades ago. This could eventually transform what are perceived as socially desirable norms.

In secure advanced industrial societies, among successful young people it is no longer socially acceptable to be sexist or a gay-basher. But older people and the publics of low-income societies remain solidly opposed to gender equality and tolerance of gays. Western motion pictures and television programs, cell phones and the internet have penetrated widely even in low-income countries, but they haven't yet had much impact on their lifestyle norms.[32] Education and mass communications may play important roles in transforming attitudes toward gender equality and tolerance of gays but so far their impact has been largely limited to societies with relatively high levels of existential security.

It seems that *both* intergenerational population replacement and value diffusion are occurring. As we will see, intergenerational change seems to play the dominant role in the shift from Materialist to Postmaterialist values, but some value diffusion also seems to be taking place: given birth cohorts not only failed to become more Materialist as they aged – they actually became slightly *more* Postmaterialist over time.

Major Predictions

The theory just discussed, generates the following predictions:

1. When a society attains sufficiently high levels of existential security that a large share of the population grows up taking survival for granted, it brings coherent and roughly predictable social and cultural changes, producing an intergenerational shift from values shaped by scarcity, toward increasing emphasis on Postmaterialist values and Self-expression values.
2. As younger birth cohorts replace older cohorts in the adult population, it transforms the societies' prevailing values – but with long time-lags. The youngest cohorts have little political impact until they reach adulthood, and even then they are still a small minority of the adult population; it takes additional decades before they become the dominant influence in their society.
3. Intergenerational value change is shaped by short-term period effects such as economic booms or recessions, in addition to population replacement, but in the long run the period effects often cancel each other out, while the population replacement effects tend to be cumulative.
4. Intergenerational value change can eventually reach a threshold at which new norms became socially dominant. At this point, conformist pressures reverse polarity, supporting changes they had

formerly opposed and bringing much more rapid cultural change than that produced by population replacement alone.

5. Cultural change is path-dependent: a society's values are shaped by its entire historical heritage, and not just its level of existential security.

The following chapters test these hypotheses.

2 THE RISE OF POSTMATERIALIST VALUES IN THE WEST AND THE WORLD

More than four decades have passed since the shift from Materialist to Postmaterialist values was hypothesized. Have the predicted changes actually taken place?

A large body of evidence, analyzed using three different approaches – (1) cohort analysis; (2) comparisons of rich and poor countries; (3) examination of actual trends observed over the past 40 years – all points to the conclusion that major cultural changes are occurring, and that they reflect a process of intergenerational change linked with rising levels of existential security.

The first empirical evidence of intergenerational value change came from surveys carried out in 1970 in six West European societies to test the hypothesized value shift. Although the Values Surveys have subsequently monitored a much broader range of value changes, this research provided the earliest quantitative evidence of intergenerational value change and the most extensive time series data base. From 1970 to 2009, representative national surveys were carried out almost every year in these six countries, providing a detailed time series covering four decades based on more than 300,000 interviews. Additional time series evidence is now available from scores of other countries on all six inhabited continents.

In testing the value change hypothesis, we asked people which goals they considered most important, choosing between such things as economic growth, fighting rising prices, maintaining order, and the fight against crime (which tap Materialist priorities); and freedom of speech, giving people more say in important government decisions, more say on the job, and a society where ideas count (which tap Postmaterialist priorities).[1] Representative national surveys in 1970 asked these questions in six West European countries (Great Britain, France, Italy, West Germany, Belgium and The Netherlands).

These surveys revealed large differences between the values of young and old in all six countries. As Figure 2.1 indicates, among those aged 65 and older, people with Materialist value priorities outnumbered those with Postmaterialist value priorities by more than 14:1. This suggests that in the early twentieth century, Materialists outnumbered Postmaterialists overwhelmingly. In that era, the Marxist claim that politics is dominated by class conflict and economic issues was a reasonably good first approximation of reality. But as one moves from older to younger cohorts, the balance gradually shifts toward a diminishing proportion of Materialists and a growing proportion of

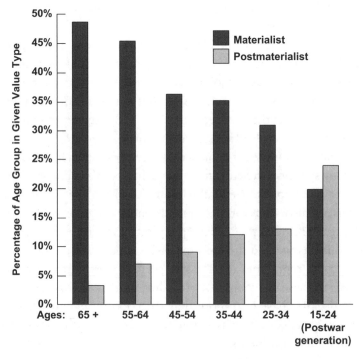

Figure 2.1 Value type by age group, among the publics of Britain, France, West Germany, Italy, Belgium and The Netherlands in 1970.
Source: European Community survey in February 1970.
Based on original 4-item Materialist/Postmaterialist values battery.
Reprinted from Inglehart, 1990: 76.

Postmaterialists. Among the youngest cohort (those 18–25 years old in 1970) Postmaterialists outnumber Materialists. This cross-sectional evidence suggests that, as the oldest birth cohorts die off and are replaced by younger cohorts during the decades following 1970, we should observe a shift in prevailing motivations, with Postmaterialists becoming increasingly numerous.

But do these age differences reflect enduring birth cohort effects or transient life-cycle effects? With data from just one time point, one can't be sure – and the two interpretations have very different implications. The life-cycle interpretation implies that the postwar cohort will become increasingly Materialist as they age, so that by the time they are 65 years old they will be just as Materialist as the 65-year-olds were in 1970 – and society as a whole won't change at all. The cohort-effects interpretation implies that the younger cohorts will remain relatively Postmaterialist over time – so that as they replace the older, more Materialist cohorts, the society's prevailing values *will* change.

Cohort analysis provides the only conclusive way to answer this question and it requires: (1) survey data covering several decades; (2) surveys carried out at numerous time points, enabling one to distinguish period effects from life-cycle and birth-cohort effects; and (3) sufficiently large numbers of respondents at each time point so that one gets accurate estimates when one breaks the sample down into several birth cohorts.

Figure 2.2 shows the results of a cohort analysis based on over 300,000 interviews. It follows given birth cohorts over four decades, using data from Euro-barometer surveys that included the Materialist/ Postmaterialist battery in almost every year from 1970 to 1997, supplemented with data from the Values Surveys from 1999 and 2007–2009.[2] This figure pools the data from all six countries in order to provide sufficiently large samples to reliably estimate each cohort's position at a given time – which is calculated by subtracting the percentage of Materialists from the percentage of Postmaterialists. Thus, at the zero point on the vertical axis, the two groups are equally numerous. The proportion of Postmaterialists increases as one moves up; and the proportion of Materialists increases as one moves down on Figure 2.2.

If the age differences shown in Figure 2.2 reflected life-cycle effects, then each of the lines on this figure would shift downward as they moved to the right, with each cohort becoming more Materialist as it aged from 1970 to 2009. If the age differences reflect stable birth

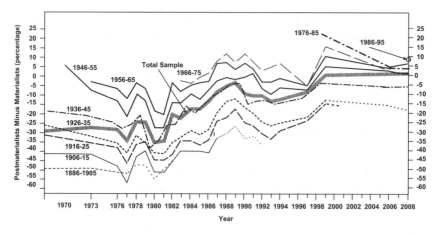

Figure 2.2 Cohort analysis: Percentage of Postmaterialists minus percentage of Materialists in six West European countries (Britain, France, West Germany, Italy, Belgium and The Netherlands), 1971–2009.

Source: data from 1970 through 1997 are from Euro-Barometer surveys; data from 1999, 2006 and 2008–2009 are from European Values Study/World Values Survey.

cohort effects, the lines would be horizontal, with each cohort remaining about as Postmaterialist at the end of the time series as it was at the start.

But we also need to take period effects into account. Our theory implies that events that diminish existential security, such as major recessions, will push all cohorts downward in response to current conditions. With recovery, they will return to their former level, so that in the long run they could remain just about as Postmaterialist as they were at the start. In the short run, a period effect that pushed all the cohorts downward would give the misleading impression that the age differences reflected life-cycle effects. But in the long run, positive and negative fluctuations are likely to cancel each other out.

With detailed data from the long time series in Figure 2.2, we can see that period effects clearly *are* present. As Inglehart and Welzel demonstrate, they reflect current economic conditions, particularly inflation.[3] During periods of economic downturn, each birth cohort moves down, becoming more Materialist; with recovery, each birth cohort moves up again, becoming more Postmaterialist – but the *differences* between given birth cohorts remain stable. Consequently, the period effects have no lasting impact: the younger cohorts remain relatively Postmaterialist despite short-term fluctuations, and over a period of four decades we find no overall tendency for the members of given birth cohorts to become more Materialist as they age.

But during this four-decade span, the three oldest birth cohorts left the sample. They were replaced by three younger cohorts, born in 1956–65, 1966–75 and 1976–85. The cohort analysis in Figure 2.2 shows no evidence of life cycle effects. It is clear that the age-related differences found in 1970 reflect lasting cohort differences. This implies that as younger, less Materialist cohorts replace older ones in the adult population, these societies will shift from Materialist toward Postmaterialist values.

This is precisely what happened. During the past four decades, there was a substantial shift toward Postmaterialist values among the six publics first surveyed in 1970 (we also found similar shifts in the USA and other Western countries). The heavy shaded line on Figure 2.2 shows the net shift toward Postmaterialist values among the adult population as a whole at various time points from 1970 to 2009. In the early 1970s, Materialists heavily outnumbered Postmaterialists in all six countries. Overall, Materialists were four times as numerous as Postmaterialists, and 14 times as numerous as Postmaterialists among the oldest cohort. Similarly, in the USA in 1972, Materialists were three times as numerous as Postmaterialists. During the ensuing years, major shifts occurred. By 2000, Postmaterialists were slightly more numerous than Materialists in Western Europe and twice as numerous as Materialists in the USA. The predicted shift toward Postmaterialist values had taken place.

But Western levels of economic security have not continued to rise during the past two decades. Economic growth has been slow and, because of rising income inequality the gains have gone almost entirely to the top; a large share of the population has experienced stagnant or declining real income. This has been reinforced by cutbacks in the welfare state and high levels of unemployment, particularly among youth. The shift toward Postmaterialist values has tapered off in these Western countries. Thus, in the most recent surveys, the youngest cohorts are no more Postmaterialist than the other postwar cohorts – though they are significantly more so than the one surviving prewar cohort, in which Materialists still outnumber Postmaterialists. As a result, intergenerational population replacement no longer brings a large shift toward Postmaterialist values.

But a major value transition has occurred: in 1970, Materialists vastly outnumbered Postmaterialists in all Western countries. By 2000 Postmaterialists were slightly more numerous than Materialists – but because Postmaterialists tend to be concentrated among the more secure, better-educated and more articulate strata of society, they set the tone: their values have become politically correct. The Postmaterialist value shift is no longer a major factor in these countries; except for the oldest cohort, young and old now have pretty similar values. But the culture of high-income Western countries has been transformed.

The logic of the Postmaterialist shift has significant implications for other countries. The world as a whole has shown unprecedented economic growth since 1980, with India and China experiencing annual growth rates from 6 to 10 percent. Only a few decades ago, most people in both countries lived just above the starvation level. In the memory of living people, at least 30 million Chinese starved to death after the failure of the Great Leap Forward. These countries now have many millionaires (and millions living in dire poverty). Their impressive growth rates mean that 40 percent of the world's population is moving from starvation-level poverty to a modest level of economic security. Evolutionary modernization theory implies that in the long run, this will bring a shift toward Postmaterialist values. But, as we have seen, multi-decade time-lags are involved. For now, Postmaterialists constitute tiny minorities in both China and India. But our theory predicts that if they continue on their present trajectories, a shift toward Postmaterialist values will take place when a younger generation emerges that has grown up taking survival for granted. Many other countries from Mexico to Singapore already have reached this threshold.

In the world as a whole, the ratio between Materialists and Postmaterialists varies tremendously according to a society's level of economic development. Low-income countries and strife-torn countries show an overwhelming preponderance of Materialists, while prosperous and secure ones are dominated by Postmaterialists. Thus, Materialists outnumber Postmaterialists in Pakistan by a ratio of 55 to 1, and in Russia by a ratio of 28 to 1; but in the USA Postmaterialists outnumber Materialists by 2 to 1, and in Sweden by 5 to 1. No one can guarantee that prosperity and peace will continue, but in countries that do attain high levels of existential security, we can expect to find intergenerational value change.

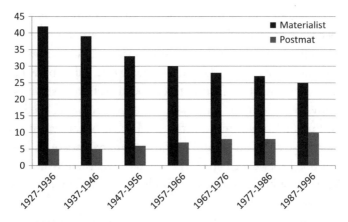

Figure 2.3 Materialist vs. Postmaterialist values by birth cohort, in 11 ex-communist countries now in the European Union (Bulgaria, Croatia, Czech Republic, Estonia, Hungary, Latvia, Lithuania, Poland, Romania, Slovakia and Slovenia), 2008–2012.

Figure 2.3 shows the distribution of Materialist and Postmaterialist values in each birth cohort that was born from 1927 to 1996 in 11 ex-communist countries that are now members of the European Union – Bulgaria, Croatia, the Czech Republic, Estonia, Hungary, Latvia, Lithuania, Poland, Romania, Slovakia and Slovenia – using the latest available survey from 2008–2012. These countries earliest available surveys (around 1990) already showed large intergenerational differences indicating a shift toward Postmaterialist values – which probably contributed to the mass demonstrations that led to the fall of communist regimes there.

The transition from state-run to market economies brought severe economic dislocations that dampened the trend toward Postmaterialist values, but this economic decline was not lasting in these countries, which soon became members of the European Union; during their first decade in the EU, these new members had economic growth rates about twice as high as those of the older members. The intergenerational shift toward Postmaterialist values has resumed, as Figure 2.3 indicates. Among the oldest cohort, born from 1927 to 1936, Materialists still outnumber Postmaterialists by a ratio of 8 to 1 – but among the youngest cohort, the ratio is only 2.5 to 1. Intergenerational value change seems to be emerging, though these countries still lag far behind Western Europe in absolute numbers of Postmaterialists.

The Russian public also showed signs of a strong intergenerational shift from Materialist to Postmaterialist values in the earliest available survey in 1990 – but the decline of existential security that the Russia people experienced with the collapse of communism was much more severe than in the ex-communist countries that are now European Union members. The Soviet Union disintegrated, per capita income fell to about 40 percent of its former level, social welfare institutions broke down, crime was rampant and male life expectancy declined by about 18 years. Equally important, faith in a Marxist belief system that once provided a sense of meaning and purpose to many people collapsed. The Russian public experienced an extraordinary malaise, in which a majority of the Russian public described themselves as unhappy and dissatisfied with their lives as a whole.

Around 2000, the Russian economy began to recover, largely due to rising oil and gas prices, and order was restored by Vladimir Putin. Subjective well-being levels are also recovering – but the youngest Russian birth cohorts have not experienced significantly higher levels of economic and physical security than their elders: their formative years were shaped by widespread poverty and disorder. Consequently, recent Russian surveys show little evidence of an intergenerational shift toward Postmaterialist values, and Materialists overwhelmingly outnumber Postmaterialists.

Figure 2.4 shows the distribution of Materialist and Postmaterialist values by birth cohort in eight Latin American countries – Argentina, Brazil, Chile, Colombia, Guatemala, Mexico, Peru

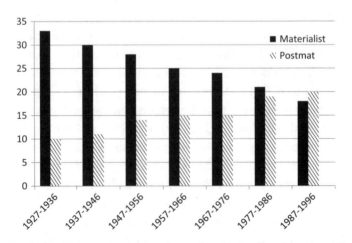

Figure 2.4 Materialist vs. Postmaterialist values by birth cohort, in eight Latin American countries (Argentina, Brazil, Chile, Colombia, Guatemala, Mexico, Peru and Uruguay, 2005–2012).

and Uruguay – based on the latest available surveys, from 2005 to 2012. During the past 25 years, most Latin American countries have experienced substantial economic growth and many have made successful transitions from authoritarian regimes to democratic governments. These countries now show signs of an intergenerational shift from Materialist to Postmaterialist values. Among the oldest cohort (born from 1927 to 1936), Materialists outnumber Postmaterialists by more than three to one. But among the youngest cohort (born from 1987 to 1996), Postmaterialists outnumber Materialists. In their overall value distributions, these countries still lag far behind the six West European countries analyzed above – and even farther behind the USA and Sweden, where Postmaterialists outnumber Materialists by wide margins. But an intergenerational transition seems to be transforming Latin American countries.

The forces of modernization are starting to transform Islamic societies, but they are still at an early stage. The 2007–2014 wave of the WVS shows evidence that a process of intergenerational value change is now at work in some Muslim-majority countries, particularly those that played leading roles in the Arab Spring. Figure 2.5 shows the shifting balance between Materialist and Postmaterialist values in nine Muslim-majority countries, Morocco, Tunisia, Libya, Palestine, Jordan, Turkey, Albania and Indonesia. Among the oldest birth cohort,

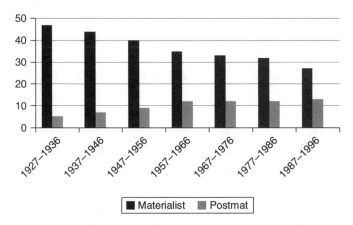

Figure 2.5 Materialist vs. Postmaterialist values by birth cohort in nine Muslim-majority countries (Morocco, Algeria, Tunisia, Libya, Palestine, Jordan, Turkey, Albania and Indonesia). N = 24,107.

Source: World Values Survey and European Values Study, 2007–2013.

Materialists outnumber Postmaterialists by a ratio of more than 10 to 1; among the youngest birth cohort, the ratio is only about 2 to 1. The ratio is shifting, but it has not yet produced a cohort in which Postmaterialists outnumber Materialists.

The age-related differences are relatively weak in 13 other Muslim-majority countries: Kazakhstan, Uzbekistan, Azerbaijan, Kyrgyzstan, Lebanon, Iran, Saudi Arabia, Qatar, Yemen, Mali, Pakistan, Bangladesh and Malaysia (median r = −.05). The countries that show evidence of relatively strong intergenerational value change do not have the highest levels of per capita GDP (which are found in the Gulf states) – but they do have significantly higher life expectancies, lower infant mortality rates and lower fertility rates than the other Islamic countries. Thus, the median life expectancy in the countries shown in Figure 2.5 is 75 years; the median life expectancy in the others is 69 years. Muslim-majority countries with relatively high life expectancies show relatively large intergenerational value differences. Moreover, apart from Indonesia, these countries are clustered on or near the Mediterranean and have relatively large population flows to and from Western Europe.

Simply holding elections will not establish effective democracy in the Muslim world. And it seems unlikely that the Arab-speaking countries will, in the near future, establish an enduring wave of democratization like the one that swept Eastern Europe in the final days of the Cold War. But there are signs that intergenerational change is beginning to transform the culture of some Muslim-majority countries.

Intergenerational Value Change Has Launched a Positive Feedback Loop

The shift from Materialist to Postmaterialist values has slowed in Western Europe, but it is spreading to many other countries. Moreover, the emergence of an intergenerational value shift in the postwar era eventually launched a positive feedback loop under which each new birth cohort grew up under more permissive conditions than those that had shaped older cohorts. For people take the world into which they are born for granted: it seems familiar and normal. And for the past 60 years, each successive birth cohort in high-income societies has been born into a world in which tolerance of gender equality and gays and other outgroups was steadily becoming more widespread and ethnic diversity was increasing. This meant that the gap between contemporary reality and the world that one was born into was greater for older birth cohorts than it was for younger ones – so older cohorts felt more threatened and disoriented by contemporary levels of social tolerance and ethnic diversity than younger ones. This process continued even when younger cohorts no longer were shaped by higher levels of economic security than their elders. For younger birth cohorts, the legalization of same-sex marriage and the election of an African American President were simply continuations of a familiar trend. For older cohorts they were shocking events that had been inconceivable in the world in which they had been born.

This principle applies to geographic differences as well as birth cohort differences. If one was born in New York or Los Angeles in 1960, ethnic and cultural diversity were familiar and relatively acceptable. If one was born in 1960 in rural Montana or West Virginia, they were not. The legalization of same-sex marriage and the election of an African American President seemed incompatible with the norms of the world into which they had been born. Consequently, both the younger birth cohorts and people born in diverse metropolitan areas are considerably more supportive of the new cultural norms than older people and those from rural areas. As younger cohorts replace older ones, major cultural changes continue.

3 GLOBAL CULTURAL PATTERNS

The shift toward Postmaterialist values is only one component of a broader process of cultural change that is reshaping the political views, religious orientations, gender roles and sexual norms of people in advanced industrial societies.[1] The emerging worldview moves away from traditional norms, especially those that limit self-expression.

We find huge cross-national differences in what people believe and value. The Values Surveys have monitored about 90 percent of the world's population. In some countries, 95 percent of the public say that God is very important in their lives, while in others only 3 percent say so. In some societies, 90 percent of the people believe that men have more right to a job than women; in others, only 8 percent think so. These cross-national differences are robust and enduring, and are closely linked with a society's level of economic development: people in low-income societies are much likelier to emphasize religion and traditional gender roles than are people in rich countries.

To identify the main dimensions of global cultural variation, Inglehart and Baker performed a factor analysis of each society's mean level on scores of variables measured in the Values Surveys.[2] The two most important dimensions that emerged reflected: (1) Traditional versus Secular-rational values and (2) Survival versus Self-expression values.

People holding Traditional values are strongly religious, have high levels of national pride and respect for authority, and low tolerance for abortion and divorce. Secular-rational values have the opposite characteristics. The Traditional/Secular-rational values dimension reflects the transition from agrarian society to industrial society. Classic modernization theory focused on this dimension, arguing that industrialization was linked with occupational specialization, urbanization, centralization, bureaucratization, rationalization and secularization – themes discussed extensively by Marx, Weber, Durkheim, Spencer and other classic modernization theorists. The evidence from the Values Surveys supports their claims: the people of agrarian societies do indeed tend to emphasize traditional values, while societies with a high percentage of industrial workers are much likelier to emphasize Secular-rational values.

Another major dimension of cross-cultural variation is linked with the transition from industrial society to postindustrial society. This is a recent development that classic modernization theory did not discuss. We examine it more closely here. The shift from a manufacturing economy to a knowledge economy is linked with pervasive value changes that can be summed up as a shift from Survival values to Self-expression values. Table 3.1 shows how strongly the responses to 20 different questions are correlated with this Survival/Self-expression values dimension. A correlation of zero indicates that responses to a given question are unrelated to this dimension. Correlations near .90 indicate that responses to a given question are linked with the underlying Survival/Self-expression dimension in an almost one-to-one relationship. This table only shows the relatively strong correlations; many other questions are also linked with this dimension.

As Table 3.1 demonstrates, whether one has Materialist or Postmaterialist values is a particularly sensitive indicator of the broader Survival/Self-expression values dimension. This is logical, since the conditions that lead to Postmaterialist values are also conducive to Self-expression values. But these values also reflect a number of issues that go beyond Postmaterialist values. For example, Self-expression values reflect mass polarization over such questions as whether "Men make better political leaders than women," and "When jobs are scarce, men have more right to a job than women." Self-expression values are also linked with tolerance of outgroups, gays and lesbians. People with Self-expression values give high priority to environmental protection, tolerance of diversity and rising demands for participation in decision-making in economic and political life.

People who emphasize Survival values tend to be significantly less satisfied with their lives and less happy than people with

Table 3.1 *Orientations linked with Survival vs. Self-expression values*

People with SURVIVAL VALUES endorse the following:	Correlation
Materialist rather than Postmaterialist values (economic and physical security are one's top priorities)	.87
Men make better political leaders than women	.86
I am not highly satisfied with my life	.84
A woman has to have children to be fulfilled	.83
I wouldn't want foreigners, homosexuals or people with AIDS as neighbors	.81
I have not and would not sign a petition	.80
I am not very happy	.79
I favor more emphasis on the development of technology	.78
Homosexuality is never justifiable	.78
I have not recycled to protect the environment	.76
I have not attended a meeting or signed a petition to protect the environment	.75
A good income and safe job are more important than a feeling of accomplishment and working with people you like	.74
I do not rate my health as very good	.73
A child needs a home with both a father and a mother in order to grow up happily	.73
When jobs are scarce, a man has more right to a job than a woman	.70
A university education is more important for a boy than for a girl	.69
The government should ensure that everyone is provided for	.69
Hard work is one of the most important things to teach a child	.65
Imagination is not one of the most important things to teach a child	.62
Tolerance is not one of the most important things to teach a child	.62
People with SELF-EXPRESSION VALUES take the opposite position on all of the above	

The original polarities vary; some statements have been reworded to reflect Survival values.

Self-expression values. This is a remarkable finding. It suggests that certain value systems may be more conducive to happiness than others. As long as a society remains near the survival level, its culture is mainly oriented toward ensuring physical survival. But as survival becomes secure, a society's culture tends to become adapted to maximizing subjective well-being. Self-expression values are conducive to subjective well-being in so far as they emancipate people from traditional constraints that are no longer necessary for survival, allowing greater freedom of choice in how to live one's life. For many groups such as women and gays, emancipation from traditional constraints makes a major contribution to life satisfaction and happiness, and in this sense the shift from Survival values to Self-expression values is an effective cultural evolution. Though it reflects the impact of complex events with unforeseen consequences, in retrospect this cultural shift looks as if the people of advanced industrial societies had consciously chosen to adopt a cultural strategy that enhances their happiness and life satisfaction.

The shift from Survival values to Self-expression values also includes a shift in child-rearing values, from emphasis on hard work toward emphasis on imagination and tolerance as important values to teach a child. Societies that rank high on Self-expression values tend to have an environment of trust and tolerance, in which people place a relatively high value on individual freedom and have activist political orientations – attributes that, the political culture literature has long argued, are crucial to democracy.

A major component of rise of Self-expression values is a shift away from deference to all forms of external authority. Submission to authority has high costs: the individual's personal goals must be subordinated to those of others. Under conditions of insecurity, people are willing to do so. Under threat of invasion, civil war or economic collapse, people tend to seek strong authority figures who can protect them from danger. Conversely, prosperity and security are conducive to tolerance of diversity and rising demands to have a say in what happens to them. This helps explain a long-established finding: rich societies are much likelier to be democratic than poor ones. Under conditions of insecurity, people may readily submit to authoritarian rule, but with rising levels of existential security, they become less willing to do so.

The rise of Self-expression values brings an intergenerational change from norms linked with survival of the species, to norms linked with the pursuit of individual well-being. Thus, younger birth cohorts are more tolerant of homosexuality than their elders, and they are more favorable to gender equality and more permissive in their attitudes toward abortion, divorce, extramarital affairs and euthanasia. Economic accumulation for the sake of economic security was the central goal of industrial society. Its attainment set in motion a process of gradual cultural change that makes these goals less crucial – and is now bringing a rejection of the hierarchical institutions that helped attain them.

Economic Development and Value Change

The central claim of classic modernization theory is that economic and technological development tend to bring coherent and roughly predictable social and political changes. Evolutionary modernization theory agrees, but argues that these societal changes are largely driven by the fact that modernization brings value changes that are causing the people of economically advanced societies to have systematically different motivations – and consequently different behavior – from the people of less developed societies.

Is this empirically true? Data from hundreds of surveys covering 90 percent of the world's population indicates that it is – to a striking degree. Figure 3.1 presents a cross-cultural map of the world, showing where the publics of given countries are located on each of the two major dimensions. Moving from the bottom to the top of this map, one moves from emphasis on Traditional values to emphasis on Secular-rational values; moving from left to right, one moves from emphasis on Survival values toward emphasis on Self-expression values.

As Figure 3.1 demonstrates, the publics of high-income societies rank high on both major dimensions of cross-cultural variation, placing relatively strong emphasis on both Secular-rational values and on Self-expression values. Conversely, the publics of low-income and lower-middle-income societies rank relatively low on both dimensions, tending to emphasize Traditional values and Survival values. The publics of upper-middle-income societies fall into an intermediate zone.[3] The zones' boundaries capture a remarkably consistent relationship between economic development and values: all of the high-income societies – without a single exception – fall into the upper-right-hand zone, ranking relatively high on both major dimensions of cross-cultural

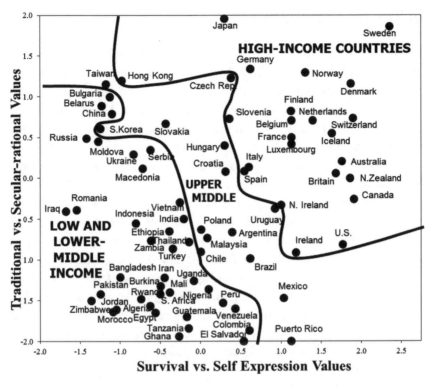

Figure 3.1 Mean scores of 75 countries on two major value dimensions, by level of development.
Source: Data from Values Surveys (median date of survey 2005); economic level based on World Bank's income categories as of 1992.

variation (each of which taps the responses to scores of questions). Conversely, all of the low-income and lower-middle-income societies – again without a single exception – fall into the lower-left-hand zone, ranking relatively low on both dimensions. The remaining societies fall into an intermediate zone.

The cross-cultural differences depicted here are huge: in relatively Traditional societies, up to 95 percent of the public say that God is very important in their lives; in Secular-rational societies, as few as 3 percent do so. In Survival-oriented societies, up to 96 percent of the public say that homosexuality is never justifiable; in Self-expression-oriented societies, as few as 6 percent say so. To a remarkable degree, a society's values and goals reflect its level of economic development. The classic Marxist emphasis on economic determinism seems justified.

The Persistence of Traditional Cultures

But reality is not quite that simple. Modernization theorists from Marx and Weber to Bell and Toffler have argued that the rise of industrial society is linked with coherent cultural shifts away from traditional value systems.[4] But other social scientists including Huntington, Putnam, Fukuyama, Inglehart and Baker, Inglehart and Welzel argue that cultural traditions are remarkably enduring and shape the political and economic behavior of their societies today. *Both* claims are true.[5]

Evidence from around the world indicates that socioeconomic development *does* tend to propel various societies in a roughly predictable direction. Socioeconomic development brings occupational specialization, rising educational levels and rising income levels; it diversifies human interaction, shifting the emphasis from command–obedience relations toward bargaining relations; in the long run this brings cultural change, including changing gender roles, changing attitudes toward authority, changing sexual norms, declining fertility rates, broader political participation and more critical, less easily manipulated publics.

But cultural change is path dependent. The fact that a society was historically Protestant or Orthodox or Islamic or Confucian gives rise to cultural zones with distinctive value systems that persist even when one controls for the effects of socioeconomic development. These cultural zones are robust. Although the value systems of different countries are moving in the same direction under the impact of powerful modernizing forces, their value systems have not been converging, as simplistic models of cultural globalization suggest.

This may seem contradictory, but it is not. If all of the world's societies were moving in the same direction at the same rate of speed, the distances between them would remain constant and they would never converge. The reality is not that simple, of course, but this illustrates an important principle: postindustrial societies *are* changing rapidly and they are moving in a common direction – but the cultural differences between them were empirically as great in 2014 as they were in 1981. Though socioeconomic development tends to produce systematic changes in what people believe and want out of life, the influence of cultural traditions does not disappear. Belief systems have remarkable durability and resilience. Though values can and do change, they continue to reflect a society's historical heritage. Cultural change is path dependent.

Nevertheless, socioeconomic development brings predictable long-term changes. One indication of this is the fact that the worldviews and behavior of the people in developed societies differ immensely from those of people in low-income societies. Another indication is the fact that the value systems of developed societies are changing in a consistent and roughly predictable direction. These changes do not reflect a homogenizing trend – they cannot be attributed, for example, to the impact of a global communications network that is transmitting a common set of new values throughout the world. If this were the case, the same value changes would occur in all societies that are exposed to global communications. But this has not been happening. These value changes are *not* taking place in low-income countries, or in societies that were experiencing sharply declining standards of living, such as the Soviet successor states from 1990 to 2000 – even though these societies were integrated into the global communications network. These changes occur only when the people of a given society have experienced high levels of existential security for long periods of time. Socioeconomic development brings predictable cultural and political changes – and its collapse tends to bring changes in the opposite direction.

These changes are probabilistic and they are not linear. Industrialization brings a shift from traditional to Secular-rational values – but with the rise of postindustrial society, cultural change starts to move in another direction. The shift from Traditional to Secular-rational values becomes slower, while another change becomes more powerful – the shift from Survival to Self-expression values, through which people place increasing emphasis on free choice, autonomy and creativity. This change was moving slowly during the transition from pre-industrial to industrial societies, but it becomes the dominant trend when industrial society gives way to postindustrial society. The classic modernization theorists focused on the rise of Secular-rational values. Quite understandably, they did not foresee the rise of Self-expression values that emerges in later stages of modernization. This trend is very different from the technocratic authoritarianism that many modernization theorists (and novelists such as George Orwell)[6] thought would shape the future. In contrast with these expectations,

Self-expression values make democracy the most likely outcome at advanced levels of modernization.

The industrial phase of modernization does not necessarily lead to democracy, but allows for authoritarian, fascist and communist versions of industrialization and mass mobilization. But in the postindustrial phase of modernization, rising Self-expression values challenge authority and raise growing demands for genuinely responsive democracy, as Chapter 7 will demonstrate.

Progress is not inevitable. Socioeconomic development brings massive and roughly predictable cultural changes, but if economic collapse occurs, cultural changes start to move in the opposite direction. Development has been the dominant trend of recent centuries: most countries are far more prosperous today than they were two hundred years ago. But this rising long-term trend shows numerous fluctuations.

The fact that a society was historically shaped by a Protestant or Confucian or Islamic cultural heritage leaves an enduring impact, setting that society on a trajectory that continues to influence subsequent development – even when the direct influence of religious institutions fades away. Thus, although few people attend church in Protestant Europe today, the societies that were historically shaped by Protestantism continue to manifest a distinctive set of similar values and beliefs. The same is true of historically Roman Catholic societies and historically Islamic or Orthodox or Confucian societies, as Figures 3.2 and 3.3 demonstrate.

Factor analysis of data from the 43 societies in the 1990 WVS/EVS found that the Traditional/Secular-rational values dimension and the Survival/Self-expression values dimensions accounted for over half of the cross-national variance on scores of variables.[7] Figure 3.2 shows the locations of 43 countries on these two dimensions, based on surveys carried out in 1990–1991. When this analysis was replicated with data from the 1995–1998 surveys, the same two dimensions emerged (see Figure A2.1 in appendix). Similarly, in analysis of the 2000–2001 surveys (see Figure A2.2 in appendix) and the 2005–2007 surveys, these same two dimensions again emerged – although the new surveys included dozens of additional countries.[8]

Figure 3.3 shows the locations of 94 countries on the global cultural map, using the latest available data from the 2008–2014 Values Surveys. Comparing this cultural map with the maps based

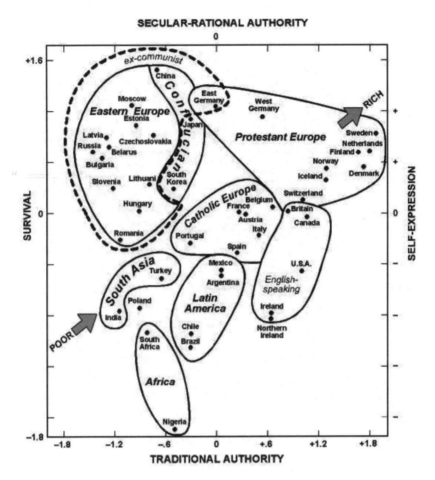

Figure 3.2 Locations of 43 societies on global cultural map, 1990–1991.
Source: Inglehart, 1997: 93.

on earlier surveys, one finds the same basic pattern, with cultural
zones consisting of Protestant Europe, Catholic Europe, the English-
speaking countries, Latin America, Africa, the Confucian countries,
South Asia and Eastern Europe/Orthodox all in similar positions on
the two cultural maps.[9] But Figure 3.3 is based on surveys carried
out more than 20 years later than those in Figure 3.2, adding scores
of new countries and dropping several countries that were included
earlier: the later map includes more than twice as many countries
as the earlier one. Nevertheless, the overall pattern is remarkably
similar. The 1990 map included only four Latin American countries;
the 2011 map contains ten – but they all fall in the same region. The

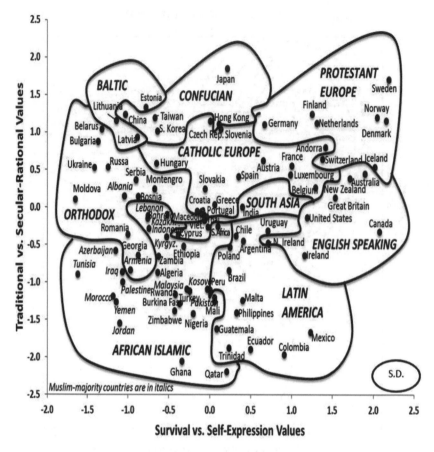

Figure 3.3 Locations of 94 societies on global cultural map, 2008–2014 (median year of survey is 2011).

Source: Values Surveys. The size of the mean standard deviation within a given country is shown on the lower right. The names of Muslim-majority societies are in italics.

1990 map had only two African countries while the 2011 map has 11 – but they too fall in the same region at the lower-left. The 1990 map had only one Muslim-majority country (and thus no Islamic zone); the 2008–2014 map has 15 Muslim-majority countries (five of which are in Africa), and they all fall into the lower-left quadrant together with the African countries. Their relative positions on these two dimensions were remarkably stable attributes of given countries from 1981 to 2014.

Welzel has developed alternative measures of cross-cultural variation that are conceptually and empirically rather similar to these two dimensions:[10] at the national level, the scores on Welzel's Sacred vs. Secular values dimension correlate with Traditional/Secular-rational values at r = .82, and his Survival/Emancipative values dimension correlates with Survival/Self-expression values at r = .80. Though his measures are constructed in a more elegant way than mine, they are correlated with each other (r = .56) which is logical, since they tap two phases of the modernization process. But this has the drawback of pulling any two-dimensional map into a long, narrow diamond shape. My two dimensions are constructed to be uncorrelated, which distorts reality somewhat (as does any two-dimensional map of the world) but makes it possible to display the relative positions of many countries on each dimension in a clearer, less crowded fashion.

Evolutionary modernization theory holds that rising levels of existential security are conducive to a shift from Traditional values to Secular-rational values, and from Survival values to Self-expression values. Accordingly, as we have seen, virtually all of the high-income countries rank high on both dimensions, falling into the upper-right region of the chart – while virtually all of the low and lower-middle-income countries rank low on both dimensions, falling into the lower-left region of the chart.

But the evidence also supports the Weberian view that a society's religious values leave a lasting imprint. The publics of Protestant Europe show relatively similar values across scores of questions – as do the publics of Catholic Europe, the Confucian-influenced societies, the Orthodox societies, the English-speaking countries, Latin America and sub-Saharan Africa. At first glance, these clusters might seem to reflect geographic proximity, but this holds true only when geographic proximity coincides with cultural similarity. Thus, the English-speaking zone extends from Great Britain and Ireland to the USA and Canada to Australia and New Zealand, while the Latin American zone extends from Tiajuana to Patagonia; and an Islamic subgroup within the African–Islamic cluster shows that Morocco is culturally relatively close to Indonesia, though they are on opposite sides of the globe. The cross-national differences found here reflect each society's economic *and* sociocultural history.

Is it justifiable to use national-level mean scores on these variables as indicators of societies' attributes? National means tell only part of the story; measures of variance and skew are also informative. But having examined them, we conclude that the most interesting statistical aspect of subjective orientations are the differences in national-level means.

One can imagine a world in which everyone with a university-level education had modern values, placing them near the upper-right-hand corner of the map – while everyone with little or no education clustered near the lower-left-hand corner of the map. We would be living in a global village where nationality was unimportant. Perhaps some day the world will look like that, but the reality today is quite different. Although individual Swedes or Nigerians can fall anywhere on the map, there is surprisingly little overlap between the prevailing orientations of large groups from one country and their peers in other countries. The cross-national cultural differences are so large that they dwarf the differences within given societies. The ellipse in the lower-right-hand corner of Figure 3.3 shows the size of the mean standard deviation on each dimension *within* given countries.[11] It occupies a tiny fraction of the map. Two-thirds of the average country's respondents fall within one standard deviation of their country's mean score on both dimensions and 95 percent fall within two standard deviations. Despite globalization, nations remain an important unit of shared experiences, and the predictive power of nationality is much stronger than that of income, education, region or sex.[12]

Modernization-Linked Attitudes Tend to Be Enduring and Cross-nationally Comparable

The two main dimensions of cross-cultural variation constitute stable attributes of given societies that are fully as stable as per capita GNP. Most attitudinal variables tap transient orientations. But the forces of modernization have impacted on large numbers of societies in enduring and comparable ways. Urbanization, industrialization, rising educational levels, occupational specialization and bureaucratization produce enduring changes in people's worldviews. They do not make all societies alike, but they do tend to make societies that have experienced them *differ* from societies that have not experienced them, in consistent ways. For example, modernization tends to make religion less influential. Specific religious beliefs vary immensely, but the worldviews of people for whom religion is important differ from those for whom religion is not important in remarkably consistent ways.

Our theory holds that Self-expression values should be strongly correlated with indicators of economic modernization. Although measured at different levels and by different methods, we find remarkably strong linkages between individual-level values and societies' economic characteristics. Across all available societies, the average correlation between Self-expression values and ten widely used economic modernization indicators, ranging from per capita GDP and mean life expectancy to educational levels, is .77.[13]

The Self-expression/Individualism/Autonomy Super-dimension

Survival/Self-expression values have been measured in hundreds of surveys in countries containing 90 percent of the world's population. This dimension is robust. In wave after wave of the Values Surveys, the relative positions of given countries on the global cultural map are remarkably stable over time. Relative scores on this dimension are much more stable than most other orientations: only religion and its close correlate, Traditional/Secular-rational values, shows even greater stability. The Values Surveys have measured over 100 orientations repeatedly in scores of countries over the last 35 years. The correlations between a country's position on the earliest and latest available surveys range from a low of .04 (in response to the question, "Do you live with your parents?") to a high of .93 (in response to the question "How important is religion in your life?"). The stability of responses concerning religion is not surprising. Whether religion is considered extremely important or completely unimportant is one of the most deeply rooted aspects of any culture. For religious people, one's views on this topic are instilled early in life, supported by religious institutions, and reinforced by weekly or even daily prayer – while secular people have the opposite experience. But Survival/Self-expression values, though not supported by any formal institutions and having no clear external label, are almost as stable as religion: r = .89.

Moreover, the Survival/Self-expression values dimension seems to tap a dimension of cross-cultural variation that psychologists have been studying for decades under the name of "Collectivism/Individualism." Oyserman, Coon and Kemmelmeier cite hundreds of studies dealing with Individualism/Collectivism. Individualism is usually seen as the opposite of Collectivism.[14] Social psychologists find that Individualism is more prevalent in Western societies than elsewhere, arguing that Protestantism and civic emancipation in Western societies led to institutions that gave greater scope to individual choice, personal freedom and self-actualization.

Hofstede defined Individualism as a focus on rights above duties, a concern for oneself and immediate family, an emphasis on personal autonomy and self-fulfillment, and basing identity on one's personal accomplishments.[15] Collectivism emphasizes conformity to group norms and goals. In collectivist societies, group membership is a central aspect of identity and collectivist goals, such as sacrifice for the common good, are highly valued. Furthermore, Collectivism implies that life satisfaction derives from successfully carrying out social roles and obligations, and restraint in emotional expression is valued to ensure in-group harmony.

Hofstede first measured "Individualism/Collectivism" in the early 1970s in surveys of IBM employees in scores of countries. Despite the lapse of several decades and although he did not use representative national samples, the relative positions of the countries Hofstede measured around 1973 correspond closely to the relative positions of countries on the Survival/Self-expression values dimension, as measured in national surveys conducted several decades later.

Furthermore, Survival/Self-expression values also seem to tap the same dimension of cross-cultural variation as does Schwartz's "Autonomy/Embeddedness" dimension. Schwartz examined a broad array of values. Factor analysis of data from scores of countries reveals an Autonomy–Embeddedness dimension that corresponds to the concept of Individualism and Collectivism. According to Schwartz:

> In autonomy cultures, people are viewed as autonomous, bounded entities. They cultivate and express their own preferences, feelings, ideas, and abilities, and find meaning in their own uniqueness... In embeddedness cultures, meaning in life comes largely through social relationships, identifying with the group, participating in its shared way of life, and striving toward its shared goals. Embedded cultures emphasize maintaining the status quo and restraining actions that might disrupt in-group solidarity or the traditional order.[16]

Table 3.2 *The Self-expression/Individualism/Autonomy factor (first principal component loadings)*

Survival/Self-expression values, national mean scores	.93
Individualism-Collectivism scores (Hofstede)	.89
Autonomy-Embeddedness scores (Schwartz)	.87

One factor emerged, which explains 80 percent of the cross-national variation. *Source*: Values Survey data; Hofstede 2001 (with additional country scores from Chiao and Blizinsky, 2009); and Schwartz (2003).

As Table 3.2 above demonstrates, despite large differences in theoretical approaches and measuring techniques, Survival/Self-expression values, Individualism/Collectivism and Autonomy/Embeddedness all tap a single underlying dimension that accounts for 81 percent of the cross-national variation. Countries that rank high on Self-expression (rather than Survival values) tend to rank high on both Individualism (rather than Collectivism) and Autonomy (rather than Embeddedness). I will refer to this underlying super-dimension as Self-expression/Individualist/Autonomy values. Survival/Self-expression values show the strongest loading on this super-dimension, correlating with it at .93, but Individualism/Collectivism and Autonomy-Embeddedness also show very strong correlations.

The fact that these three dimensions go together so closely at the national level is a remarkable finding for several reasons. First, because Hofstede did not measure Individualism/Collectivism using representative national samples – his studies were based on surveys of IBM employees.[17] Furthermore, although Hofstede covered scores of countries, his surveys were conducted around 1973 – but the cross-national differences he found then correspond closely to those found in representative national surveys in the twenty-first century. Clearly, IBM employees are not representative of their national populations, so the absolute levels of their values do not provide accurate measures of the national means. Nevertheless, if they deviate from the national mean in the same direction, and by roughly the same amount, then the *relative* positions of given societies will be in the right ball park. Furthermore, most of Hofstede's fieldwork was carried out in the early 1970s. As Inglehart and Welzel have demonstrated, in recent decades there has been a systematic shift toward growing emphasis on Self-expression values.[18] Being linked with rising levels of existential security, this shift has been strongest in high-income countries, but it has also affected other societies to some extent.

Nevertheless, the *relative* positions of given societies that Hofstede found around 1973 correspond closely to those of the same societies measured in recent representative national surveys. This may seem astonishing. But if – as Inglehart and Welzel have found – virtually all developed countries are moving in the same direction at roughly the same pace, their *relative* positions will remain roughly constant.[19] A growing gap has been opening up between the values of the people in high-income countries and those in low-income countries, but this has left the rank order of their positions largely unchanged. The positions of given countries on the global cultural map in the earliest available survey are strongly correlated with their positions in the latest available survey, as measured thirty years later.

The same principles apply to Schwartz's measures of Autonomy/Embeddedness values. They were not measured with representative national samples – Schwartz studied students, who clearly are not a representative sample of their countries' populations. But if the students deviate from their national means in the same direction, and by roughly the same amount, then the *relative* positions they show for given societies will be reasonably accurate. Accordingly, the relative positions of given countries on the Autonomy/Embeddedness dimension correspond closely to those found on both Survival/Self-expression values and Individualism/Collectivism. As Table 3.2 indicates, the correspondence is astonishingly strong. Survival/Self-expression values, Individualism/Collectivism and Autonomy/Embeddedness all tap a common underlying dimension, with Survival/Self-expression values showing the highest loading.[20] Individualism-Collectivism, Autonomy-Embeddedness and Survival/Self-expression values all reflect variation in the extent to which given societies allow people a narrow or broad range of free choice. Scarcity and insecurity impose severe constraints on human choice but modernization gradually frees people from the rigid cultural constraints that prevail under insecure conditions.

An additional reason why this Self-expression/Individualism/Autonomy super-dimension is so robust may be because its cross-national differences reflect genetic variation – which in turn is rooted in different levels of historic vulnerability to disease and starvation as Gelfand et al. and Thornhill and Fincher have argued.[21] Examining the impact of biological factors on culture, Chiao and Blizinsky find linkages between genetic factors and collectivist attitudes, arguing that cultural values have evolved, adapting to the social and physical environments under which genetic selection operates.[22] The evidence suggests that certain populations evolved in environments that were relatively vulnerable to disease, giving a survival advantage to genetic variations linked with avoidance of strangers and strict conformity to social taboos – while other populations evolved in environments that were less vulnerable to disease, which gave a survival advantage to genetic variation linked with greater openness to strangers and different social norms. This led to the emergence of a pattern of cross-cultural variation in which some societies were relatively closed to outsiders and cultural diversity, while other societies were relatively open. Empirically, the Individualism/Collectivism dimension that Chiao and Blizinsky use is rather closely correlated with Self-expression values.[23]

Economic development, the emergence of the welfare state and other historic factors can change people's values considerably – but the process is path dependent, with the influence of genetic differences persisting to some degree. With technological development, human vulnerability to disease has diminished dramatically – but its historic impact has not disappeared. Even today, cross-national differences on this cultural super-dimension are so robust that any competently designed study seems likely to uncover them.

The work of Acemoglu and Robinson also points in this direction.[24] They trace the roots of economic development and democracy back for 500 years, attempting to determine which came first. They conclude that both economic development and democracy can be traced to enduring fixed national effects – which they claim reflect institutional differences. But calling them institutions is arbitrary: fixed national effects capture any enduring attribute of given countries, from institutions to language to culture to climate and topography and historic vulnerability to disease. Recent research has produced additional relevant evidence, with Shcherbak finding that cross-national differences in lactose intolerance have a genetic basis and are strongly correlated with cross-national differences on this cultural super-dimension.[25] Meyer-Schwarzenberger analyzes the structure of 166 languages, finding strong and robust correlations between Self-expression values and a measure of Linguistic Individualism that may also be rooted in genetic differences.[26] Inglehart et al. find strong correlations between cross-national variation on certain genes, and the extent to which a given society emphasizes tolerance and Self-expression values.[27]

Building on earlier exercises in genetic mapping, Inglehart et al. gathered data on 79 STR allele frequencies of five genetic markers used in forensic genetic testing to identify people's ethnic origins.[28] They obtained data from 39 countries (countries such as the USA, Canada, Australia, Uruguay and Argentina – populated mainly by immigrants from other countries – were not included). A principal components factor analysis of each country's mean score on the 79 STR alleles produces two main dimensions. When we map the 39 countries on these two dimensions, they fall into five geographic clusters, grouping countries in Europe, sub-Saharan Africa, South America, South Asia and North Africa, and East and Southeast Asia – replicating some of the clusters found on the global cultural maps shown above. The first principal component could be interpreted as reflecting the degree of historical parasite prevalence, with which it is correlated at r = −.86. It seems possible that historical vulnerability to disease may, over the course of many centuries, have given a survival advantage to certain genetic variations over others.

I do *not* view a country's score on this genetic variation dimension as reflecting genetic variation and nothing else: like Acemoglu and Robinson's Fixed Country Effects, this score is a black box that reflects not only genetic variation but also anything else that co-varies with geography. But since this score is directly derived from measures of genetic variation, it would be rash to deny that it *includes* genetic variation – along with differences in culture, language, institutions, topography, climate and anything else linked with a country's geographic location.

Benjamin et al. analyzed a sample of comprehensively genotyped subjects with data on economic and political preferences, finding evidence of significant heritability of these traits – but also finding evidence that the heritable variation on these traits is explained by many genes with small effects.[29] Coupled with the fact that genetic variation goes in clusters, this has important implications. At this stage, we don't know which genes (if any) are shaping cross-cultural variation on the Self-expression/Individualism/Autonomy Super-dimension. But a growing body of evidence suggests that genetic factors may be involved – in a complex causal chain linked with climatic conditions and historic vulnerability to disease.

Cultural differences reflect a society's entire historical heritage – and this heritage can be reshaped by dynamic societal processes. In other words, Individualism is not a static individual-level psychological attribute – it is shaped by a society's level of development. Self-expression values, Autonomy values and Individualism all tap a set of orientations that become more widespread as existential constraints on human choice recede. Modernization facilitates a shift away from Collectivism, toward Individualism, bringing increasing emphasis on individual autonomy and weakening traditional hierarchical norms. This cultural shift, in turn, is conducive to societal changes such as the emergence and flourishing of democratic institutions. Possibly because of linkages with genetic variation, this pattern of cross-cultural variation is so robust and so deep-rooted that almost any competently designed empirical study of cross-cultural differences is likely to uncover it – and researchers in a wide range of fields have done so.

Value Change on Two Major Dimensions

Evolutionary modernization theory holds that the pervasive differences we have found between the values of rich and poor societies reflect a process of intergenerational value change that occurs when societies attain such high levels of existential security that the younger birth cohorts grow up taking survival for granted. If so, we would expect to find more intergenerational value change in high-income societies than in low-income societies.

As Figure 3.4 indicates, empirical evidence supports this expectation. The vertical axis on this graph reflects the extent to which given birth cohorts in given types of countries emphasize Survival values or Self-expression values. As it demonstrates, the publics of high-income societies emphasize Self-expression values much more strongly than the publics of low-income or middle-income countries. But we also find that the *intergenerational differences* are much greater in high-income societies than elsewhere: the oldest cohort (born in 1927 or earlier) is only slightly above the global mean on Survival versus Self-expression values (the zero point on the vertical scale); but among the youngest cohort (born since 1978), Self-expression values are almost one standard deviation above the mean for the world as a whole.

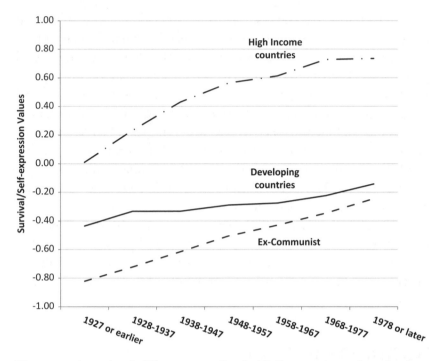

Figure 3.4 Age-related differences on Survival/Self-expression values, in three types of societies.
Source: Values Surveys, 1981–2014. The countries included in each of the three types of societies are listed in Appendix 2.

Among the publics of developing countries, we find much less emphasis on Self-expression values – and only a slight increase in emphasis on Self-expression values as we move from old to young: these countries are still approaching the threshold at which a substantial share of the population has grown up taking survival for granted.

The publics of ex-communist societies show even lower levels of emphasis on Self-expression values – but we find a relatively strong intergenerational increase in emphasis on these values as we move from old to young. The publics of these societies attained relatively high levels of existential security during the decades after World War II, producing a substantial amount of intergenerational value change. But the collapse of communism and existential security around 1990 produced strong period effects that drove down all birth cohorts' absolute levels of Self-expression values to levels from which they have not yet recovered.

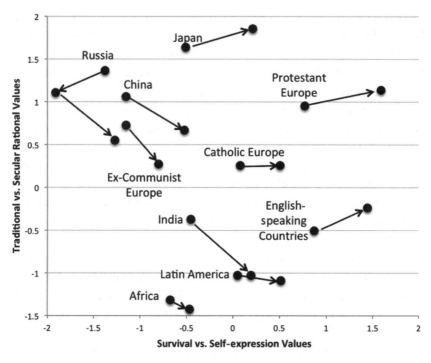

Figure 3.5 Net change on two major dimensions of cross-cultural variation from earliest to latest available survey (1981–2014) in ten types of societies.
The countries included in each of the ten types of societies are listed below in Appendix A2.4.

This pattern of age differences, together with the strong linkage found between value systems and per capita GDP, suggests that economic development brings systematic changes in a society's beliefs and values. Time-series evidence supports this expectation. Tracing given countries' positions in successive surveys from 1981 to 2014, one finds that the publics of virtually all high-income countries moved in the predicted direction. As Figure 3.5 demonstrates, the publics of eight Protestant European countries, eight Catholic European countries plus seven English-speaking countries and Japan, all moved toward greater emphasis on Secular-rational values and Self-expression values.[30]

In striking contrast, the publics of Russia, China and a group of 21 other former communist countries moved toward greater emphasis on Traditional values. This reflects the resurgence of religion that occurred following the collapse of the communist belief system. Although Africa, Latin America and the Islamic countries show the highest *levels* of religiosity, they changed very little from 1981 to 2014. By far the largest *gains* in religiosity occurred in the ex-communist world, where religion and nationalism moved in to fill the ideological vacuum left by the collapse of a communist belief system that once gave a sense of meaning and purpose to millions of people.

Despite this increasing emphasis on Traditional values, rising economic security brought a significant overall increase in emphasis on Self-expression values. Russia was a particularly dramatic case: initially, it experienced a much sharper decline in existential security than most other ex-communist countries, with real per capita income falling to about 40 percent of its previous high, along with rising crime, and declining male life expectancy. These conditions began to reverse themselves around 2000, when Putin restored order and oil and gas prices recovered, bringing strong economic recovery. The Russian public shifted from rising emphasis on Survival values and moved toward growing acceptance of Self-expression values – but traditional values continued to fill the vacuum left by the collapse of the communist belief system.

The values of African publics show very little change. Sub-Saharan Africa has recently begun to enjoy strong economic growth, but because cultural change involves long time-lags, we would not expect to see them emerge in the adult population for some time.

Conclusion

We have found that rising levels of existential security tend to bring coherent and roughly predictable social and cultural changes, leading the people of relatively secure societies to have systematically different values from those of less developed societies. Though globalization has undermined the bargaining position of workers in high-income countries, it is transferring capital and technology to other countries throughout the world, raising their levels of existential security and bringing greater openness to new ideas and more egalitarian social norms.

Cultural change is path-dependent: a society's values reflect its entire historical heritage. But despite approaching it from different theoretical perspectives and using completely different measurement methods, researchers in many different fields have found a pattern in which existentially secure societies consistently rank high on an underlying Individualism/Autonomy/Self-expression super-dimension, while less secure societies consistently rank low on it. How this dimension is labeled and how it is interpreted is shaped by one's theoretical expectations, but this pattern of cross-cultural variation is so robust and deep-rooted that a variety of empirical studies of cross-cultural differences, carried out by researchers from a wide range of disciplines, have uncovered it. This super-dimension of cross-cultural variation seems to be shaping contemporary levels of democracy and legislation concerning gender equality, gays and lesbians and many other topics, as succeeding chapters will demonstrate.

4 THE END OF SECULARIZATION?*

The leading social thinkers of the nineteenth century – Comte, Spencer, Durkheim, Weber, Marx and Freud – all believed that religious beliefs reflected a pre-scientific worldview that would gradually disappear as scientific rationality became increasingly widespread.[1] And ever since the Enlightenment, leading figures in philosophy, anthropology and psychology have postulated that theological superstitions, liturgical rituals and sacred practices will be outgrown in the modern era. During most of the twentieth century, many social scientists assumed that religion was disappearing, and secularization was ranked with bureaucratization, rationalization and urbanization as an inherent aspect of modernization.

More recently, this thesis has been challenged. The growth of fundamentalist[2] movements and religious parties in the Muslim world, the evangelical revival sweeping through Latin America and many former communist countries, and the prominence of fundamentalist politics in the USA demonstrate that religion has not died out and shows no sign of doing so. It remains a powerful factor in social and political life. Prominent critics suggest that it is time to bury the secularization thesis, arguing that religion is a permanent feature of human society. The decisive factor in whether religion flourishes or decays, they claim, is whether religious leaders energetically build and maintain their congregations.[3]

Religious market theory provides the most prominent challenge to the secularization thesis. It suggests that supply-side factors, notably denominational competition and state regulation of religious

---

* This chapter draws on Norris and Inglehart, 2011.

institutions, shape levels of religious participation. In recent decades, many social scientists have advanced this account, although it has encountered sustained criticism.[4] Market-based theories of religion assume that the demand for religious products is constant, based on the otherworldly rewards of life after death promised by most faiths. Dissimilar levels of religious behavior in various countries are said to result less from "bottom up" demand than from "top down" variance in religious supply. Established churches are said to be complacent monopolies taking their congregations for granted, with a fixed market share due to state regulation and subsidy for the established faith. By contrast, where a free religious marketplace exists, energetic competition between churches expands the supply of religious "products," thereby mobilizing religious activism among the public.

The theory claims to be a universal generalization, but the evidence supporting it is mainly drawn from the United States and Western Europe. The proliferation of diverse churches in the United States is claimed to have maximized choice and competition among faiths, stimulating religiosity among the American public. American churches are subject to market forces, depending on their ability to attract clergy, volunteers and financial resources. Competition produces diversity, stimulates innovation and compels churches to actively recruit congregations by responding to public demands. Starke and Finke argue that most European nations, by contrast, sustain what they term "a *socialized* religious economy," with state subsidies for established churches. Religious monopolies, they claim, are less innovative, responsive and efficient. Where the clergy enjoy secure incomes and tenure regardless of their performance, they will grow complacent, slothful, and lax: "when people have little need or motive to work, they tend not to work, and subsidized churches will therefore be lazy."[5] Finke and Stark believe that if the "supply" of churches was expanded in Europe through disestablishment (deregulation), and if churches made more effort, this would lead to a resurgence of religious behavior among the public: "Faced with American-style churches, Europeans would respond as Americans do." In short, they conclude, "To the extent that organizations work harder, they are more successful."[6]

Were Comte, Durkheim, Weber and Marx completely wrong in their beliefs about the decline of religion in industrialized societies? We think not. The supply-side critique relies on selected anomalies and focuses heavily on the United States (which happens to be a deviant case) rather than comparing systematic evidence across a broad range of rich and poor societies. This theory fails to explain why virtually all Muslim-majority societies are much more religious than the USA, though one religion not only holds a monopoly in most of these societies but can sometimes even impose the death penalty on anyone converting to another faith.

There is no question that the traditional secularization thesis needs updating. It is obvious that religion has not disappeared from the world, nor does it seem likely to do so. Nevertheless, the concept of secularization captures an important part of what is going on. Evolutionary modernization theory emphasizes the importance of a sense of existential security: when people feel that survival is so secure that it can be taken for granted, religion becomes less important. If this is true, we should find religiosity to be strongest among vulnerable populations, especially those facing survival-threatening risks. We argue that economic and physical insecurity is a key factor driving religiosity and will demonstrate that the process of secularization – a systematic erosion of religious practices, values and beliefs – has moved farthest among the most prosperous strata of secure postindustrial nations.

Religion is not an unchanging aspect of human nature. Anthropological studies have found that the belief in a creator God who is concerned with human moral conduct is rarely found in hunting and gathering societies. Instead of accepting this core concept of contemporary world religions, the people of hunting and gathering societies tend to have animist beliefs that local spirits inhabit trees, rivers, mountains and other natural features. The concept of a God concerned with moral conduct remains rare among horticultural societies; it only becomes prevalent with the emergence of agrarian societies.

Since the Biblical era, changing concepts of God have evolved – from an angry and punitive tribal God who could be placated by human sacrifice, and who not only accepted but demanded genocide against outsiders – to a benevolent God whose laws applied to all of humanity. Moral concepts are also evolving, in ways that are linked with socioeconomic development. Prevailing moral norms have changed gradually throughout history, but in recent decades the pace of change has accelerated sharply.

The decline of xenophobia, racism, sexism and homophobia are part of a long-term trend away from inward-looking tribal moral norms, under which large parts of humanity were excluded from moral

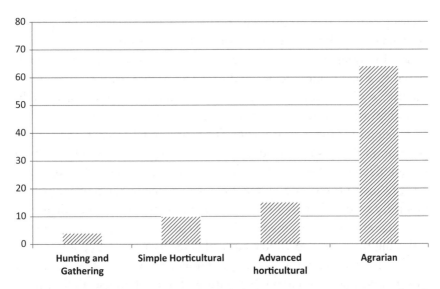

Figure 4.1 Percentage of societies with a belief in a creator God concerned with human moral conduct.
Source: Nolan and Lenski, 2011: 72, based on data from George Peter Murdock *Ethnographic Atlas* (1962–1971).

citizenship, and genocide and slavery were standard practice. The distinction is fading between an in-group, who merits just treatment, and outgroups, to whom moral norms do not apply. Globalization and the emergence of knowledge societies is linked with a trend toward universal moral norms in which formerly excluded groups, such as foreigners, women and gays, are believed to have human rights. And war is becoming less acceptable for a growing part of the world's population.

Rights have existed for centuries, but they originally applied only to given individuals or social classes.[7] After World War II, the United Nations Charter included the concept of universal human rights, though some of the founding members were dictatorships that blatantly ignored human rights. But with the spread of democracy, support for the idea of universal human rights has become increasingly widespread.

Evolutionary modernization theory suggests that economic and political changes go together with cultural developments in coherent and consistent ways. As societies develop from agrarian to industrial economies and then to postindustrial societies, growing existential security reduces the importance of religion in people's lives. The greater economic and physical security, longevity and health found in postindustrial nations mean that fewer people in these societies view traditional spiritual values, beliefs and practices as vital to their lives, or to the lives of their community. This does not imply that all forms of religion disappear; some elements may remain, such as formal adherence to religious identities, even when their emotional impact and central position in life has dwindled. But people living in advanced industrial societies tend to become less obedient to traditional religious leaders and institutions, and less inclined to engage in religious activities. Contrary to the claims of the religious markets school, the "demand" for religion is far from constant; instead striking variations are evident, reflecting the degree to which survival is secure or insecure.

In pre-industrial societies, humanity was at the mercy of inscrutable and uncontrollable natural forces. Because their causes were dimly understood, people tended to attribute whatever happened to anthropomorphic spirits or gods. When the majority of the population began to make their living from agriculture, they were largely dependent on things that came from heaven, like the sun and rain. Farmers prayed for good weather, for relief from disease, or from plagues of insects.

Industrialization brings a cognitive mismatch between traditional normative systems, and the world which most people know from their first-hand experience. The symbols and worldview of the established religions are no longer as persuasive or compelling as they were in their original setting. In industrial society, production moves indoors into a man-made environment. Workers do not passively wait for the sun to rise and the seasons to change. When it gets dark, people turn on the lights; when it gets cold, people turn up the heating. Factory workers do not pray for good crops – production depends on machines created by human ingenuity. With the discovery of germs and antibiotics, even disease ceases to be seen as a divine visitation; it becomes a problem that is increasingly under human control.

Such profound changes in people's daily experience lead to changes in the prevailing cosmology. In industrial society, where the factory is the center of production, a mechanistic view of the universe seems natural. Initially, this gave rise to the concept of God as a great watchmaker who had constructed the universe and then left it to run largely on its own. But as human control of the environment increased, the role ascribed to God dwindled. Materialistic ideologies arose that proposed secular interpretations of history, and secular utopias to be attained by human engineering. As knowledge societies evolved, the mechanical world of the factory became less pervasive. People's life experiences dealt more with ideas than with material things. In the knowledge society, productivity depends less on material constraints than on information, innovation, and imagination. Concern about the meaning and purpose of life has not dwindled. But under the conditions of existential insecurity that dominated the lives of most people throughout most of history, the great theological questions concerned a relatively narrow constituency; the vast majority of the population was more concerned with the need for reassurance in the face of a world where survival was uncertain, and this was the dominant factor motivating the grip of traditional religion on mass publics.

Virtually all of the world's major religious cultures provide reassurance that, even though the individual alone can't understand or predict what lies ahead, a higher power will ensure that things work out. Both religion and secular ideologies assure people that the universe follows a plan, which guarantees that if you follow the rules, everything will turn out well, in this world or the next. This belief reduces stress, enabling people to cope with anxiety and focus on dealing with their immediate problems. Without such a belief system, extreme stress tends to produce withdrawal reactions. Under conditions of insecurity, people have a powerful need to see authority as both strong and benevolent – even in the face of evidence to the contrary.

Individuals under stress yearn for rigid, predictable rules. They want to be sure of what is going to happen because survival is precarious and their margin for error is slender. Conversely, people raised under conditions of relative security can tolerate more ambiguity and have less need for the absolute and rigid rules that religions provide. People with relatively high levels of existential security can more readily accept deviations from familiar patterns than people who are uncertain that their survival needs will be met. In economically secure industrial societies, with an established social safety-net insuring people against the risks of poverty, an increasing sense of security brings a diminishing need for absolute rules, contributing to the decline of traditional religious institutions.

The Values Surveys ask each respondent to rate the importance of six major aspects of life, family, work, religion, friends,

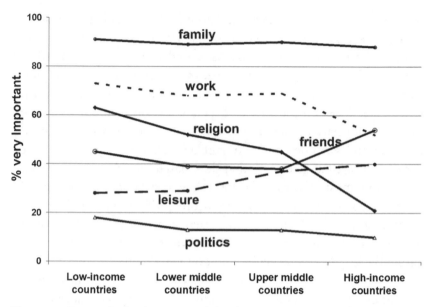

Figure 4.2 Economic development and the changing importance of major aspects of life.

leisure and politics. Figure 4.2 shows the percentage saying that a given domain is "Very important" in their life, based on hundreds of thousands of interviews in countries containing most of the world's population. Virtually everyone views the family as very important – this seems to be a constant across rich and poor societies. But the importance attached to religion drops sharply as we move from low-income societies (where 62 percent of the population consider it very important) to high-income societies (where only 20 percent consider it very important). In low-income societies, only family and work are rated as more important than religion. In high-income societies, both friends and leisure are rated as more important than religion. The cross-sectional evidence in Figure 4.2 suggests, but does not prove, that the importance of religion declines in high-income societies (the time-series evidence presented below in Figure 4.3 does so). The demand for religion is far from constant.

Emphasis on friendship shows a curvilinear pattern, declining as one moves away from the face-to-face communities of low-income countries, and then showing a renewed emphasis on friendship in high-income societies. In low-income societies, religion is considerably more important than friends and vastly more important than leisure.

Conversely, a central characteristic of high-income societies is the fact that both friends and leisure are more important than religion.

The linkage between economic security and secularization is a tendency, not an iron law. One can easily think of striking individual exceptions, such as Osama bin Laden who was very rich and fanatically religious. But when we go beyond anecdotal evidence, we find that the overwhelming bulk of evidence points in the opposite direction: people who experience threats to themselves and their families or their community during their formative years tend to be far more religious than those who grow up under safer and more predictable conditions. In relatively secure societies, religion has not disappeared. In surveys most West Europeans still say they believe in God, or identify themselves as Protestants or Catholics on official forms. But the importance and vitality of religion, and its influence on how people live their daily lives, has eroded markedly. During the twentieth century in nearly all postindustrial nations – from Canada and Sweden to France, Britain and Australia – official church records show that where church attendance once was high, it has declined to the point where today, churches are being converted to museums or hotels. Public opinion surveys monitoring European church-going during the last fifty years confirm this phenomenon.

The overall trend is clear: in advanced industrial societies, church attendance has fallen during the past several decades; moreover, the clergy have largely lost their authority over the public and are no longer able to dictate to them concerning birth control, divorce, abortion, sexual orientation and the necessity of marriage before childbirth. Secularization is not limited to Western Europe, as some critics have claimed. It is occurring in most advanced industrial societies including Australia, New Zealand, Japan and Canada. The United States remains an outlier among postindustrial societies, with a public that holds more traditional worldviews than that of any other high-income country except Ireland. But even in America, there has been a clear trend toward secularization; this trend has been weakened by the country's relatively weak social welfare institutions and high levels of economic inequality, and partly masked by massive Hispanic immigration, bringing in people with relatively traditional worldviews and high fertility rates. But despite these factors, even the USA shows a clear trend toward secularization. Weekly church attendance declined from about 35 percent in 1972 to 25 percent in 2002, while the percentage saying that they never attend church rose from 9 percent to about 20 percent.[8]

Nevertheless, religion is unlikely to disappear in the foreseeable future. In a previous book, Norris and I argued that:

1. The publics of virtually all advanced industrial societies have been moving toward more secular orientations during the past fifty years. Nevertheless,
2. The world as a whole now has more people with traditional religious views than ever before – and they constitute a growing proportion of the world's population.

> Though these two propositions initially seem contradictory, they are not. As we will see, the fact that the first proposition is true helps account for the second – because secularization reduces human fertility rates. Practically all of the countries in which secularization is most advanced, show fertility rates far below the replacement level – while societies with traditional religious orientations have fertility rates that are two or three times the replacement level. They contain a growing share of the world's population.[9]

Due to these demographic trends, the world as a whole now has more people with traditional religious views than ever before – and they constitute a growing proportion of the world's population. Rich societies are secularizing but they contain a declining share of the world's population; while poor societies are not secularizing and they contain a rising share of the world's population. Thus, modernization does indeed bring a de-emphasis on religion within virtually any country that experiences it – but the percentage of the world's population for whom religion is important, is rising.

The differential fertility rates of religious and secular societies is by no means coincidental; it is directly linked with secularization. The shift from traditional religious values to Secular-rational values brings a cultural shift from emphasis on traditional roles for women, largely limited to producing and raising many children, to a world in which women have an increasingly broad range of life choices, and most women have careers and interests outside the home. This cultural shift is linked with a dramatic decline in fertility rates, as Chapter 5 will demonstrate.

Classic secularization theory held that religion would gradually disappear, with the spread of education and scientific knowledge. But influential recent work that we have cited claims that the human demand for religion is fixed and only requires energetic religious entrepreneurs to be revitalized – or even that there has been a global resurgence of religion.[10] What has actually been happening?

Has religion been disappearing, or are we witnessing a global resurgence of religion? Figure 4.3 shows the changes that have taken place in response to the question, "How important is God in your life?" This question has been asked in every wave of the Values Surveys since 1981 and is a particularly sensitive indicator of religiosity, being strongly correlated with the responses to a score of other questions concerning religion. It uses a ten-point scale on which "1" indicates that God is not at all important in the respondent's life, and "10" indicates that God is very important. This figure shows the changes in the percentage choosing "10" on this scale, from a country's earliest available survey to its latest available survey in all 60 countries from which we have a time series of at least ten years (the median time-span being 21 years). As this figure indicates, as many societies experienced declining religiosity as rising religiosity. Because of widely differing human fertility rates, a larger share of the world's population is religious today than it was 30 years ago, but among the 60 countries examined here, religiosity rose in 30 countries and fell in 30. And the pattern of changes was far from random.

People living in Africa, Latin America and countries with Muslim majorities are far more religious than people living in most other countries, as Figure 3.3 in the previous chapter suggests (virtually all such countries are located on the lower half of the map, reflecting their emphasis on Traditional values). They already ranked high on religiosity in the earliest available survey and they continue to do so – but Figure 4.3 focuses on *change*, and most of these countries showed little change.

Around 1990, most ex-communist countries experienced the collapse of their political, social and economic systems, the breakdown of order and the collapse of a communist ideology that once gave a sense of predictability and meaning to the lives of many people. This opened an ideological vacuum that is being filled by a resurgence of religion and nationalism. Consequently, we find growing emphasis on religion in those societies that were hardest hit by the collapse of the communist order.

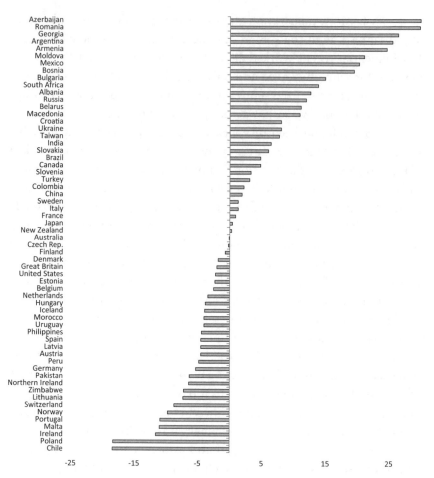

Figure 4.3 Change in percentage saying God is very important in their life, from earliest to latest survey.

Source: World Values Survey and European Values Study surveys carried out from 1981 to 2012, including all countries providing at least a ten-year time series. The median change is zero; the median time-span covered is 21 years.

Thirteen of the 16 countries showing the largest gains in religiosity are ex-communist (including China, still ruled by a communist party but now having one of the world's most competitive market economies and a Gini economic inequality index even higher than that of the USA). Sixteen of the 22 ex-communist countries show increased religiosity – and all six exceptions (Poland, Hungary, the Czech Republic and the three Baltic countries) made relatively smooth transitions to market economies and are now members of the European Union and NATO: if existential security is conducive to secularization, these are countries that would be expected to secularize. Poland is the most extreme exception to the tendency for ex-communist countries to become more religious, showing one of the most dramatic declines in religiosity to be found among these 60 countries. For most of its history since 1792, Poland was ruled by Russia, Austria and Prussia, and then by the Soviet Union. The Roman Catholic church became a center of resistance to rule by the Protestant Prussians and Orthodox Russians, and finally by Atheist Soviet oppressors. Being a practicing Catholic was a way to show support for Polish independence. The Polish population became hyper-Catholic, in much the same way as the Irish became hyper-Catholic in resistance to domination by Protestant England. During the last 25 years Poland has been free from Soviet domination and is now a relatively secure member of the European Union and NATO. Without the stimulus of oppression by neighbors of another religion, religiosity has receded toward the level found in other high-income countries – as has also happened in Ireland. At the other extreme, Azerbaijan is a historically Muslim country where religion was firmly repressed under Soviet Rule. It is considerably less prosperous than Poland or Ireland and, like most ex-communist societies, it has become increasingly religious – and its protracted territorial struggle with neighboring Armenia has probably contributed to the fact that it shows the largest increase in religiosity to be found among these 60 countries.

Increasing emphasis on religion is found mainly in Soviet successor states that experienced traumatic transitions to market economies (and war with their neighbors, as with Azerbaijan, Georgia and Armenia); countries that emerged from the bloody breakup of Yugoslavia; or continuing political instability. In addition to the economic stress that accompanied the transition from state-run economies, ex-communist countries have experienced the collapse of a Marxist belief system. To a considerable extent, its place is being filled by growing religiosity.

Conversely, 20 of the 21 high-income countries (as defined by the World Bank in 1990)[11] in Figure 4.3 show decreases in religiosity, or statistically insignificant increases; only one such country shows an increase of more than three percentage points. The overall pattern is clear: low-income countries tend to be much more religious than economically secure ones; but the countries showing the largest increases in religiosity since 1981 are mainly ex-communist countries in which economic and physical security broke down and the communist ideology collapsed. Conversely, the importance of religion has declined in almost all high-income countries – including the USA which, despite the offsetting influence of heavy Hispanic immigration, shows a decline.

Other indicators of religiosity show similar patterns. Changes in religious service attendance and changes in the percentage identifying themselves as strong believers, increased in most former communist countries, and declined in most high-income societies.

Secularization Moves at the Pace of Intergenerational Population Replacement

Generally, deep-rooted values change at the pace of intergenerational population replacement. For example, the shift from Materialist to Postmaterialist values mainly reflects intergenerational population replacement. Figure 2.2 showed a cohort analysis of changes in these values in six West European countries from 1970 to 2009. Although one finds substantial short-term fluctuations linked with period effects, the long-term pattern is clear: a given birth cohort's mean score on the Materialist/Postmaterialist values index changed very little across this 39-year time span. But among the population as a whole, we *do* find a substantial shift toward Postmaterialist values: the mean score on this index rose by 30 points for the combined six-nation sample. This change was overwhelmingly due to intergenerational population replacement: *within* a given birth cohort, the average net change from the earliest to the latest available measure was an increase of only five points. This may reflect the increasing social acceptability of Postmaterialist responses, but it accounts for only one-sixth of the net change.

Changes in religiosity show a similar pattern. Though religiosity has remained strong in most low-income and middle-income countries, and increased in most ex-communist countries, in recent decades it has declined in almost all high-income countries – and this decline is largely due to intergenerational population replacement. Figure 4.4 shows the relationship between birth cohort and religiosity in 14 high-income countries that were surveyed in 1981 and again around 2009. One line shows the 1981 levels for all cohorts,

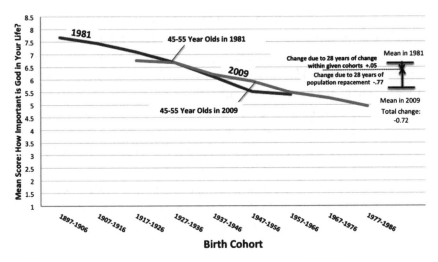

Figure 4.4 Changes in Importance of Religion, as measured by the question "How important is God in your life?" due to intergenerational population replacement, and due to within-cohort changes, in 14 high-income societies.

Source: Combined data from EVS and WVS surveys in following high-income countries: Australia (1981 + 2012), Belgium (1981 +2009), Canada (1981 + 2006), Denmark (1981 + 2008), France (1981 + 2008), Great Britain (1981 + 2009), Iceland (1984 + 2009), Ireland (1981 + 2008), Italy (1981 + 2009), Netherlands (1981+ 2008), Norway (1982+ 2008), Spain (1981 + 2011), Sweden (1981 + 2011), USA (1982 +2011). Median span=28 years.

and the other line shows the 2009 levels. Both lines show a downward slope as we move from older to younger birth cohorts, reflecting the fact that younger respondents are less religious than their older compatriots. Five of these birth cohorts are present in substantial numbers in both 1981 and 2009, and their levels of religiosity are almost identical at both points in time: the intergenerational differences do not reflect life-cycle effects – the religiosity of given birth cohorts remained almost unchanged across this 28-year period, so the two lines overlap where they are based on the same birth cohorts. But the 1981 line includes two highly religious older birth cohorts (on the left side of the graph) that had dropped out of the sample by 2009. They were replaced by two much more secular younger birth cohorts (on the right side). This process of intergenerational population replacement brought a substantial decline in emphasis on religion in these 14 high-income countries, producing a net decline of .77 points on the religiosity index – a change that was almost entirely due to intergenerational population replacement.

As Figure 4.5 demonstrates, changes in attendance at religious services show a similar pattern, with given birth cohorts showing almost exactly the same levels in both 1981 and 2009, causing the lines to overlap where they are based on the same birth cohorts – even though the 2009 line measures these cohorts 28 years later than the 1981 line. But because the older cohorts dropped out by 2009 and were replaced by younger, more secular cohorts, intergenerational population replacement brought a substantial decline in attendance. The decline in religiosity in high-income countries is almost entirely due to intergenerational population replacement.

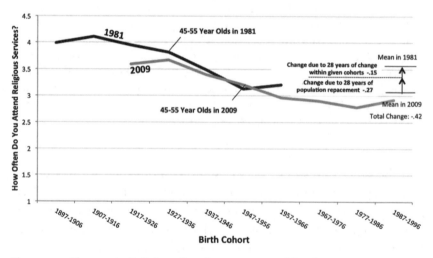

Figure 4.5 Changes in Religious Practice, as measured by the question "… How often do you attend religious services these days?" due to intergenerational population replacement, and due to within-cohort changes, in 14 high-income societies. Mean factor scores on Individual-choice norms factor based on tolerance of homosexuality, divorce and abortion.

Source: Combined data from EVS and WVS surveys in following high-income countries (according to World Bank categories as of 2001): Australia (1981 + 2012), Belgium (1981 +2009), Canada (1981 + 2006), Denmark (1981 + 2008), France (1981 + 2008), Great Britain (1981 + 2009), Iceland (1984 + 2009), Ireland (1981 + 2008), Italy (1981 + 2009), Netherlands (1981 + 2008), Norway (1982+ 2008), Spain (1981 + 2011), Sweden (1981 + 2011), USA (1982 + 2011). Median span = 28 years.

The End of Secularization?

Although economic modernization tends to bring secularization within any country that experiences it, I see no prospect of religion disappearing in the foreseeable future. There are several reasons:

First, secularization brings a sharp decline in human fertility rates, which remain relatively high in religious societies – so the world as a whole has a larger proportion of people with strong religious beliefs today than it did 30 years ago.

Second, while industrialization was linked with an increasingly materialistic, mechanical secular worldview, the rise of the knowledge society brings growing interest in ideas, innovation and Postmaterialist concerns. Hierarchical authoritarian religious institutions are losing their ability to tell people how to lead their lives but spiritual concerns, broadly defined, are becoming more widespread in postindustrial societies. The shift from an industrial economy to a knowledge economy brings a shift from the materialist, mechanistic world of the factory, to a world where ideas are central. A new version of religion that allowed space for individual autonomy could provide a growing market for an enterprising religious entrepreneur.

Such entrepreneurs undoubtedly can help promote religion. But the supply-side hypothesis doesn't provide an adequate explanation for what has been happening in the world unless one assumes that both the Muslim-majority countries and the ex-communist countries are teeming with energetic religious entrepreneurs – while high-income countries (including the USA) are devoid of them. The USA obviously does have plenty of energetic religious entrepreneurs, but religion is nevertheless losing ground. It seems pretty clear that the demand for religion is diminishing in high-income countries.

Moreover, there has been a reaction against the perceived decadence of secular Western societies in preindustrial societies, leading them to reject secularization. In addition, one might expect the recent global economic crisis to undermine existential security, leading to increasing emphasis on religion. Whether religion expands or erodes partly depends on the extent to which the trend toward growing prosperity that has been shaping the world for the past three centuries, resumes or disappears.

There is another reason why I do not expect that religion will disappear in the foreseeable future: as Chapter 7 will demonstrate, having a clear belief system is conducive to happiness. This belief system need not be religious – but some firm set of convictions is crucial. With the collapse of communism, the twentieth century's main alternative to religion disappeared in many countries – and to a considerable extent, the void this opened up, is being filled by the spread of religious beliefs.

5 CULTURAL CHANGE, SLOW AND FAST: THE DISTINCTIVE TRAJECTORY OF NORMS GOVERNING GENDER EQUALITY AND SEXUAL ORIENTATION*

Introduction

As we have seen, high levels of economic and physical security encourage a shift from Materialist to Postmaterialist values. This makes people more favorable to a variety social changes, ranging from greater emphasis on environmental protection to democratization. It is also bringing growing acceptance of gender equality and homosexuality.[1]

Throughout history, most societies instilled norms limiting women to the roles of wife and mother, and stigmatizing homosexuality and any other sexual behavior not linked with reproduction.[2] High levels of security bring growing acceptance of gender equality and other behavior that was discouraged by agrarian societies, which require high fertility rates to maintain their populations. During the past century these cultural norms have been changing slowly in high-income societies, mainly through intergenerational population replacement – but this process recently reached a threshold at which rapid cultural change began, leading to major societal-level changes such as growing numbers of women holding positions of authority and the legalization of same-sex marriage.

---

* This chapter is based on Inglehart, Ponarin and Inglehart, 2017.

Advanced industrial societies no longer require high fertility rates, and they have dropped sharply. Effective birth control technology, labor-saving devices, improved childcare facilities and very low infant mortality make it possible for women to have full-time careers and children – with or without a husband. Traditional Pro-fertility norms are no longer needed and they are giving way to Individual-choice norms, which allow people to choose their own behavior.

But basic cultural norms don't change immediately. As the persistence of religion demonstrates, they generally change slowly. Although leading nineteenth-century social theorists agreed that religion was heading toward extinction, a larger share of the world's population held traditional religious values in 2004 than in 1980.[3] But, as we will see, norms concerning gender equality, divorce, abortion, and homosexuality are now changing with remarkable speed, although this shift from Pro-fertility norms to Individual-choice norms is opposed by virtually all major religions.

People are reluctant to give up traditional norms governing gender equality and sexual behavior, as is evident from persistent opposition to abortion, same-sex marriage and gender equality even in such economically secure societies as the USA. Adherence to traditional lifestyle norms is stronger still in countries suffering from insecure conditions that make people cling to familiar norms. But when a society attains high levels of existential security, and survival comes to be taken for granted, people become increasingly open to new norms.

If economic development is conducive to the emergence of individual-choice norms, we would expect these norms to be more widespread among the publics of rich countries than poor ones –which is precisely what we find.

When a society reaches a sufficiently high level of economic and physical security that younger birth cohorts grow up taking survival for granted, it launches an intergenerational shift from survival-norms to individual-choice norms. But the effects of reaching this threshold do not manifest themselves immediately: until they reach adulthood, the birth cohorts formed under the new conditions have little influence. Even when they begin to enter adulthood, they are still a minority and it takes additional decades before they become a majority of the adult population. Consequently, we are not dealing with a phenomenon in which economic growth in one year brings a corresponding increase in emphasis on individual-choice norms the next year. Instead, we are dealing with a process of intergenerational population replacement that may reflect thresholds reached forty or fifty years earlier.

Nevertheless, intergenerational population replacement has gradually made individual-choice norms increasingly acceptable in high-income societies – and they seem to have reached a tipping point at which the prevailing outlook shifts from rejection to acceptance of new norms. At this point, the influence of conformism reverses polarity: instead of inhibiting tolerant attitudes, it encourages them, sharply accelerating the pace of cultural change.

Thus when a society attains high levels of existential security, rapid cultural changes can occur – but this happens only after a lag of several decades between the time when secure conditions emerge, and the time when new norms become predominant. For example, Western economic miracles, welfare states and the Long Peace all emerged fairly soon after 1945. But the political consequences of these events only began to manifest themselves twenty years later, when the first postwar birth cohort became politically relevant as young adults: the Student Protest Era erupted in 1968, when those born from 1945 to 1955 were in their teens and early twenties.[4] Student protest in advanced industrial societies continued throughout the 1970s but was still a minority phenomenon that evoked strong negative reactions. But by the 1980s, the older members of the postwar birth cohorts were in their thirties and forties, occupying influential positions in society. By the 1990s, Postmaterialists had become as numerous as Materialists, and norms that were considered deviant in the 1960s became politically correct. Conformist influences began to reverse polarity among growing segments of the adult population of high-income countries, bringing rapid cultural change. As we will demonstrate:

1) These value changes involve very long time-lags between the onset of the conditions leading to them, and the societal changes they produce. There was a time-lag of 40–50 years between when Western societies first attained high levels of economic and physical security after World War II, and the occurrence of such relevant societal changes as legalization of same-sex marriage.

2) One distinctive set of norms concerning gender equality, divorce, abortion and homosexuality supports a pro-fertility strategy that was essential to the survival of pre-industrial societies but eventually became superfluous. This set of norms is now moving on a trajectory that is distinct from that of other cultural changes.

3) Although basic values normally change at the pace of intergenerational population replacement, the shift from Pro-fertility norms to Individual-choice norms has reached a tipping-point where conformist pressures have reversed polarity and are now accelerating value changes they once resisted, bringing major societal changes such as legalization of same-sex marriage.

Theory and Hypotheses

Our analysis deals with two distinct phenomena:

1. The first is a shift from "Pro-fertility Norms" (emphasizing traditional gender roles and stigmatizing any sexual behavior not linked with reproduction) to "Individual-Choice Norms" (supporting gender equality and tolerance of homosexuality). Decades ago, Lesthaeghe and Surkyn[5] and Van de Kaa,[6] demonstrated that the intergenerational shift from Materialist to Postmaterialist values led to lower human fertility rates in Western Europe. This chapter deals with another, more recent shift in societal norms concerning gender equality and tolerance of gays and lesbians. This cultural change has important political consequences, encouraging new legislation concerning gender and sexual orientation.

2. The second phenomenon involves the speed of cultural change – which normally moves at the glacial pace of intergenerational population replacement. When the conditions shaping a society's younger generation's pre-adult years differ substantially from those shaping older groups, intergenerational value change occurs. It proceeds with a multi-decade time-lag between the emergence of the societal conditions conducive to the change, and the time when a society as a whole has adopted new values.

But the process can reach a tipping point at which prevailing opinion becomes favorable to the new norms and conformist pressures reverse polarity. In high-income countries, the shift from Pro-fertility norms to Individual-choice norms recently reached this point. Instead of resisting the effect of intergenerational population replacement, conformism now reinforces it, bringing rapid cultural change.

The Values Surveys have monitored norms concerning gender equality and sexual orientation in successive waves of surveys from 1981 to 2014. Although deep-seated norms limiting women's roles and stigmatizing homosexuality persisted from Biblical times to the twentieth century, these surveys now show dramatic changes in high-income countries from one wave to the next, with growing support for gender equality and tolerance of gays and lesbians.

This is changing society. For most of recorded history, same-sex marriage did not exist in large societies. In 2000 it was legalized in The Netherlands, followed by a growing number of other countries. Similarly, until recently women were second-class citizens in most countries, not obtaining the vote (even in developed countries) until well into the twentieth century. In recent years, women have been elected to top political office in many countries.

Cultural Evolution and the Shift to Individual-Choice Norms

Many thousands of societies have existed, most of which are now extinct. They instilled a wide variety of norms concerning gender equality and reproductive behavior. Some agrarian societies encouraged having large numbers of children, while others emphasized higher investment in fewer children. But all pre-industrial societies that survived for long, encouraged much high human fertility rates than those of today's high-income societies. Preindustrial societies encouraged high fertility rates because they faced high infant mortality rates and low life expectancies, making it necessary to produce large numbers of children in order to replace the population. Even West European societies (which emphasized higher investment in fewer children), produced six to eight children per woman.[7] In striking contrast, contemporary West European societies now produce from 1.1 to 1.9 children.

Economic factors reinforced the tendency for agrarian societies to have high fertility rates: having many children was economically beneficial, but as development proceeded, having many children became an economic liability.

Not all pre-industrial societies encouraged high fertility rates. From Biblical times to the twentieth century, some societies (such as the Shakers) required celibacy – but these societies have disappeared. Virtually all societies that survive as independent nations today, inculcated gender roles and reproductive norms encouraging high fertility rates. Accordingly, the public of every low-income or lower-middle-income society included in the Values Surveys – without a single exception – places relatively strong emphasis on Pro-fertility norms. These norms encourage women to cede leadership roles to men and devote themselves to bearing and raising children. They also stigmatize any form of sexual behavior that is not linked with reproduction, such as homosexuality, abortion, divorce or masturbation.

In some countries the daughters or widows of kings, from Cleopatra to Catherine the Great, could inherit the throne, with one woman ruling the country while the rest were second-class citizens. Because tiny numbers of women were involved, this had a negligible impact on the society's human fertility level, making it compatible with traditional Pro-fertility norms. Much more recently, women's suffrage movements emerged, with women winning the right to vote around 1920 in historically Protestant democracies and around 1945 in historically Catholic democracies. This was a major advance, but allowing women to vote once every few years still had little impact on fertility rates. Traditional Pro-fertility norms began to erode noticeably in the 1960s and 1970s when the post-war birth cohorts first became politically relevant.

Rising Existential Security and Cultural Change

Survival has become increasingly secure. Life expectancies, incomes and school attendance rose from 1970 to 2010 in every region of the world.[8] Poverty, illiteracy and mortality are declining globally.[9] And war, crime rates and violence have declined dramatically for many decades.[10]

The world is now experiencing the longest period without war between major powers in recorded history. This, together with the postwar economic miracles and the emergence of the welfare state, produced conditions under which a large share of those born since 1945 in Western Europe, North America, Japan, Australia and New Zealand grew up taking survival for granted, bringing intergenerational shifts toward Postmaterialist values and Self-expression values (as Chapter 2 demonstrated). Most societies no longer require high fertility rates, which have dropped dramatically – especially in high-income societies where life-expectancy rates have almost doubled in the past century[11] and infant mortality rates have fallen to one-thirtieth of their 1950 level.[12] For many years, it has no longer been necessary to women to produce six to eight children in order to replace the population.

But deep-rooted cultural norms change slowly. Virtually all major world faiths emphasize pro-fertility norms – and they do so vigorously. Pro-fertility norms are not presented as matters of individual judgment. They are held to be absolute values, violation of which will bring eternal damnation. It was necessary to make these cultural sanctions strong because Pro-fertility norms require people to suppress strong natural urges. "Thou shalt not commit adultery" goes against deep-rooted desires; requiring women to devote their lives to child-bearing and child-rearing entails major sacrifices; and defining homo-sexuality as sinful, unnatural behavior imposes severe self-repression and self-hatred on gays and lesbians.

These norms are no longer necessary for societal survival, but deep-rooted values resist change. Nevertheless, modernization brings high levels of economic and physical security.[13] People grow up taking survival for granted, making them increasingly open to new ideas. As Chapters 3 and 4 demonstrated, Self-expression values – which include tolerance of homosexuality – have become widespread in societies with secure living conditions.

Evolutionary Modernization Theory

Evolutionary modernization theory argues that the degree to which people experience threats to their survival has pervasive effects on their society's cultural norms. Western Europe's postwar economic miracles and welfare states led to the emergence of a predominantly Postmaterialist generation born after 1945, but this generation did not become politically visible until 20 years later, when they reached adult-hood – contributing to the student protest era of the late 1960s and 1970s. At that point, there was a huge gap between the values of this first postwar birth cohort and all older cohorts.

But the 20-year-olds eventually became 30-year-olds and then 40-year-olds and then 50-year-olds. As postwar birth cohorts replaced older cohorts, their values gradually spread. Today, Western Europe's social norms are profoundly different from those of 1945. In 1945, homosexuality was still criminal in most West European countries; it is now legal in virtually all of them. Church attendance has declined dramatically, fertility rates have fallen below the replacement level, and women have won high political office. But there was a time-lag of 40 to 50 years between the onset of the conditions conducive to these changes, and the point where new values were accepted by society as a whole.

The long time-lags between the onset of conditions conducive to deep-rooted cultural changes and the time when they transform a society means that current socioeconomic conditions don't explain current cultural changes. The intergenerational shift to Individual-choice norms in Western countries has now attained enough momentum that it seems unlikely to reverse itself. But, as we have seen, these countries are currently experiencing economic stagnation, rising inequality and high unemployment, which is often blamed on massive immigration. Many recent immigrants are Islamic and hostility to them is compounded by highly publicized Islamic terrorism. Today, women and gays do not seem threatening, but Muslim immigrants do. Accordingly, in recent years, ethnocentric populist parties have won unprecedentedly large shares of the vote in national elections. Clearly, not all aspects of cultural change are moving at the same pace.

In pre-industrial societies, tolerance of abortion, homosexuality and divorce remains extremely low and conformist pressures inhibit people from expressing tolerance. In Egypt, for example, fully 99 percent of the public condemned homosexuality in recent surveys – which means that even the homosexuals were condemning homosexuality.

But intergenerational population replacement has gradually made individual-choice norms increasingly acceptable in high-income societies – initially among the student population and then among society as a whole. A tipping point is being reached where the prevailing outlook shifts from rejection to acceptance of new norms, and instead of inhibiting tolerant attitudes, conformism and social desirability begin to encourage them. As attitudes become more tolerant, gays and lesbians come out. Growing numbers of people realize that some of the people they know and like are gay, leading them to become more tolerant – encouraging more gays to come out, in a positive feedback loop.[14]

In short, when a society attains high levels of existential security and people grow up taking survival for granted, rapid cultural changes can occur – but this happens with a time-lag of several decades between when secure conditions first emerge, and when new norms become predominant.

Hypotheses

This theory generates the following hypotheses:

Hypothesis 1. A syndrome of Individual-choice norms exists, in which the publics of some societies endorse a coherent set of traditional Pro-fertility norms, while the publics of others support a set of Individual-choice norms concerning gender equality and divorce, abortion and homosexuality. **Support or opposition to the various components of this syndrome go together.**

Hypothesis 2. High levels of existential security are conducive to Individual-choice norms. The publics of societies with high per capita GDP, high life expectancy and low infant mortality (the three indicators of existential security used here) will be likelier to support Individual-choice norms than those with low levels. Similarly, within given countries, the most secure strata will be likeliest to support Individual-choice norms.

Hypothesis 3. Over the past 50 years, existential security levels have risen substantially in developed countries, producing large differences between the values of younger and older cohorts. Consequently, as younger cohorts replace older ones, we should observe an intergenerational shift from Pro-fertility norms to Individual-choice norms.

Hypothesis 4. Because this shift reflects the level of existential security that prevailed during the pre-adult years of people who were born several decades ago, **the strongest predictor of a society's level of support for new values will not be its current levels of per capita GDP, life expectancy and infant mortality, but levels that prevailed several decades ago.**

Hypothesis 5. Although intergenerational population replacement involves long time-lags, **cultural change can reach a tipping point at which new norms become perceived as dominant.** Social desirability effects then reverse polarity: instead of retarding the changes linked with intergenerational population replacement, they accelerate them – **bringing rapid cultural change.**

Hypothesis 6. When they become dominant, the new norms can have major societal-level consequences, such as gender quotas on electoral lists, or legalization of same-sex marriage.

Data and Methods

We test these hypotheses against data from the Values Surveys, which cover the full range of economic development, including 22 low-income countries, 29 lower-middle income countries, 20 upper-middle income countries and 28 high-income countries, as classified by the World Bank in 2000 (these countries are listed in Appendix A3.1).[15] The Values Surveys also cover all major cultural zones, including the

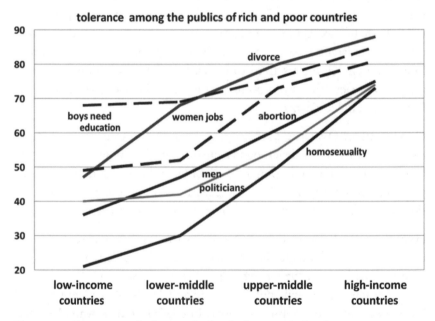

Figure 5.1 Six aspects of tolerance, by level of economic development.
Percentage expressing tolerant views on given topic. Question wording is shown in Table 5.1.
The questions concerning divorce, abortion and homosexuality are measured on 10-point scales, with codes 6 through 10 being coded as tolerant. The questions concerning gender equality have tolerant and intolerant responses. The countries included in each category are listed in Appendix A3.1.

most populous countries in each group. The questions analyzed here were asked in identical form in successive waves of these surveys.

Our dependent variable is Individual-choice norms. Although value change occurs at the individual level, we are primarily interested in how this leads to societal-level changes. Value change does not automatically change a society's laws and institutions, but it does make such changes increasingly likely. Individual-level cultural change leads to societal-level change in two ways: first, democratic elites and institutions are necessarily responsive to mass preferences, but even autocratic leaders are not immune to them. Moreover, because elites grow up within a given society, in the long run they tend to reflect its prevailing norms.

It is sometimes suggested that aggregating individual-level data to the societal-level is somehow tainted. This interpretation is mistaken. Over 60 years ago, in his classic article on the ecological fallacy, Robinson pointed out that the relationships between two variables at the individual level are not necessarily the same as those at the aggregate level.[16] This is an important insight, but it does not mean that aggregating is wrong – it simply means that one can't assume that a relationship that holds true at one level also holds true at another level. Social scientists have been aggregating individual-level data to construct national-level indices such as fertility rates for so long that they seem familiar and legitimate – but they are no more legitimate than aggregated subjective data. Its infant mortality rate is an important national-level attribute of any country – but all of the living or dying is done by individuals. Similarly, income inequality is a valid and meaningful national-level variable, although it is based on the incomes of individuals.

In this chapter, Individual-choice norms are measured at both the individual level and the societal level. We happen to find similar causal relationships at both levels: relatively secure individuals and relatively secure countries rank highest on these norms. But because this chapter focuses on how cultural change leads to sociopolitical changes, our key analyses are done at the societal level.

Table 5.1 shows a national-level factor analysis that demonstrates that three questions concerning acceptance of divorce, abortion and homosexuality and responses to three questions concerning acceptance of gender equality have a strong tendency to go together. Each question's factor loading shows how strongly responses to

Table 5.1 *Pro-fertility norms vs. individual-choice norms (Principal component factor analysis)*

Response:	Factor loading:
Homosexuality is never justifiable	−.90
When jobs are scarce, men have more right to a job than women	−.89
Divorce is never justifiable	−.89
On the whole, men make better political leaders than women do	−.88
Abortion is never justifiable	−.80
A university education is more important for a boy than for a girl	−.78

High *positive* scores indicate support for Individual-choice norms.
Source: National-level data from 80 countries included in the Values Surveys.

that question are correlated to an underlying Pro-fertility versus Individual-choice dimension. Loadings around .90 indicate that they go together in an almost one-to-one relationship. The publics of some societies tend to be strongly favorable to gender equality and relatively tolerant of divorce, abortion and homosexuality, while the publics of other societies tend to have unfavorable attitudes toward all six questions. Consequently, we used the responses to these six questions to measure the extent to which a society (or an individual) supports traditional Pro-fertility norms or Individual-choice norms.[17]

Our key independent variable is an index of Existential Security, based on factor scores from a principal components analysis of each country's levels of life expectancy, infant mortality and GDP/capita.[18] They also tap a single dimension, showing loadings of .97, −.97 and .90 respectively in 1960. Reliable cross-national data are available since 1960, enabling us to construct this index at various time points.

Although people who emphasize Individual-choice norms also tend to emphasize Postmaterialist values, the shift from Pro-fertility to Individual-choice norms shows distinctive behavior and is moving at a much more rapid pace than the shift from Materialist to Postmaterialist values.[19]

Empirical Analyses and Findings

Hypothesis 1. A syndrome of Individual-choice norms exists, in which the publics of some societies endorse traditional Pro-fertility norms, while others support Individual-choice norms concerning gender equality and divorce, abortion and homosexuality.

As Table 5.1 demonstrates, acceptance or rejection of all six indicators of Individual-choice norms **does** go together, with the publics of some societies being relatively favorable to gender equality, divorce, abortion and homosexuality, while others reject them. One dimension emerges, with Pro-fertility norms and Individual-choice norms at opposite poles.

Hypothesis 2. High levels of existential security are conducive to Individual-choice norms.

As Figure 5.1 demonstrates, the publics of high-income countries are much likelier than those of low-income countries to hold tolerant attitudes toward all six indicators of Individual-choice norms. Averaged across the six items, in low-income countries only 38 percent of the public has tolerant attitudes, compared with 80 percent in high-income countries.[20] These findings support the hypothesis that high levels of existential security are conducive to Individual-choice norms – but before testing this hypothesis more conclusively, let us explore a key characteristic of our main independent variable, Existential Security:

Hypothesis 3 holds that, in so far as societies have attained high levels of existential security, support for Individual-choice norms will become more widespread over time. This has indeed happened, as Figure 5.2 demonstrates. Support for these norms increased in 40 of the 58 countries from which we have at least ten years of time-series data – and, in keeping with the claim that these changes are linked with existential security, it increased in 23 of the 24 high-income countries, with the one deviant case (Italy) showing only a minuscule decline.

Hypothesis 3 also holds that the strongest predictor of a society's support for Individual-choice norms will not be its *current* level of Existential Security (as measured by per capita GDP, life expectancy and infant mortality) but the level that prevailed several decades before these norms were measured.

Figure 5.3 compares the predictive power of a country's level of Existential Security as measured at various time-points before the

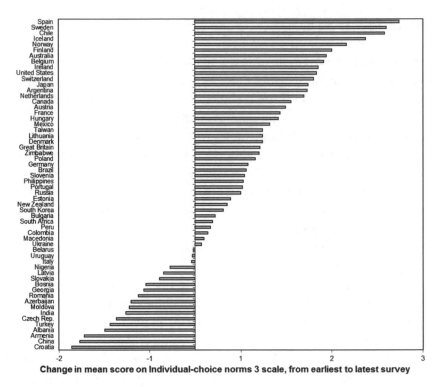

Figure 5.2 Changes in Individual-choice norms from earliest available survey to latest available survey in all countries having time series of at least ten years.

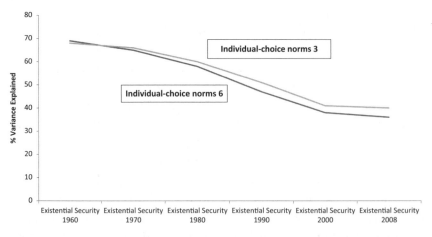

Figure 5.3 Impact of a country's level of Existential Security at various time points on adherence to Pro-fertility norms vs. Individual-choice norms around 2009.

Cell entry is the percentage of variance in Individual-choice norms in latest available survey that is explained by a country's score on the Existential Security index measured in given year.

survey in which Individual-choice norms were measured (around 2009).[21] Our two earliest measures – Existential Security in 1960 and 1970 – are the strongest predictors of Individual-choice norms around 2009 (each explaining almost 70 percent of the cross-national variation). Surprising as it may seem – but as predicted by Hypothesis 3 – these much-earlier measures explain far more variance than does Existential Security measured in 1980, 1990, 2000 or at the time of the survey. This is remarkable. Normally, the strongest version of a predictor is one measured shortly before the dependent variable.[22] Thus, voting intentions measured a week before an election are usually stronger predictors of the actual vote than voting intentions measured a month before the election – which are a stronger predictor than voting intentions six months or a year before the election. As Silver demonstrates, if a survey carried out one year before the election indicates that a US Senate candidate has a five-point lead over her opponents, the probability that she will actually win is only slightly better than would be predicted by a random coin flip.[23] But as the survey gets closer to the election, its predictive power gets steadily stronger. A survey carried out one week before the election showing the same five-point lead has an 89 percent likelihood of accurately predicting the result, and a survey carried out one day before the election has a 95 percent likelihood of being accurate. The appropriate time-lag depends on the topic being explored, but time-lags of more than a few years are unusual.[24]

Here, our strongest predictor of a public's acceptance of Individual-choice norms in 2009, is an index of Existential Security based on their country's Life Expectancy, Infant Mortality and per capita GDP almost *50 years* before the dependent variable. Why?

We are dealing with exceptionally deep-rooted cultural norms that were already established in Biblical times and showed little change for many centuries. The usual time series analysis approach, in which change on the dependent variable is predicted by slightly earlier changes in the independent variables is not appropriate here, for the dependent variable – Individual-choice norms – is linked with religious and cultural traditions that strongly resist change and largely do so through intergenerational population replacement. The emergence of low levels of infant mortality and high levels of life expectancy and economic security in 1960 were conducive to change in these norms – but it took decades for their impact to become manifest at the societal level.

All three components of the Existential Security index show this same unusual pattern: recent measures of life expectancy (and infant mortality and GDP/capita) have a much weaker impact on acceptance of new norms governing gender equality and reproductive behavior than do earlier measures – with the levels that existed in 1960 or 1970 explaining far more of the variance in Individual-choice norms in 2009, than more recent measures.

This also holds true of religiosity (as measured by the perceived importance of God in one's life). Religiosity is one of the most deep-rooted of all mass attitudes and is very resistant to change. Here again, Existential Security in 1960 or 1970 is a significantly stronger predictor of religiosity in 2009, than is Existential Security in 2000 or 2008, as Figure 5.4 demonstrates.

This also holds true of Postmaterialist values. Existential Security in 1960 or 1970 explains about twice as much of the variance in a country's level of Postmaterialism in the latest survey (around 2010), as does Existential Security in 2000 or 2008, as Figure 5.4 also demonstrates. These values reflect the level of security that prevailed during a given birth cohorts' pre-adult years.[25]

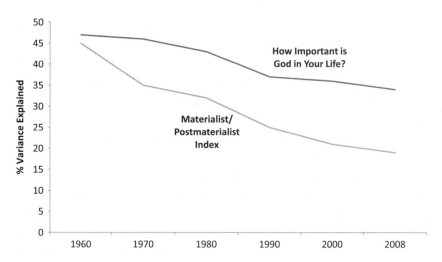

Figure 5.4 The impact of Existential Security measured at various time points, on religiosity and on Materialist/Postmaterialist values as measured in latest available survey.

Importance of God and Postmaterialist values were measured in the latest available survey for each country (the median year being 2008), in 96 and 94 countries respectively.

A recent article tested the hypothesis that high levels of existential security are conducive to Individual-choice norms, using regression analysis – a statistical technique designed to help sort out what is causing what.[26] The results of these analyses support Hypothesis 2, indicating that a society's level of Existential Security in 1970 explains fully 65 percent of the cross-national variation in its acceptance of Individual-choice norms around 2009. The findings also show that Postmaterialist values explain additional variance in support for Individual-choice norms. Postmaterialist value priorities emerge if one grows up taking survival for granted. They tap aspects of existential security, such as declining violence rates that are not captured by our Existential Security index. Accordingly, Existential Security in 1970 plus a nation's level of Materialist/Postmaterialist values explain 73 percent of the cross-national variation in support for Individual-choice norms. Since virtually all major religions instill Pro-fertility norms, we would expect religiosity to have a negative impact on Individual-choice norms. It does: adding religiosity to the equation modestly increases the explained variance, in the predicted negative direction.

This article also uses multi-level regression analysis to explore the cross-level interactions effects of existential security with individual-level variables. It finds that, while education has no effect on support for Individual-choice norms in countries with low levels of Existential Security, education has a strong effect on support for Individual-choice norms in countries with high levels of Existential Security. In other words, we can't attribute the rise of Individual-choice norms to rising education levels per se: in less secure societies, education has little effect – but in countries with high levels of Existential Security, education is strongly linked with support for Individual-choice norms. This suggests that high-income societies have reached a tipping point where the new norms have become prevalent among the more educated strata. Other interaction effects indicate that religiosity has a stronger (negative) effect on support for Individual-choice norms in *less* secure countries, while income and Postmaterialist values have stronger effects on support for Individual-choice norms in *more* secure countries. In other words, religion plays a major role in reinforcing traditional Pro-fertility norms in societies with low levels of Existential Security, but gradually loses its power to do so as societies attain higher levels of security. Conversely, both income and Postmaterialist values have little impact on norms governing gender roles and reproductive behavior in less-secure societies, but have increasing impact in societies with high levels of Existential Security.

What is causing these changes? Analysis of the *changes* in support for Individual-choice norms from the earliest to the latest available survey indicates that a society's level of Existential Security is the strongest single predictor – by itself, accounting for 40 percent of the net change.[27] A country's level of Materialist/Postmaterialist values also has a significant impact on changing support for Individual-choice norms, and a country's level of religiosity also has a significant (negative) impact on change in support for Individual-choice norms.

Although a country's economic growth rate from 1990 to 2010 is a change indicator, it does not have a significant impact on changes in support for Individual-choice norms – in fact, high growth rates are *negatively* linked with changing support for Individual-choice norms. Though it may seem surprising, a country's *level* of existential security is a stronger predictor of changes in support for Individual-choice norms than its recent rate of economic *growth* – which actually points in the wrong direction.

Despite the maxim that only change can explain change, broader empirical evidence confirms this finding. High-income countries are likelier to show growing support for Individual-choice norms on all six of the Individual-choice indicators than less-prosperous countries. But countries with high economic *growth* rates in recent years were *less* likely to show growing support for Individual-choice norms than countries with low growth rates: high economic *levels* are a better predictor of increasing support for Individual-choice norms than high economic *growth* rates.

This is true because we are dealing with exceptionally deep-rooted norms. Change does not begin until a high-security-level threshold is reached, and the results become manifest much later, through intergenerational population replacement. Ultimately, of course, the process *does* reflect change, since attaining this threshold reflects many decades of economic growth that contributed to high levels of existential security. Change *is* caused by change. But such long time-lags are involved that in the interim (which may be 50 years or more), a country's *level* of existential security provides a more accurate predictor of change than does its recent economic growth rate – or recent *changes* in life expectancy, infant mortality, and per capita GDP.

In recent decades, low-income and middle-income countries have had much higher economic growth rates than high-income
countries: the countries with the highest growth rates are below the
threshold at which people start adopting Individual-choice norms. This
explains why high recent economic growth rates are *negatively* correlated with rising support for Individual-choice norms.

When support for Individual-choice norms reaches a level
where the dominant opinion in a given social milieu comes to support Individual-choice, it can reverse the polarity of social desirability
effects – producing much more rapid changes than those from intergenerational value change alone. This is unusual.

For example, as we saw in Chapter 2, the shift from
Materialist to Postmaterialist values is mainly due to intergenerational population replacement. Although substantial short-term fluctuations occur, a given birth cohort's mean score on the Materialist/
Postmaterialist values index changes very little from the earliest to
the latest reading across a 38-year time span. But among the population as a *whole*, there was a substantial shift toward Postmaterialist
values: the mean score on the Materialist/Postmaterialist index
rose by 30 points for the combined six-nation sample. This change
was overwhelmingly due to intergenerational population replacement: *within* a given birth cohort, the average net change was an
increase of only five points.

The shift from Materialist to Postmaterialist values was almost
entirely driven by intergenerational population replacement. Changes
in religiosity show a similar pattern. Though religiosity has increased
in most ex-communist countries, in recent decades it has declined in
almost all high-income countries – and this decline almost entirely
reflects intergenerational population replacement, as the preceding
chapter demonstrated.

Changes in Individual-choice norms show a very different pattern, as Figure 5.5 (based on the same 14 high-income countries) demonstrates. Here, the effects of intergenerational population replacement
are reinforced by large changes *within* given birth cohorts – with each
cohort becoming substantially more supportive of Individual-choice
norms in 2009 than it was in 1981.[28] Though intergenerational population replacement is linked with a .265 increase on the Individual-
choice norms index, changes within given cohorts account for an even
larger increase of .435 points. We can't prove that these intra-cohort

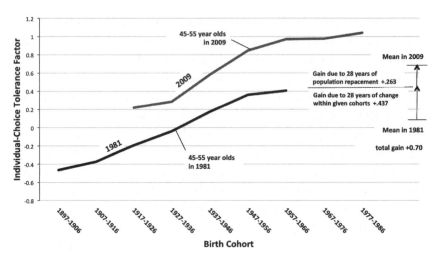

Figure 5.5 Changes in Individual-choice norms due to intergenerational popula-
tion replacement, and to within-cohort changes, in 14 high-income societies.
Based on mean factor scores on Individual-choice norms 3.
Source: Values Surveys in the 14 high-income countries listed in Figure 6.3.

shifts reflect changes in social desirability effects (which are inherently
difficult to measure since they imply that one can't take one's measure-
ments at face value) but this explanation seems plausible. If true, it
supports the hypothesis that exceptionally rapid changes in Individual-
choice norms are occurring in high-income societies because conformist pressures have reversed polarity.

   Historical evidence also suggests that this was the case. During
the 2004 US presidential election, same-sex marriage was so unpop-
ular that, in order to increase turnout among social conservatives,
Republican strategists put referenda banning same-sex marriage on
the ballot in key swing states. The ban was approved in every case.
From 1998 through 2008, there were 30 statewide referenda seeking
to ban same-sex marriage, and all 30 of them succeeded. But the tide
suddenly turned. In 2012, there were five new statewide referenda on
the topic – and in four out of five cases, the public voted in favor of
legalizing same-sex marriage. In recent cases, appellate courts generally struck down restrictions on same-sex marriage and in 2015 the
US Supreme Court ruled that the Constitution guarantees a right to
same-sex marriage: even elderly judges seemed to sense that a water-
shed social change is occurring and wanted to be on "the right side
of history."

Hypothesis 6 holds that when new norms become culturally dominant they can have major societal-level consequences, such
as growing numbers of women gaining positions of authority, or the
legalization of same-sex marriage.

The spread of Individual-choice norms can bring important
societal-level changes. As Figure 5.6 demonstrates, legislation concerning homosexuality is closely linked with the degree to which Individual-
choice norms have emerged among given publics. The scale used here

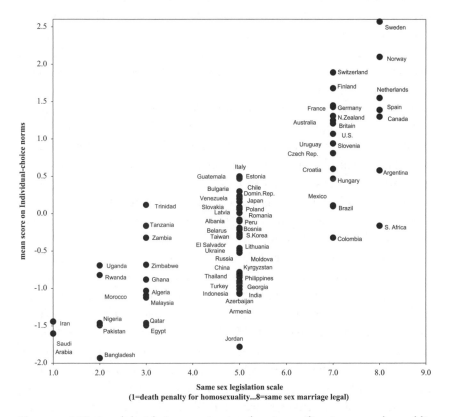

Figure 5.6 National legislation concerning homosexuality in 2012, by public
acceptance of gender equality, divorce, abortion and homosexuality (r = .79).
Based on country's mean score on 6-item Individual-choice norms index. Legislation
concerning homosexuals in 2012 downloaded from LGBT Portal (original scale's
polarity reversed to make high scores reflect tolerant legislation).
Scale: 1 = death penalty for homosexuality, 2 = heavy penalty, 3 = minimal penalty,
4 = homosexuality illegal but not enforced, 5 = same sex unions not recognized,
6 = some form of same sex partnership but not marriage, 7 = same sex unions recognized but not performed, 8 = same sex marriages performed. No cases available
with codes 4 or 6.

ranges from a score of "1" in countries where homosexuality is punishable by the death penalty, to a score of "8" in countries where same-sex marriage is legal. Countries that rank high on Individual-choice norms are much likelier to have adopted legislation favorable to gays and lesbians ($r = .79$).

It seems unlikely that this strong correlation between mass-level values and societal legislation exists because the legislation shaped the values. Same-sex marriage first became legal in 2000, but the relevant values had been spreading for decades. In 2001 The Netherlands experienced a sudden surge in same-sex marriages. The proximate cause was the fact that the Dutch parliament had just legalized same-sex marriages. But the root cause was the fact that a gradual shift had taken place in the Dutch public's attitudes toward homosexuality. In the 1981 Values Surveys, almost half of the Dutch expressed disapproval of homosexuality (the old being much less tolerant than the young) – but the Dutch were more tolerant than any other public surveyed. In most countries, 75–99 percent of the public disapproved of homosexuality. These attitudes gradually become more tolerant through an intergenerational value shift. By 1999, disapproval among the Dutch public had fallen to less than half its 1981 level. A year later, the Dutch parliament legalized same-sex marriage, soon followed by a growing number of other countries – all of which had relatively tolerant publics.[29]

As Figure 5.7 demonstrates, countries that rank high on Individual-choice norms also tend to rank high on the UN Gender Empowerment Measure (reflecting the extent to which women hold high positions in political, economic and academic life). The correlation between the six-item Individual-choice index and the UN Gender Empowerment measure is .87. Legislative changes (such as the adoption of gender quotas) probably help legitimate Individual-choice norms, but here again, the underlying norms have been changing for 50 years, while the legislative changes are relatively recent. The cultural changes clearly preceded the institutional changes, and seem to have contributed to them.

The claim that institutions determine culture does not hold up in the light of historical evidence, which suggests that culture and institutions influence each other, with cultural change sometimes preceding institutional change.

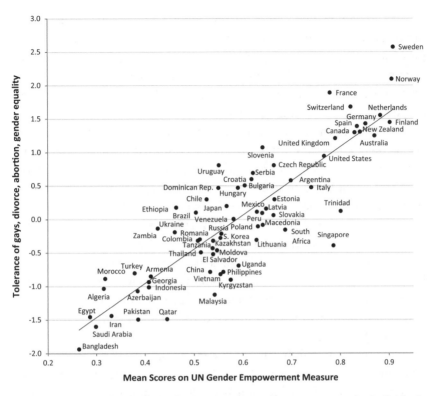

Figure 5.7 Societal levels of Gender Empowerment, by mass support for Individual-choice norms (r = .87).

Conclusion

We hypothesized that high levels of existential security are contributing to an intergenerational shift from Pro-fertility norms to Individual-choice norms, and evidence from the past three decades indicates that these changes have indeed occurred. A handful of variables linked with Existential Security explain most of the cross-national variation in support for Individual-choice norms – and they also explain most of the *change* in support for Individual-choice norms levels from 1981 to 2014. Though in high-income countries, the more educated and secure strata are likeliest to hold the new norms, education itself is not driving these changes: these norms are not linked with education in low-income countries.

Although the rise of Postmaterialist values and the declining importance of religion in high-income countries have moved at the pace of intergenerational population replacement, Individual-choice norms are now spreading much more rapidly. This seems to reflect a reversal of the social conformity effects linked with Pro-fertility norms among the publics of high-income societies.

During the past century, sharply falling infant mortality and rising life expectancy rates produced conditions where women no longer needed to devote their lives to producing and rearing large numbers of children in order to replace the population. The repression and self-denial linked with traditional Pro-fertility norms was no longer needed for societal survival – and the shift toward Individual-choice norms was conducive to higher levels of subjective well-being, as Chapter 8 will demonstrate. After long time-lags linked with intergenerational population replacement, the spread of Individual-choice norms seems to have reached a tipping point where conformist pressures reversed polarity – greatly accelerating the rate of change.

Future research on intergenerational value change should take into account the remarkably long time-lags between the onset of conditions conducive to individual-level changes and the point at which they produce societal-level changes. It should also probe into the conditions under which value change does not move at the pace of generational replacement. The evidence examined here suggests, but does not prove, that value change can reach a tipping-point at which conformist pressures reverse polarity, accelerating changes they once retarded. As Chapter 9 demonstrates, xenophobia shows the opposite pattern: although younger birth cohorts in high-income countries are less xenophobic than older ones, xenophobia has not been declining in many high-income countries – apparently because of a large-scale influx of immigrants and refugees, and widespread fear – stoked by massive media coverage of terrorist activities – that foreigners may be terrorists.

The rapid shift from Pro-fertility norms to Individual-choice norms has stimulated strong negative reactions among social conservatives in many countries. In the 2016 election Donald Trump mobilized xenophobic and sexist sentiments to win the US Presidency. But the social base for the sexist component of such appeals seems to be dwindling. The evidence examined here suggests that, after centuries of stability, traditional norms concerning gender equality and sexual orientation are rapidly eroding in high-income societies, in a cultural shift that has already begun to transform legislation concerning homosexuality and the extent to which women hold positions of authority. Though she didn't win the Presidency, Hillary Clinton was the first woman to win the Presidential popular vote – by a margin of almost three million votes. If the USA operated on the principle of one person, one vote, Clinton would be President.

6 THE FEMINIZATION OF SOCIETY AND DECLINING WILLINGNESS TO FIGHT FOR ONE'S COUNTRY: THE INDIVIDUAL-LEVEL COMPONENT OF THE LONG PEACE*

Overview: The Feminization of Society

The shift from Pro-fertility norms to Individual-choice norms that we have just examined is part of a broader feminization of society that occurs at advanced stages of modernization. This reduces the extent to which people are willing to engage in war, contributing to one of the most dramatic developments of recent decades: the virtual disappearance of war between major powers.

Societies dominated by Pro-fertility norms are patriarchal, but the rise of Individual-choice norms is linked with rising gender equality – and declining rates of violence. In 2013, one third of all murders in the USA were committed by young men 17–29 years of age, although this group was less than 10 percent of the population. Virtually everywhere, young men are much likelier to commit violent acts than the rest of the population. This seems to reflect both biological factors (high testosterone levels, linked with violent behavior) and cultural norms (violence being much more acceptable among men than among women). The testosterone levels seem to be fairly constant, but the cultural norms are changing.

---

* This chapter draws on Inglehart, Puranen and Welzel, 2015.

Societies dominated by Pro-fertility norms allow sex only within marriage, imposing severe sexual repression on unmarried young men. Throughout history, societies have encouraged young men to demonstrate their fitness through heroic acts of violence on behalf of their tribe or country, motivating them to risk their lives in war. The ideal leader was the Alpha Male who fought fearlessly and demanded unquestioning obedience in combat. Gat has argued that war sometimes provided almost the only opportunity for young men to have sex, with rape being a fringe benefit of war.[1]

Knowledge societies need a less hierarchical leadership style: innovation and creativity become crucial, and people need to think for themselves. The shift toward Individual-choice norms has a better fit with the functional needs of a Knowledge Society, where a supportive, stereotypically feminine style of leadership is more effective than a command-obedience model. Violence is discouraged and non-Alpha males like Bill Gates become desirable marriage partners. Lower fertility rates and longer life expectancies bring an aging population in which young males constitute a smaller percentage, and sexual repression diminishes. The public becomes less willing to fight for their country, reinforcing macro-societal trends linked with modernization and globalization.

Since the end of World War II, war between major powers has virtually disappeared. In an early attempt to explain this phenomenon, Doyle described it as the "Democratic Peace," presenting evidence that democracies almost never fight each other.[2] But more recent work shows that only the rich democracies of modern times have been at peace with each other – earlier democracies fought each other regularly.[3] These findings support the argument that the "democratic peace" exists because most modern democracies are prosperous and interrelated through trade.[4]

Mueller,[5] Gat[6] and Pinker[7] present massive evidence of a long-term decline in rates of murder, war and other forms of violence; these trends suggest that there has been a diminishing acceptance of violence and war among the publics of developed countries, but these authors do not provide any individual-level evidence of such changes. This chapter does, presenting the results from representative national surveys covering 90 percent of the world's population. This evidence demonstrates that, over the last 30 years, willingness to fight for one's country has been diminishing among the publics of most countries, particularly among the publics of high-income countries. The reasons for this declining willingness to fight are complex, but one major factor seems to be the spread of Individual-Choice norms discussed in the preceding chapter. Our species is gradually adopting more peaceful, feminine orientations. The Long Peace is gaining an increasingly solid mass basis.

For decades after World War II, hard-headed realists took it for granted that it was only a question of time before World War III broke out, possibly eradicating civilization. But events took an unexpected turn. The world became unexpectedly peaceful. By 1984, the world had already experienced the longest period without war between major powers since the Roman Empire, and this long peace now extends over more than thirty additional years.

Much earlier, liberal thinkers had argued that expanding markets and trade would make war unprofitable. In 1909, Angell predicted the end of war between European powers because of their extensive economic interdependence.[8] But the two world wars that followed discredited the claim that development and trade would make war obsolete.

Decades later, the enduring peace among major powers led a new generation of scholars to reconsider this seemingly disproven idea. Penetrating analyses of large bodies of evidence suggests that the classic liberals were right.[9] While this view has become widely accepted among political scientists, disputes continue over the question of whether modern democracies' prosperity and interdependence accounts for their peacefulness,[10] or whether there is something inherent in democracy itself that makes democracies less warlike.[11]

Theory

Since the end of World War II, peaceful interstate relationships have become increasingly prevalent.[12] As Pinker argues, this trend is part of a long-term decline of violence. In the seventeenth and eighteenth centuries, societies began to abolish slavery, dueling, witch burning, torture and other cruelties.[13] Murder rates in developed countries have been declining dramatically for centuries. Since World War II, developed states have stopped waging war on one another and the number

of wars and war casualties worldwide has declined.[14] Since the end of
the Cold War, civil wars have also been declining.[15] Even mass insurrections have become less violent in recent decades, and non-violent
insurrections have been more successful in ending oppression than
violent ones.[16]

The decline in violence parallels rising levels of existential security. By 2010, the world as a whole had attained the highest level of
prosperity ever experienced.[17] During the past two decades, Western
societies have had relatively slow growth rates, but material well-being
remains high; life expectancies have reached unprecedentedly high levels and continue to increase, as do levels of education and access to
information.[18] The rest of the world has been catching up with the
West.[19] China and India – with almost 40 percent of the world's population – have had exceptionally high rates of economic growth, and
many other developing societies have made impressive gains, and sub-
Saharan Africa is now beginning to catch up in life expectancies, education and per capita incomes.[20] From 1970 to 2010, people in all regions
of the world experienced growing material well-being, increased access
to education and rising life expectancies.[21]

These changes have been accompanied by growing emphasis
on human rights and democracy.[22] For the past two centuries, democracy has become increasingly widespread – with each surge being followed by a decline, but with a long-term upward trend. Despite the
recent revival of authoritarianism, human rights and democracy have
made massive progress since the late 1980s.[23]

Pinker suggests that the decline of violence reflects the spread
of markets and trade, which depend on nonviolent human transac-
tions, as well as increasing education and access to information, which
enable people to see the world from the perspective of people unlike
themselves.[24] As this happens, 'enlightenment values' begin to dominate people's worldviews.

As this book argues, economic development, together with
declining vulnerability to starvation, disease and violence, bring a rising
sense of existential security. Young generations grow up taking survival
for granted and feel less threatened by people from other countries and
less eager to fight them.

The negative relationship between pro-choice values and tolerance of violence and war reflects an evolutionary principle: sexual

freedom and physical violence are at opposite poles of the existential security continuum. At one pole, life is full of threats, making violence and rigid sex norms a necessity of survival. At the opposite pole, violence becomes counter-productive and sexual repression becomes less crucial.[25]

Cultural evolution is also shaped by historical learning. Thus, defeat and devastation in World War II left a legacy among the publics of the former Axis powers. From the earliest available surveys to the latest ones, the Japanese, German and Italian publics have expressed the lowest willingness to fight for their country among any of the publics for which we have data. Conversely, the publics of the five Nordic countries show an anomalously high level of willingness to fight for their country that reflects the evolution of a new role for the military in those countries. Sweden played a leading role in this development. In 2000 the Swedish parliament made important changes in the role of the Swedish Armed Forces. Previously, the Swedish Armed Forces were mainly oriented toward repelling an invasion of Swedish territory, but by 2000 the risk of invasion was seen as low. The new policy held that, "Defending a nation has historically been equivalent to protecting its borders. Today, defending a nation can take place far away, through creating peace, stability and prosperity in turbulent parts of the world. In this manner, defending a nation has come to include defending its values, and protecting democracy or human rights."[26] Accordingly, Swedish military personnel are now mainly involved in international peace support operations, which have been carried out in Afghanistan, Kosovo, Bosnia, Liberia, the Congo and Lebanon. The Swedish military has close ties with those of the other Nordic countries, which hold common military exercises and share camps at missions in troubled countries. The publics of the Nordic countries have become aware of these changes, and military service has taken on connotations of serving international development and peace-keeping – in much the same way as serving in the Peace Corps has positive and prestigious connotations in the USA.[27] It seems possible that in the long run, this outlook might spread to other European countries; for now, it is almost exclusively a Nordic phenomenon. In the world as a whole, willingness to fight for one's country is still motivated by xenophobic fears, more than by the goal of defending democratic values.

Our evolutionary modernization theory suggests three hypotheses:

(1) *Cross-sectionally*, the publics of more developed societies will place more emphasis on Individual-choice values and be less willing to risk their lives in war.

(2) *Longitudinally*, in societies in which Individual-choice values are most widespread, people's willingness to risk lives in war will fall most sharply.

(3) In *multi-level perspective*, individuals who live in societies with widespread Individual-choice values will be less willing to risk their lives in war.

Since historical learning is also an influence on cultural evolution, this adds a fourth hypothesis:

(4) *Historically*, the former Axis powers' devastating defeat in World War II sharply diminished their people's willingness to fight for their country; while the exceptionally strong prevalence of Self-expression values in the Nordic countries led to the emergence of a military primarily geared to peace-keeping missions and developmental aid; this, in turn, led to the emergence of a distinctive and positive view of the role of the military among the Nordic publics, making them more willing to fight for their country.

Methods, Samples, Measurements

To test our hypotheses, we use Values Survey data from societies around the world. Surveys at multiple time points are not available from all countries, so our sample size drops to 41 countries when analyzing change in people's willingness to fight. Our dependent variable is measured by the following question:

> "Of course, we all hope that there will not be another war, but if it were to come to that, would you be willing to fight for your country?"
>
> The response options were "yes" and "no." Respondents who did not answer this question (30 percent of all respondents) are treated as missing.

Findings

As Figure 5.1 in the preceding chapter demonstrated, all six components of Individual-choice norms are strongly linked with levels of economic development, rising as we move from low-income societies to lower-middle-income societies, to upper-middle societies and reaching their highest level among high-income societies. Since economic levels have been rising during recent decades in most of the world, this suggests that Individual-choice values should have been spreading, particularly in high-income countries. This has indeed been the case, as Figure 5.4 demonstrates: Support for these norms increased 40 of the 58 countries from which we have at least ten years of time-series data – and, in keeping with the claim that these changes are linked with existential security, it increased in 23 of the 24 high-income countries.

The graphs in Figures 6.1a and 6.1b show the proportion of a public that is unwilling to fight for their country, in the latest available survey from 84 societies. The levels vary widely, from lows of 2 percent in Vietnam and Qatar and 3 percent in Turkey and China, to a high of 74 percent in Japan. The publics of Germany, Japan and Italy – the Axis Powers of World War II – show some of the world's highest rates of unwillingness to fight for their country.

Willingness to fight for one's country also varies with levels of development. In low-income societies[28] the mean figure is 20 percent, in middle-income societies 25 percent and in high-income societies, an average of 37 percent of the public is unwilling to fight for their country.

These findings suggest a link between existential security and willingness to fight for one's country, but this link is mediated by the tendency for economic development to encourage Individual-choice values. Figure 6.1 shows how a public's average willingness to fight in war is linked to the prevalence of Individual-choice values. Figure 6.1a shows the relationship in all countries from which data are available. It demonstrates that the overall correlation between Individual-choice values and unwillingness to fight ($r = .44$) is fairly strong and in the predicted direction.[29]

Andorra provides a critical test case of the inverse relationship between Individual-choice values and willingness to fight. A majority of Andorra's population now consists of prosperous French and Spanish citizens who maintain residence there to take advantage of low taxes.

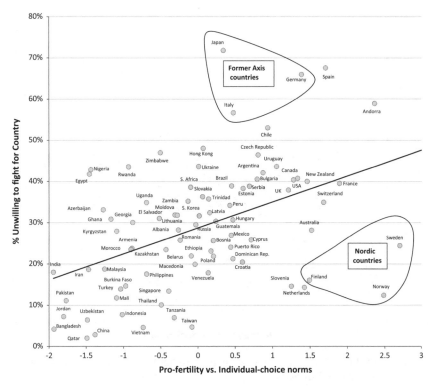

Figure 6.1a Individual-choice and willingness to fight for country (with former Axis and Nordic countries).
Based on each country's latest available survey, median year being 2007.
r = .44, r2 = .20, N = 84 countries.

It has one of the world's highest per capita incomes and no perceived military threat, and accordingly, its public shows some of the strongest pro-Individual-choice orientations among all surveyed publics – and very little willingness to fight.

There are two coherent groups of outliers, as Figure 6.1a indicates. The first group consists of the Germans, Italians and Japanese – all of whom are even more unwilling to fight than their strong pro-choice orientation predicts. This reflects the historical learning experience of their history under fascist regimes that led to devastating defeat in World War II. This left a lasting aversion to militarism that shows up in all available surveys since 1981. A contrasting group of outliers are the Nordic countries: Norway, Sweden and Finland.[30] Although their publics exhibit some of the world's strongest pro-choice orientations, their willingness to fight is much higher than this would predict because

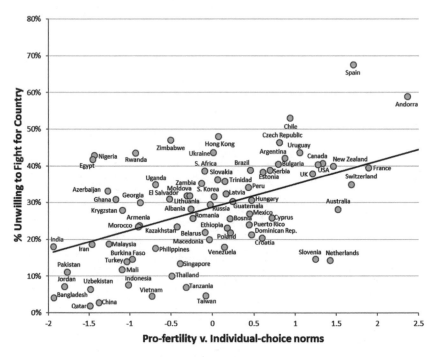

Figure 6.1b Individual-choice and willingness to fight for country (without former Axis and Nordic countries).

$r = .55, r^2 = .31$

military service has taken on very different connotations from what it has in other countries.

Because of their distinctive historic experiences, these two groups of societies deviate from the overall pattern, weakening the otherwise strongly negative relationship between Individual-choice values and willingness to fight. Accordingly, if we drop these two groups from the analysis, the impact of choice values on willingness to fight becomes stronger, as Figure 6.1b demonstrates: the overall relationship between Individual-choice norms and unwillingness to fight for one's country rises to $r = .55$.

Regression analyses demonstrate that a multivariate index of existential security explains 26 percent of the variance in willingness to fight for one's country: moving from societies with the lowest levels of existential security to those with the highest increases a public's unwillingness to fight by 28 percentage points.[31] Adding dummy variables for the former Axis and Nordic groups has an additional powerful effect, raising the explained variance to 55 percent. Adding Individual-choice values to the analysis raises the explained variance still further, to 65 percent. Moreover, while the effects of historic experiences remain strong and highly significant when we drop existential security from the analysis, choice values almost entirely absorb the pacifying effect of existential security – in keeping with the hypothesis that existential security diminishes willingness to fight largely through its tendency to produce an Individual-choice-oriented culture. Consequently, a model with only two explanatory variables – historical learning experiences and Individual-choice values – explains 65 percent of the cross-national variance in willingness to fight.

Longitudinal Evidence

Individual-choice values are linked with low willingness to fight for one's country at both the national and individual levels, but this does not demonstrate a causal linkage. To move toward a causal interpretation, we must establish that a dynamic relationship exists between Individual-choice values and willingness to fight. Figure 5.2 in the preceding chapter demonstrated that pro-choice values have been rising in most societies. This suggests that people's willingness to fight for one's country should have fallen as these values were rising.

As Figure 6.2 demonstrates, this is indeed what we find – overwhelmingly. This figure covers all 41 societies from which data is available across a span of at least ten years.[32] As it demonstrates, the public's willingness to fight fell in 36 societies, showed no change in two societies, and increased in three societies. Among societies showing any change, 92 percent became less willing to fight for their country. The mean change was a six-point decline per decade in the percentage saying they were willing to fight.

The two countries showing the largest *increases* in willingness to fight are Italy and France. Throughout the postwar period, both countries had powerful communist parties that opposed their countries' participation in NATO, which was seen as directed against the Soviet Union. After 1990, both communist parties collapsed, opening the way for modest increases in willingness to fight for one's country.

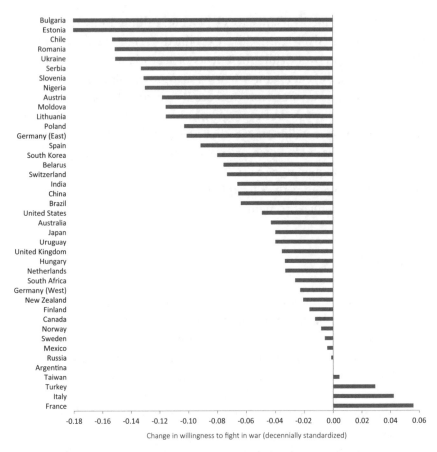

Figure 6.2 Change in people's willingness to fight for their country in war. Bars show average change scores per national population, from the earliest to latest, for all 41 countries covered by a time series of at least ten years (WVS/EVS, 1981–2012). Since length of time in change measures varies from country to country, all changes are standardized to the length of a decade.

Longitudinal analyses[33] demonstrate that willingness to fight is a relatively stable characteristic of given societies: it changes, but does so at a glacial pace. Contrary to the original version of the "democratic peace" thesis, this analysis shows that rising democracy from Time 1 to Time 2 does *not* significantly diminish willingness to fight at Time 2. Nor does rising existential security show a significant diminishing effect. The strongest effect – and the only one that is highly significant besides the Nordic experience – reflects rising emphasis on Individual-choice values.[34] When these values rise from their minimum to their maximum levels, a public's willingness to fight falls by 55 percentage points from time 1 to time 2.[35] Although only limited longitudinal evidence is available, these findings converge with those from the broader cross-sectional data, suggesting that rising Individual-choice values play a major role in reducing a public's willingness to fight.

Conclusion

Cross-sectional evidence, longitudinal evidence and multi-level evidence from societies containing most of the world's population indicates that rising existential security gives rise to Individual-choice values. As these values become widespread, people's willingness to fight other countries dwindles.

Without full experimental controls, one cannot prove causality. But evidence from countries around the world suggests that rising existential security encourages a shift toward Individual-choice orientations and reduces tolerance of human casualties, bringing a diminishing willingness to fight for one's country. The evidence suggests that this transformation has been going on over the last thirty years, strengthening the factors supporting international peace.

Cultural evolution is also driven by historic learning experiences. World War II left a lasting legacy: from the earliest available surveys to the present time, only a minority of the German, Japanese and Italian publics say that they would be willing to fight for their country. Conversely, a distinctive role for the military has emerged in the Nordic countries, endowing military service with connotations of peace-keeping among the publics of the Nordic countries.

These trends are reversible. Russia's seizure of Crimea and intervention in the Eastern Ukraine evoked widespread concern, bringing economic sanctions, capital flight from Russia and impelling Nordic political leaders to reassess the role of their countries' military forces. But so far, no influential Western leaders – not even the Hawks – have advocated military action against Russia. The norms of the Long Peace continue to prevail for now.

7 DEVELOPMENT AND DEMOCRACY*

Overview

In recent years, a democratic boom has given way to a democratic recession. Between 1987 and 1995, scores of countries made transitions to democracy, bringing widespread euphoria about democracy's future. But since then, democracy has retreated in many countries and attempts to establish democracy in Afghanistan and Iraq have left both countries in chaos. Moreover, democracy is in disarray in many high-income countries, for reasons discussed in Chapter 9. This, together with growing authoritarianism in China and Russia, has led many observers to argue that democracy has reached its high-water mark and is in long-term retreat.

That conclusion is mistaken. The underlying conditions of societies around the world point to a more complicated reality. The bad news is that it is unrealistic to assume that democratic institutions can be set up easily, anywhere. Although the outlook is never hopeless, democracy is most likely to emerge and survive when certain social and cultural conditions are present. The US government ignored this reality when it attempted to establish democracy in Iraq without considering cultural cleavages that endangered the effort.

---

* This chapter includes material from Inglehart and Welzel, 2005; Inglehart and Welzel, 2009; Welzel and Inglehart, 2008; and Inglehart and Welzel, 2010.

The good news, however, is that the conditions conducive to democracy can and do change – and abundant evidence indicates that the process of modernization advances them. Modernization is a syndrome of social changes linked with industrialization. Once set in motion, it tends to penetrate all aspects of life, bringing occupational specialization, urbanization, rising educational levels, rising life expectancy and rapid economic growth. This transforms social life and political institutions, bringing rising mass participation in politics and – in the long run – making democratic political institutions more likely.

The long-term trend toward democracy has always moved in surges and declines. At the start of the twentieth century only a handful of democracies existed, and even they were not full democracies by today's standards. There was a large increase in the number of democracies immediately after World War I, another surge following World War II, and a third surge at the end of the Cold War. Each of these surges was followed by a decline, such as the spread of fascism during the 1930s – and each period of decline stimulated widespread belief that the spread of democracy had ended, and that the wave of the future was fascism (or communism; or bureaucratic authoritarianism). But the number of democracies never fell back to its original base line, and in the long run, each decline was followed by a renewed spread of democracy. By the early twenty-first century, about 90 countries could be considered democratic.[1]

Although many of them are flawed democracies, the overall trend is striking: in the long run, the cognitive mobilization and changes in mass values linked with modernization tend to bring democracy. There is no reason to believe that this does not apply to contemporary Russia and China. Although Russia experienced a period of sharp decline following the collapse of the Soviet Union, with per capita GDP falling to 40 percent of its former peak, and life expectancy falling rather than rising, Russia's long-term trend has been toward rising economic and physical security.

Though China has had rapid economic growth since 1980, its public has not forgotten that, as recently as the 1960s, more than 30 million Chinese citizens starved to death: for now, prosperity takes top priority for most of the Chinese public, and economic success helps legitimate one-party rule by the Chinese Communist Party. The Chinese leadership is currently cracking down on dissent – partly because they are aware that economic development tends to bring demands for an increasingly open and democratic political system, as is already true in China's most prosperous region, Hong Kong. There is no need to panic about the fact that democracy is currently in retreat. The dynamics of modernization and democracy are becoming increasingly clear, and it is unlikely that they will fail to function in the long run.

Development and Democracy

Over half a century ago, Seymour Martin Lipset pointed out that rich countries are much likelier to be democracies than poor countries. Although this claim was contested for many years, it has held up against repeated tests. Why are economic development and democracy so closely linked? Simply reaching a given level of economic development does not automatically produce democracy; it can do so only by bringing changes in how people act. Accordingly, Lipset suggested that development leads to democracy because it produces certain sociocultural changes that shape human actions.[2] The empirical data needed to test this claim did not exist then, so his suggestion remained a passing comment.[3] But it has a very real basis.

A century and a half ago, Karl Marx argued that industrialization leads to the rise of the bourgeoisie, the bearer of democracy. Karl Deutsch argued that urbanization, industrialization and rising mass literacy transform geographically scattered and illiterate peasants into participants who become increasingly able to play a role in politics.[4] But representative democracy is only one possible outcome – industrialization can also lead to fascism or communism.[5]

The causal direction of the linkage between economic development and democracy has been questioned: are rich countries likelier to be democratic because democracy makes countries rich, or is development conducive to democracy? Today, it seems clear that the causal sequence works mainly from economic development to democratization. During early industrialization, authoritarian states are just as likely to attain high rates of economic growth as are democracies. But beyond a certain level, democracy becomes increasingly likely to emerge and survive. Thus, among the scores of countries that democratized around 1990, most were middle-income countries: almost all of the high-income countries already *were* democracies, and few low-income countries made the transition.

The strong correlation between development and democracy reflects the fact that economic development is conducive to democracy. The question of *why* development leads to democracy has been debated intensely. It does not result from some mysterious force that causes democratic institutions to emerge automatically when a country attains a certain level of GDP. Instead, economic development brings democracy *if* it changes people's values and behavior. Economic development is conducive to democratization insofar as it (1) creates a large and articulate middle class and (2) transforms people's values and motivations, so that they give higher priority to free choice and freedom of expression.

Today, we have better measures than ever before of what the key changes are, and how far they have progressed in given countries. Multivariate analysis of the data from the Values Surveys makes it possible to sort out the relative impact of economic, social and cultural changes, and the results indicate that economic development is conducive to democracy insofar as it brings specific structural changes (particularly the rise of a well-educated, articulate population that is accustomed to thinking for themselves) and certain cultural changes (particularly the rise of Self-expression values).[6] Wars, depressions, institutional changes, elite decisions and specific leaders also influence what happens – but cultural change is a major factor in the emergence and survival of democracy.

Modernization brings rising educational levels as the workforce moves into occupations that require independent thinking, making people more articulate and more skilled at organizing political action. As knowledge societies emerge, people become accustomed to using their own initiative and judgment on the job, and become increasingly likely to question hierarchical authority.

Modernization also makes people economically more secure, and Self-expression values become increasingly widespread when a large share of the population grows up taking survival for granted. The desire for freedom and autonomy are universal aspirations. They may be subordinated to the needs for subsistence and order when survival is precarious, but they take increasingly high priority as survival becomes secure. The basic motivation for democracy – the universal human desire for free choice – starts to play an increasingly important role. People place growing emphasis on free choice in politics and demand civil and political liberties and democratic institutions.

Effective Democracy

During the explosion of democracy that took place from 1987 to 1995, democracy spread rapidly throughout the world. Strategic elite agreements played an important role in this process, facilitated by an international environment in which the end of the Cold War opened the way for democratization. Initially, there was a tendency to view any regime that held competitive elections as a democracy. But many of the new democracies suffer from massive corruption and fail to provide the rule of law that is needed to make democracy effective. A growing number of observers now emphasize the inadequacy of "electoral democracy," "hybrid democracy," "authoritarian democracy," and other forms of sham democracy in which mass preferences – instead of being a decisive influence on government decisions, as democratic theory holds – are largely ignored by elites. It is crucial to distinguish between effective and ineffective democracies.

The essence of democracy is that it empowers ordinary citizens. Effective democracy reflects not only the extent to which civil and political rights exist on paper, but also the degree to which officials actually respect these rights. The first of these two components – the existence of rights on paper – is measured by the annual Freedom House rankings: if a society holds free elections, Freedom House tends to rate it as "free," giving it scores near or at the top of its scale. Thus, soon after they emerged, the new democracies of Poland, Hungary, Bulgaria and Romania received scores as high as those of the long-established Western democracies, although closer analysis showed that widespread corruption made these new democracies far less responsive to their citizens' choices.

If one uses the minimalist definition of electoral democracy, the characteristics of mass publics *are* relatively unimportant: one can hold elections almost anywhere. But generally accepted standards of what constitutes democracy have become increasingly demanding over time. When representative democracy first emerged, property qualifications existed and excluding women and slaves from voting was viewed as compatible with democracy. Today no one would accept that definition. Scholars of democracy have become increasingly critical of narrow electoral definitions of democracy. If one views democratization as a process by which political power moves into the hands of ordinary citizens, one needs a broader definition of democracy – and one finds that the orientations of ordinary citizens play a crucial role in democratization.

Effective democracy is linked with high levels of societal development. One can establish electoral democracy almost anywhere, but it may not be deep-rooted or long-lasting if it does not transfer power from the elites to the people. Effective democracy is most likely to exist with a relatively developed infrastructure that includes not only economic prosperity but also widespread participatory habits and emphasis on free choice among the public.

Democracy emerges when economic development increases people's resources, leading to (1) cognitive mobilization and (2) the emergence of Self-expression values. Since material sustenance and physical security are the most immediate requirements for survival, people give them top priority when they are scarce – but with growing prosperity, they become more likely to emphasize autonomy and Self-expression values that give high priority to free choice and participation in decision-making. Socioeconomic development makes people more likely to *want* democratic institutions – and cognitive mobilization makes them more skilled at organizing in order to *get* them.

In response to survey questions about whether democracy is desirable, strong majorities endorse democracy, even in countries where Self-expression values are weak – but in such cases, both the priority placed on self-expression, and the propensity to engage in political action are weak, leaving elites free to ignore mass preferences. Outside pressures from agencies such as the World Bank may prompt elites to adopt democratic institutions, but if they are not under strong domestic pressure to make these institutions effective, elites are likely to corrupt them, rendering democracy ineffective. Economic development tends to make Self-expression values increasingly widespread, both in democracies and in authoritarian societies.

The Role of Self-Expression Values

The political culture literature has always assumed that certain mass attitudes are conducive to democracy, but until recently this assumption was simply an act of faith. The influential *Civic Culture* study covered only five countries so it could not perform statistically significant tests of whether certain individual-level attitudes were linked with democracy (which exists only at the societal level). Today, the Values Surveys cover more than 100 countries, making it possible to measure whether countries where certain attitudes are relatively widespread actually *are* more democratic than other countries. The findings indicate that certain mass attitudes are strongly linked with democracy.

But face-validity is an unreliable guide concerning which attitudes have the most impact on democracy. Much research on democracy is based on the assumption that societies in which the public says favorable things about democracy are most likely to be democratic. This assumption seems perfectly plausible – until one discovers that the percentage of the public expressing favorable attitudes toward democracy is higher in Albania and Azerbaijan than it is in Sweden or Switzerland. At this point in history, most people are ready to give lip service to democracy, and in public opinion surveys strong majorities of the public in almost every country say that democracy is the best form of government. But this does not necessarily tap deep-rooted orientations or strong motivations – in some cases it simply reflects social desirability effects.

Explicit mass-level endorsement of democracy shows a fairly strong correlation with the existence of democracy at the societal level. But, surprising as it may seem, Self-expression values – which do not even mention democracy – are a much stronger predictor of democracy than is explicit support for democracy.[7] For endorsement of democracy does *not* necessarily go with the interpersonal trust, tolerance of other groups and political activism that are core components of Self-expression values – and empirical analysis demonstrates that these are far more important to the emergence and survival of democratic institutions than mere lip service. Consequently Self-expression values are much more strongly linked with democratic institutions than is explicit endorsement of democracy.

One reason why this is true is because Self-expression values are conducive to pro-democratic mass action. Self-expression values place a high value on freedom and autonomy. Explicit endorsement of democracy, on the other hand, may reflect various other motivations, such as the belief that democracy brings prosperity. Thus, survey questions concerning whether democracy is preferable to authoritarian alternatives are substantially weaker predictors of whether democratic institutions are actually present at the societal level than are Self-expression values.

These findings help us understand why economic development is linked with democracy: development brings rising education and employment in knowledge-sector jobs that make people more articulate and skillful in organizing to make effective demands; it also makes them more secure, encouraging Self-expression values that give high priority to freedom of choice. Since democratic institutions provide greater free choice than authoritarian institutions, people with Self-expression values generally want democracy. Elites do not choose in a vacuum whether to adopt democracy. As publics become increasingly articulate, well-organized and place higher priority on freedom, elites have less choice in the matter.

To construct an index of effective democracy, we multiply the Freedom House measures of civil and political rights by the World Bank's anti-corruption scores,[8] which is an indicator of "elite integrity," or the extent to which state power actually follows legal norms. When we examine the linkage between this measure of genuine democracy and mass Self-expression values, we find an amazingly strong correlation of $r = .90$ across 73 nations, as Figure 7.1 demonstrates. This pattern reflects a powerful cross-level linkage, connecting mass values that emphasize free choice, and the extent to which societal institutions actually provide it.

Figure 7.1 shows the relationship between this index of effective democracy and mass Self-expression values. The extent to which Self-expression values are present in a society explains over 80 percent of the cross-national variance in the extent to which liberal democracy is actually practiced. These findings suggest that the importance of the linkage between individual-level values and democratic institutions has been underestimated. Today, mass preferences seem to play a crucial role in the emergence of genuine democracy.[9]

The linkage between mass Self-expression values and democratic institutions is remarkably strong and consistent, showing only a few outliers – but these outliers are significant. China and Vietnam show considerably lower levels of democracy than their publics' values would predict. Both countries have authoritarian regimes that have greatly increased the latitude for individual choice in the economic realm, and have been experimenting with local-level democracy – but their one-party regimes are extremely reluctant to allow competition at the national level. In the long run, the success of their economic reforms tends to give rise to societal pressures that erode one-party dominance.

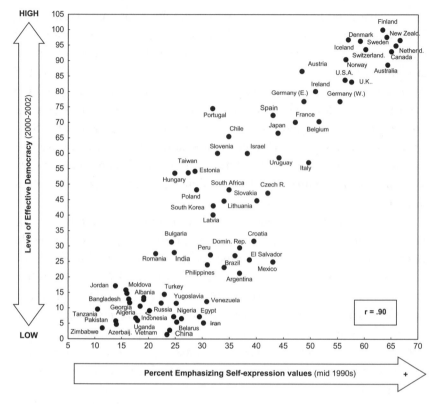

Figure 7.1 Effective democracy around 2000 by a country's mean level of Self-expression values in mid 1990s.

Source: Inglehart and Welzel, 2005: 155.

Authoritarian rulers of some Asian societies have claimed that the distinctive "Asian values" of these societies make them unsuitable for democracy (Zakaria and Lee, 1994; Thompson, 2000). In fact, the position of most Asian countries on Figure 7.1 is about where their level of socioeconomic development would predict. Japan ranks with the established Western democracies, both on the Self-expression values dimension and on its level of democracy. And South Korea's position on both dimensions is similar to those of other relatively new democracies such as Chile and Uruguay. The publics of Confucian societies are more supportive of democracy than the "Asian values" school assumes.

On the other hand, in the Muslim-majority societies from which we have data, less than 30 percent of the public ranks high on Self-expression values. The goal of democracy is attractive to these publics, but their levels of tolerance and trust and the priority they give to self-expression fall short of what is found in all established democracies. But we do not find an unbridgeable chasm between Islamic societies and the rest of the world. The belief systems of these Islamic countries also fall roughly where their level of socioeconomic development would predict them to be. The most developed of them, Turkey, is near the transition zone along with other countries such as the Philippines, South Africa, Poland, South Korea and Slovenia that experienced relatively recent transitions to democracy. Iran is a significant exception insofar as it has a lower level of democracy than its public's values would predict. Among all Islamic countries, Iran shows the strongest liberalizing pressures from its public. This tension leads us to expect that growing mass support may eventually help the country's liberalizing forces overcome theocratic rule, bringing the country on a path to liberal democracy. In recent national elections, strong majorities of the Iranian public voted in favor of regimes seeking closer relations with Western democracies – but their ability to move in this direction was blocked by unelected theocratic elites who control the military and police.

Which comes first – a democratic political culture or democratic institutions? The extent to which people emphasize Self-expression values is closely linked with the flourishing of democratic institutions. But what causes what? Previous research indicates that socioeconomic development leads to democracy, rather than the other way around. Thus, the causal direction of the relationship between socioeconomic development and democracy has been analyzed by Burkhart and Lewis-Beck (1994), using empirical data from 131 countries. They conclude that socioeconomic development causes democracy, but that democracy does not cause socioeconomic development. Helliwell (1993) reaches similar conclusions. Let us pursue these finding further.

The Impact of Self-Expression Values

Empirically, one finds a remarkably strong correlation between Self-expression values and effective democracy. But do Self-expression values lead to democracy, or does democracy cause Self-expression values to emerge? The evidence indicates that the causal flow moves mainly from Self-expression values to democracy.[10] One strong indication is the fact that democratic institutions do not need to be in place for Self-expression values to emerge. In the years preceding the 1990 wave of democratization, Self-expression values had emerged through a process of intergenerational value change – not only in Western democracies, but also within many authoritarian societies.[11] By 1990, the publics of East Germany and Czechoslovakia – living in two of the world's most authoritarian regimes – had developed high levels of Self-expression values. Although their political system were authoritarian, these countries were among the most economically advanced countries within the communist world, with highly developed educational systems and advanced social welfare systems – and high levels of Self-expression values. Thus, when the threat of Soviet military intervention was removed, they moved swiftly toward democracy.

Self-expression values emerge when a large share of the population grows up taking survival for granted. As countries develop, this worldview tends to emerge even under authoritarian political regimes. People become economically and physically more secure and more articulate. They seek more freedom of choice concerning how to spend time and money, what to believe, and with whom to interact. Even repressive regimes find it difficult to check these tendencies, for they are intimately linked with modernization, and repressing them hinders the emergence of an effective knowledge sector. Self-expression values seem to emerge in any regime where modernization increases people's sense of existential security.

In knowledge societies, people become accustomed to using their own initiative and judgment in their daily lives. They become increasingly likely to question hierarchical authority, for the desire for free choice and autonomy are universal aspirations. They may be subordinated to the needs for subsistence and order when survival is precarious, but they take increasingly high priority as survival becomes more secure. The specific democratic institutions that emerged during the past two hundred years are largely a product of Western history. But the basic motivation for democracy – the human desire for free choice – is the natural product of an environment in which rising existential security leads to the spread of Self-expression values.

Elites almost always seek to stay in power. Accordingly, democratic institutions generally emerge only when people struggle to attain them; this has been true from the liberal revolutions of the eighteenth century to the democratic revolutions of the late twentieth century. People's motivations and values played an important role in the past and they are becoming increasingly important. Self-expression values place an inherent value on freedom and self-expression, and in recent decades these values have been spreading across most of the world. Does this mean that authoritarian systems will inevitably crumble? Not automatically. Rising emphasis on Self-expression values erodes the legitimacy of authoritarian systems, but as long as determined authoritarian elites control the army and secret police, they usually can repress pro-democratic forces.

But modernization tends to bring both cognitive mobilization and growing emphasis on Self-expression values. A growing share of the people becomes motivated to demand democratic institutions, and increasingly effective in doing so. The costs and risks of repression become increasingly high. Finally, with intergenerational replacement, the elite itself may become less authoritarian and repressive, as its younger cohorts emerge from a society that places increasing value on self-expression. Social change is not deterministic, but modernization brings a growing probability that democratic institutions will emerge.

Explaining Shifts to and away from Democracy

Let us test the thesis that Self-expression values are conducive to democracy, from another perspective, building on a central premise of the political culture approach – the congruence thesis. Prominent social scientists claim that the stability of political regimes depends on the congruence between political institutions and mass values:[12] political institutions must be consistent with the citizens' value orientations or they will lack legitimacy, and their stability will be low. The greater the incongruence between mass values and political institutions, the more unstable the regime will be. If this claim is true, shifts to and away from democracy should reflect the incongruence between institutions and culture: the larger the incongruence, the larger subsequent change will be.[13] If changes occur, they should be greatest in countries that start out with the largest gaps between culture and institutions: regime changes adjust the discrepancy between culture and institutions.

One can view the linkage between democratic institutions and Self-expression values as reflecting the congruence between the supply and the demand for freedom. Democratic institutions provide a high supply of freedom since they institutionalize civil and political liberties; and Self-expression values create a cultural demand for freedom because these values emphasize freedom of choice. This means that there are two varieties of congruence: (1) an authoritarian state has congruent institutions and culture if its people emphasize Survival values rather than Self-expression values; and (2) democracies have congruence if their people emphasize Self-expression values, creating a strong mass demand for freedom that is consistent with their societies' broad institutional supply of freedom.

Conversely, if the citizens of an authoritarian state place strong emphasis on Self-expression values, moving toward democracy would reduce incongruence, bringing it into closer correspondence with the underlying cultural demand. Similarly, a society with high levels of democracy but low emphasis on self-expression would have an institutional oversupply of freedom, so one would expect a shift *away* from democracy.

During the Third Wave of democratization, in the late 1980s and early 1990s, dozens of countries made transitions from authoritarian to democratic regimes. This provides an opportunity to analyze the dynamics of the relationship between cultural values and democratic institutions.

The incongruence between the institutional supply of democracy and the cultural demand for democracy is calculated by subtracting the demand from the supply. In order to measure the incongruence that was present before the Third Wave transition, we use the pre-transition levels of democracy, as measured during 1981–1986, to indicate the supply. To calculate the cultural demand for democracy, we use Self-expression values measured around 1990 as an indication of how strong these values were *before* the transition.[14]

The more Self-expression values surpass a society's level of democracy, the greater the unmet demand. In the analysis shown on Figure 7.2, a score of −1 indicates the strongest possible *lack* of demand for more democracy, while a score of +1 indicates the maximum demand for more democracy. Our sample includes a number of stable Western democracies in which the levels of democracy have been constant since measurement began. These 16 democracies are in an equilibrium where supply and demand for democracy are in balance; accordingly, they are at the zero-point on the incongruence scale. They also are at the zero-point on the vertical dimension, which measures how much *change* a country experienced in its level of effective democracy from the early

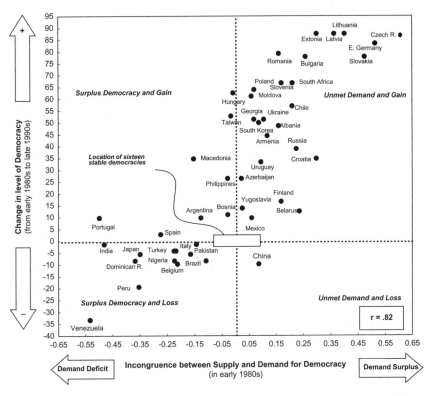

Figure 7.2 Change in level of effective democracy from early 1980s to late 1990s, by unmet demand for (or surplus supply of) democracy in early 1980s.
Source: Inglehart and Welzel, 2005: 189.

1980s to the late 1990s: since the supply and demand for democracy were in balance, they experienced no change.

The horizontal incongruence scale on Figure 7.2 reflects the extent to which the demand for democracy exceeds, or falls short of, its supply. We hypothesize that a society's score on this scale in the early 1980s will predict both the direction and the extent to which a society experienced subsequent changes towards more or less democracy: countries with unmet demand should move toward more democracy; while countries with more democracy than their culture demands should move toward *less* democracy. Moreover, moves toward democracy should be largest among the countries with the highest positive scores on the incongruence scale.

These predictions are right on target, as Figure 7.2 demonstrates. Unlike Figure 7.1, which shows the relationship between levels of Self-expression values and levels of democracy, this figure analyzes the impact of the *discrepancy* between mass values and levels of democracy, on *changes* in levels of democracy from the mid-1980s to the mid-1990s.[15] As Figure 7.2 demonstrates, the more the cultural demand for democracy exceeded its institutional supply around 1986, the greater were the subsequent moves towards democracy, from 1987 to 2002. The reverse relationship also holds also true: the more the cultural demand for democracy fell short of its actual supply, the larger the moves *away* from democracy.

We interpret scores on the horizontal axis as reflecting *unmet mass demand for democracy* – which created a political tension that was released when the blocking factors were removed around 1990. As the data demonstrate, the countries that had the highest unmet mass demand for democracy, were the ones that made the largest subsequent movement toward democracy.

Self-expression values exert pressure for *change* in levels of democracy. These values emerge through long-term intergenerational changes, while democracy often emerges suddenly after long periods of institutional blockage. Consequently, it is the *level* of Self-expression values at the time of the breakthrough, not recent *changes* in these levels, that determines the magnitude of subsequent changes toward democracy. The analysis shown in Figure 7.2 is not the usual way to analyze change, but it is an appropriate way to analyze processes involving thresholds and blocking factors, as applies here. The results indicate that a society's unmet demand for democracy in 1990 accounts for 67 percent of the change in levels of democracy from the mid-1980s to the mid-1990s.

But do Self-expression values lead to democracy, or does democracy bring Self-expression values? It seems to be mainly the former, for democratic institutions do not need to be in place for Self-expression values to emerge. Time series evidence from the Values Surveys indicates that in the years preceding the 1988–1992 wave of democratization, Self-expression values had emerged through a process of intergenerational value change – not only in Western democracies, but also in many authoritarian societies. By 1990, the publics of East Germany, Czechoslovakia, Estonia, Latvia and Lithuania – living under strongly authoritarian regimes – had developed high levels of Self-expression values despite their authoritarian political systems, reflecting the fact that they were among the most economically advanced countries in the communist world, with high levels of prosperity, education and advanced social welfare systems. In the decades before 1990, Self-expression values had been spreading, making people more likely to intervene directly in politics. Thus, when Gorbachev withdrew the threat of Soviet military intervention, unprecedented numbers of people participated in the demonstrations that helped bring about the wave of democratization that took place from 1988 to 1992. As long as determined authoritarian elites control the army and police, they can repress pro-democratic forces. But even repressive regimes find it costly to do so, for it tends to block the emergence of an effective knowledge sector.

There was only one case of the opposite phenomenon, where levels of democracy declined although the demand exceeded the supply – China being the sole exception. The Chinese government provided an extremely low supply of democracy, but mass demands gradually built up, erupting in the Democracy Movement of 1989, when demonstrators took over Tiananmen Square in Beijing, demanding greater freedom of expression. For a few months the government wavered – but in June 1989 China's top leaders ordered the army to repress the movement, using tanks to do so. The repression of the Democracy Movement illustrates the fact that mass demands for freedom do not always succeed. Determined authoritarian elites can repress mass pressures as long as they control the military. But sheer repression is costly. In 1989, the Democracy Movement was mainly concentrated among the younger and more educated segments of the urban population, in a society that was still predominantly rural. If socioeconomic development continues at its current pace, mass emphasis on self-expression will eventually become more widespread. In the long run it is likely to permeate the ranks of the younger military and party elites, making it increasingly difficult to resist democratization.

There were far more societies where the demand for freedom exceeded its supply, than societies where the demand for freedom fell short of its supply. But there *were* some countries in the latter category, such as Venezuela and Peru – and these were precisely the cases that showed *declining* levels of democracy.

The overall pattern is dominated by a strong tendency for the balance between mass demands for democracy, and a society's supply of democracy, to become congruent. This tendency explains fully 67 per cent of the variance in changes towards higher or lower levels of democracy during the Third Wave. This dynamic model explains *changes* in levels of democracy, and not just static levels of democracy.

It is virtually impossible to interpret the relationship depicted in Figure 7.2 as reflecting the impact of democratic institutions on Self-expression values. As we have seen, changes in Self-expression values built up steadily over long periods of time. The level of Self-expression values measured around 1990 had been accumulating over many years, and it existed before democratization occurred. Democratization around 1990 could not have created the levels of Self-expression values that existed in the 1980s. The causal arrow can only run from accumulated Self-expression values toward the sudden societal changes: the supply of democracy moved toward greater congruence with the societies' underlying demands for freedom.

This confirms a point made by Inglehart and Welzel:[16] controlling for other variables, the relation between Self-expression values and liberal democracy operates primarily from values to democracy. Previous levels of democracy show no impact on Self-expression values, when one controls for the temporal autocorrelation[17] of Self-expression values; but Self-expression values *do* have a substantial impact on democracy levels – even controlling for the temporal autocorrelation of democracy.

Though elite bargaining was central when representative democracy first emerged, and still plays an important role, effective democracy increasingly emerges when ordinary people develop values and skills that enable them to put effective pressures on elites. Modernization not only brings growing emphasis on Self-expression values – it also leads to social and cognitive mobilization. These two sets of changes make people more likely to *want* democracy, and increasingly effective in organizing to *get* it. Let us discuss the cognitive mobilization factor in more detail.

Social Mobilization and Cognitive Mobilization: The Shifting Balance of Political Skills

In early face-to-face political communities such as the tribe or city state, political communication was by word of mouth and dealt with things one knew first hand. Virtually everyone possessed the skills necessary for political participation, so politics could be relatively democratic, with decision-making often taking place in councils where every adult male had a voice.

The emergence of extensive political communities, governing millions rather than thousands of people, required special skills such as literacy. Word of mouth communications were no longer adequate; written messages had to be sent and received across great distances. Human memory was no longer capable of recording such details as the tax base of thousands of villages or the military manpower they could raise; written records were needed. And personal chains of loyalties were inadequate to hold together large empires; legitimating myths or ideologies had to be propagated.

The extensive political community had a greatly enlarged population and resource base, which enabled it to drive smaller competitors out of existence. But a price was paid. Elites with specialized skills were needed to coordinate the system. A wide gap opened between the illiterate masses, who did not have the specialized training needed to cope with politics at a distance, and a small elite who dealt with national politics. The peasant masses became almost irrelevant to the politics of large agrarian nations.

Industrialization makes it possible to narrow again the gap between elites and masses. As parochial people become urbanized, literate, and in contact with mass media, they gain the skills needed to relate to the national political community rather than just their village.[18] Deutsch analyzed the process of "social mobilization," which occurs when people are uprooted from physical and intellectual isolation, and from old traditions, occupations, and places of residence.[19] Gradually they became integrated into modern organizations and extensive communications networks – expanding their horizons beyond the scope of word-of-mouth communications and increasingly coming in touch with national politics.

Advanced industrial societies have long since completed the outwardly visible stages of social mobilization, such as urbanization, industrialization, mass literacy, mass military service and universal suffrage. But the core of the process continues: the dissemination of the skills needed to cope with an extensive political community. The term "cognitive mobilization" refers to this aspect of the process. Though formal education is only one component of cognitive mobilization, it is the best readily available indicator (though having a job that requires thinking for oneself is equally important).

As Figure 7.3 indicates, the proportion of the population of 18–25-year-olds receiving higher education has risen dramatically

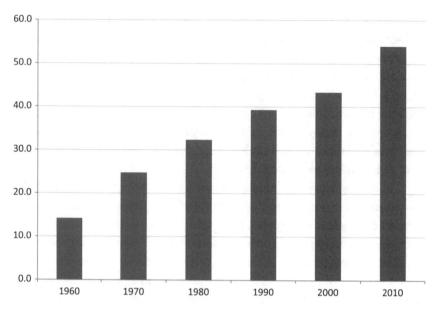

Figure 7.3 Mean percentage of college-age population enrolled in higher education in the USA, Germany and Japan, 1960–2010.
(columns show mean percent for the three countries, equally weighted).
Sources: US data from National Center of Education Statistics, 2012; Snyder, 1993 and US Census Bureau, 2012. Japan data from: Ministry of Education, Culture, Sports, Science and Technology – Japan, 2012. German data from: Kehm, 1999 and Statistisches Bundesamt (2012). Size of relevant age group is based on UN Department of Economic and Social Affairs, 2012.

during the past half-century in advanced industrial societies: in 1960, only 16 percent of the people in the relevant age-group in the USA, Germany and Japan were enrolled in higher education. The figure increased steadily, to the point where in 2010, well over half of this age-group were enrolled in higher education. This is just one indication of the extent to which the general population is gaining skills that enable them to communicate and organize for effective political action. Educated people are more likely to have a sense of "subjective political competence" and to take part in politics.[20] Numerous other studies have found that people with higher socioeconomic status are also likelier to participate in politics. But is this due to cognitive mobilization or to social status itself? In other words, are the better educated more likely to have more say in politics because they have the skills needed to press their demands more effectively – or simply because they have

better social connections, and more money with which to induce officials to bend the rules on their behalf?

It would be naive to think that wealth and personal connections are unimportant. But skills and information are important too.
By definition, there will always be an upper third, a middle third and
a lower third in socioeconomic status. But ordinary citizens' levels of
education and information have risen greatly, shifting the balance of
political skills between elites and mass, increasing the citizens' ability
to make effective political demands.

Economic development tends to increase the size of the middle class, bringing higher rates of membership in formal organizations.
Education is an indicator of one's social status, but it is also an indicator of communication skills. The distinction is important, for in multivariate analysis, cognitive variables such as education and political
information prove to be much more powerful predictors of political
participation than do relatively pure social-class indicators such as
income or occupation.[21] Communication skills seem to be even more
conducive to political participation than is social status per se.

Participation springs from two fundamentally different processes, one underlying an older mode of political participation, the
other a newer mode.[22] The institutions that mobilized mass political
participation in the late nineteenth and early twentieth century – labor
unions, churches and mass political parties – were hierarchical organizations in which a small number of leaders or bosses led a mass of
disciplined troops. They were effective in bringing large numbers of
newly enfranchised citizens to the polls in an era when universal compulsory education had just taken root and the average citizen had a
low level of political skills. But while these elite-directed organizations could mobilize large numbers, they usually produced only a relatively low qualitative level of participation, generally the simple act of
voting.

A newer elite-directing mode of participation expresses the
individual's preferences with greater precision than the old. It is issue-
oriented, and based on ad hoc groups rather than on established
bureaucratic organizations. And it aims at effecting specific policy
changes rather than simply supporting the representatives of a given
group. This mode of participation requires relatively high skill levels.

Thus, if we take one's formal education as an indicator of political skills, we find that sheer literacy seems sufficient for voting. Most

Western citizens reached this threshold generations ago. But while literacy alone may be sufficient to produce high rates of voting, higher educational levels are closely associated with more active forms of political action, such as signing petitions or participating in demonstrations. But high levels of political *skills* are a much stronger predictor of active participation than are education or social class.[23]

The rise of the knowledge society also leads to a growing potential for citizen participation in politics. In knowledge societies, one's job experience develops politically relevant skills. The traditional assembly-line worker produced material objects, working in a hierarchical system that required (and allowed) little autonomous judgment. Workers in the service and information sectors deal with people and concepts; operating in an environment where innovation is crucial, they need autonomy to use their own judgment. It is inherently impossible to prescribe innovation from above. Accustomed to working in less hierarchical decision structures in their job life, people in the information and service sectors are relatively likely to have both the skills and the inclination to take part in decision-making in the political realm as well.

Strong organizational networks can help less advantaged groups attain higher participation rates, and situational factors are also important. But in the long run, rising levels of skills are even more significant. In politics, exciting periods tend to alternate with dull ones; in the long run, people tend to lose interest. But the long-term effects of Cognitive Mobilization – that is, rising individual-level political skills – tend to be cumulative. Cognitive Mobilization is gradually raising the baseline of mass political participation.

The emergence of postindustrial society brings social and cultural changes that make democracy increasingly probable. Knowledge societies cannot function effectively without highly educated publics, who become increasingly accustomed to thinking for themselves – on the job and in political life. Furthermore, rising levels of economic security bring a growing emphasis on Self-expression values, which give high priority to free choice and motivate political action. Beyond a certain point, it becomes difficult to avoid democratization, because repressing mass demands for more open societies becomes increasingly costly and detrimental to economic effectiveness. Thus, in its advanced stages, modernization brings social and cultural changes that tend to bring democratic institutions.

Redistribution and Democracy

Some highly influential literature treats democracy as something that elites grant, if the costs in terms of economic redistribution are not excessive. This approach largely ignores the impact of cognitive mobilization and changing mass values.

Empirically, we find tremendous variation in the degree to which given publics give high priority to obtaining democratic institutions, and in their ability to organize effective demands for them. Economic development dramatically increases people's material and cognitive resources, enabling them to mount more powerful collective actions, and putting increasingly effective pressure on elites.[24] Moreover, it is not the have-nots who desire democracy most strongly. Instead, when people have relatively ample economic and cognitive resources, and move from emphasizing Survival values toward emphasizing Self-expression values, they strive most strongly for democratic institutions.

Accordingly, the survival of authoritarian regimes is not simply a question of whether elites choose to repress the masses. It reflects the balance of forces between elites and masses – which changes over time. The massive wave of democratization around 1990 was, in large part, a story of effective mass mobilization, motivated by strong emphasis on Self-expression values among people who had become increasingly articulate and skilled at organizing mass movements. The most important effect of modernization is not that it makes democracy more acceptable to elites. It is that modernization increases ordinary citizens' capabilities and willingness to struggle for democratic institutions.

An analysis of income and democracy carried out by Acemoglu et al. is a penetrating attempt to understand why rich countries are much likelier to be democratic than poor ones.[25] Using a massive historical data base, Acemoglu and his colleagues probe far back in time to see if increasing wealth preceded increasing democracy. Only when they push their analysis back fully 500 years do they find a positive correlation between changes in income and changes in democracy – which weakens or disappears when they control for fixed country effects. They conclude that both economic development and the rise of democracy are strongly path-dependent and that five centuries ago, certain European countries and their colonists embarked on a development path linked with both democracy and economic growth, while other countries moved on a path that led to political repression and less economic growth.

Their analysis indicates that nation-specific effects play a decisive role, but they do little to clarify the nature of these all-important effects. The remarkable durability of these effects suggests that they are deep-rooted cultural and institutional factors similar to those that Putnam uncovered in his analysis of the differences between the political cultures of Northern and Southern Italy – which also could be traced back to patterns that have persisted for centuries.[26] His findings also indicate that deeply rooted cultural and institutional factors play a decisive role.

Acemoglu, Robinson and their colleagues are right: economic development alone does *not* bring democracy. It does so only in combination with certain cultural and institutional factors. But these factors are not necessarily unique to certain European countries and countries populated mainly by their emigrants. Evidence from the Values Surveys indicates that in recent years, these cultural and institutional factors have been spreading through much of the world.

The model used by Acemoglu and Robinson treats mass desire for democracy as a constant that cannot explain why democracy emerges. Consequently, it leaves an unexplained elephant in the room: at the start of the twentieth century, there were only a handful of democracies in the world; by the end of the century there were scores of democracies. If economic development didn't bring this change, what did? Their model indicates that certain countries have long had a lead in both economic development and democracy, but doesn't explain what caused this immense *increase* in democracy. I argue that the root cause was economic and social modernization, which brought changes in values and social structure that made democracy increasingly likely.

Evolutionary modernization theory implies – and data from many countries confirms – that emphasize on Self-expression values has grown in recent decades, increasing the strength of mass demands for democracy. Around 1990, changes on the international scene opened the way for dozens of countries to democratize.[27] The extent to which given countries then moved toward higher levels of democracy reflects the strength of the unmet demand for democracy in these societies when this window of opportunity opened.

Acemoglu et al. don't treat mass values and skills as having an autonomous impact on democratization: mass protest is simply assumed to be something that happens whenever economic inequality is high. These assumptions fit earlier historical data relatively well, when the masses were illiterate peasants, but they are inadequate to explain the most recent wave of democratization. Political motivations have been changing massively and the propensity to participate in demonstrations in postindustrial societies has more than doubled since 1974.[28] Thus, in the 1987–1995 wave of democratization, historically unprecedented numbers of demonstrators participated in demands for democratization from Seoul and Manila to Moscow and East Berlin. Moreover, this time the struggle was not primarily about economic redistribution but about political liberty. To a striking degree, democratization in the ex-communist world was *not* motivated by mass pressures for greater economic equality – it shifted power from elites who strongly emphasized economic equality, to groups that emphasized it *less* strongly.

Democracy does not simply emerge from the desire for economic redistribution. It emerges from a struggle for democratic freedoms that go far beyond the right to vote. Throughout most of human history, despotism and autocracy prevailed. This was not simply because elites chose to repress the masses, but also because until the modern era, the masses lacked the organizational skills and the resources needed to mobilize effective demands for democratic institutions – and obtaining them was not their top priority. To understand how democracy emerges, it is not sufficient to focus solely on elites – increasingly, one must also study mass-level developments.

Conclusion

Modernization theory has both positive and negative implications. It holds that high levels of existential security are conducive to the spread of democracy – and that declining economic security has the opposite effect. And as Chapter 9 demonstrates, for the past three decades, a large share of the population of high-income societies has experienced declining real income and sharply declining relative income in comparison with their country's top 10 percent. This has stimulated the rise of xenophobic authoritarian populist parties in many European countries, and the election of a US President who attacks the mass media as "the enemy of the American people" and attempts to intimidate "so-called judges" who refuse to carry out his edicts – threatening freedom of the press and an independent judiciary.

Democracy is currently in retreat. The question is: "Is this the end of the line, or is it a temporary decline comparable to the declines experienced earlier?" The long-term trend is clear: since the Industrial Revolution, the world has become richer and safer, with declining rates of both war and domestic violence. Even today, the world as a whole is becoming richer, though the high-income countries are currently experiencing an Authoritarian Reflex – not because of objective scarcity (their economic resources are abundant and growing) but largely because of steeply rising economic inequality that is ultimately a political problem. If it were reversed, the long-term spread of democracy probably would resume.

Economic development is strongly linked with the rise of effective democracy because it tends to bring rising Self-expression values and mass mobilization. Modernization is a process based on industrialization that brings rising education, a modern occupational structure and rising levels of existential security – which eventually leads mass publics to give increasing high priority to democracy.

Evolutionary modernization theory has both encouraging and cautionary implications for US foreign policy. Iraq provides a cautionary lesson. Contrary to the appealing view that democratization can readily be established almost anywhere, this theory implies that democracy is much likelier to flourish under certain conditions than others. A number of factors made it unrealistic to expect that democracy would be easy to establish in Iraq, including deep ethnic cleavages that had been exacerbated by Saddam's policies. And after Saddam's defeat, allowing physical security to collapse was a fatal mistake. Interpersonal trust and tolerance flourish when people feel secure. Democracy is unlikely to survive in a society torn by distrust and intolerance, and in recent surveys, the Iraqi public manifested the highest level of xenophobia of any society for which data are available.[29]

Evolutionary modernization theory also has positive implications for US foreign policy. Supported by a large body of evidence, it points to the conclusion that economic development is a basic driver of democratic change – meaning that the US government should do what it can to encourage development. If it wanted to bring democratic change to Cuba, for example, isolating it was counterproductive. Lifting the embargo, promoting economic development, and fostering social engagement and connection to the world are likely to be more effective. Nothing is certain, but empirical evidence suggests that a growing sense of security and growing emphasis on Self-expression values tend to erode authoritarian regimes.

Similarly, although many observers have been alarmed by the economic resurgence of China, it has positive long-term implications. Beneath China's seemingly monolithic political structure, the social pre-conditions for democratization are emerging, and have progressed far-ther than many observers realize. In terms of the public's orientations, China is moving toward the level of mass emphasis on Self-expression values at which Chile, Poland, South Korea and Taiwan made tran-sitions to democracy. As long as the Chinese Communist Party con-trols the security forces, democratic institutions will not emerge at the national level. But mass pressures for liberalization are likely to emerge, and repressing them will have growing costs in terms of eco-nomic efficiency and public morale. In the long run, growing prosperity for China is favorable to the US national interest. More broadly, mod-ernization theory implies that the United States should welcome and encourage economic development around the world.

8 THE CHANGING ROOTS OF HAPPINESS*

Overview

Cultural change is a process through which societies adapt their survival strategies. The process operates as if evolutionary forces were consciously seeking to maximize human happiness.

In agrarian societies with little or no economic growth or social mobility, people's options are severely limited and religion makes people happier by lowering their aspirations and promising upward social mobility in an afterlife. But modernization brings changes that are conducive to happiness because they give people a broader range of choices in how to live their lives. Consequently, although *within* most countries religious people are happier than non-religious people, the people of modernized but secular countries are happier than the people of less modernized but religious countries: the modern strategy seems to be more effective than the traditional strategy to maximize happiness.

But *can* human happiness be maximized? Until recently, it was widely held that happiness fluctuates around fixed set-points – possibly genetically determined ones – so neither individuals nor societies can lastingly increase their happiness. Recent evidence undermines that conclusion. Data from representative national surveys carried out from 1981 to 2014 show that happiness rose in an overwhelming

---

* This chapter draws on material from Inglehart, Foa, Peterson and Welzel, 2008; Inglehart, 2010; and Inglehart, 1997.

majority of the 62 countries for which substantial time series data are available. Why?

Extensive empirical evidence indicates that the extent to which a society allows free choice has a major impact on happiness. From 1981 to 2007, economic development, democratization and rising social tolerance increased the extent to which the people of most countries had free choice in economic, political and social life – leading to higher levels of happiness and life satisfaction.

Development, Freedom and Happiness: A Global Perspective

Psychologists, economists, biologists, sociologists and political scientists have investigated human happiness for many years and until recently one claim found widespread acceptance: happiness remains constant. An influential body of research holds that neither rising prosperity nor severe misfortune permanently affect happiness. After a period of adjustment, it is claimed, individuals return to their baseline levels of well-being, leaving humanity on a "hedonic treadmill."[1] Similarly, as entire countries become richer, relative gains and losses neutralize each other across populations, bringing no overall increase in the happiness of their citizens.[2]

Moreover, biological factors are closely linked with a sense of well-being,[3] and research on genetic factors suggest that happiness is largely heritable.[4] Individual differences in happiness may be more or less permanent.[5] A widely accepted view is that happiness fluctuates around a fixed set-point.[6] Insofar as this set-point is biologically determined, neither individual efforts nor social policy can bring lasting changes in happiness.

In keeping with this belief, a large body of evidence indicates that the mean subjective well-being levels of given countries tend to be remarkably stable over long periods of time.[7] Social comparison theory claims to explain this stability, arguing that happiness stays the same in the face of rising income because of shifts in reference. If happiness is shaped by one's *relative* position in a society, then even if a nation's overall economy grows, only those with above-average gains will experience rising happiness, and these increases will be offset by decreases among those with below-average gains.[8]

The strongest support for the claim that the happiness levels of countries remains constant comes from the United States, which provides the longest and most detailed time series. Hundreds of surveys have measured happiness and life satisfaction among the American public since 1946, and the data show a flat trend from then to the present. Because the happiness levels of given societies do not seem to change over time, the idea that economic development brings rising happiness has been widely rejected.

Can Happiness Change?

But recent research demonstrates that the subjective well-being levels of some people can and do change over time.[9] Individuals are not necessarily trapped on a hedonic treadmill.

What about nations? Findings that happiness can change for individuals do not necessarily mean that the happiness levels of given societies change. If the relative gains and losses of different individuals cancel each other out, there will be no discernible shifts, upward or downward, for a society as a whole.

But cross-sectional comparisons of nations show a great deal of variation in happiness and life satisfaction that seems to reflect their prosperity. In 1990, I analyzed data from 24 countries covering the full range from rich to very poor, and found a .67 correlation between per capita GNP and life satisfaction. I interpreted this as implying that economic development *is* conducive to rising happiness.[10] Sufficient longitudinal evidence was not then available to provide compelling support for this interpretation. Although rich nations clearly do show higher levels of subjective well-being than poor countries, it was claimed that this simply reflects idiosyncratic cultural differences.

We now have compelling evidence. The Values Surveys have measured the happiness and life satisfaction levels of representative national surveys in scores of countries containing most of the world's population, tracing changes from 1981 to 2014. This massive time series demonstrates that the happiness levels of entire countries can and *do* rise or fall substantially – and that rising or falling prosperity helps explain these changes.

Theoretical Frame: Human Development and Happiness

Important as it is to determine if the happiness of nations has changed, it is even more important to understand *why* it has changed. I argue that cultural changes operate as if evolutionary forces were employing a strategy consciously designed to maximize human happiness.

Escaping from starvation-level scarcity brings a dramatic increase in subjective well-being. But there is a threshold at which economic growth no longer increases subjective well-being significantly. At this level, starvation is no longer a real concern for most people and survival begins to be taken for granted. Sizeable numbers of Postmaterialists begin to emerge and for them, further economic gains no longer produce substantial increases in subjective well-being. If people (or societies) behaved rationally, one would expect this to bring a shift in survival strategies. It does.

Figure 8.1 suggests how this works. At low levels of economic development, even modest economic gains bring a high return in terms of caloric intake, clothing, shelter, medical care and ultimately, in life expectancy itself. For individuals to give top priority to maximizing economic gains, and for a society to give top priority to economic growth, is an effective survival strategy for people just above the starvation level. But eventually, one reaches a point at which further economic growth brings only minimal gains in both life expectancy and subjective well-being. There is still a good deal of cross-national variation, but from this point on non-economic aspects of life become increasingly important influences on how long, and how well, people live. Beyond this point, a rational strategy is to place increasing emphasis on these non-economic goals, rather than to continue giving top priority to economic growth, as if it were the ultimate goal itself.

This strategy actually seems to work. As we will see, economic development tends to bring a shift toward Self-expression values that encourages rising gender equality, growing tolerance of gays and other outgroups, and democratization – all of which tend to increase a society's levels of happiness and life satisfaction.

This societal-level shift reflects individual-level value changes, from giving top priority to economic and physical security toward giving top priority to Self-expression values that emphasize freedom of expression and free choice. As long as a society is just above the

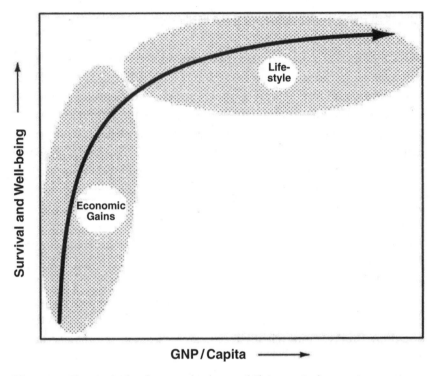

Figure 8.1 Economic development leads to a shift in survival strategies.
Source: Inglehart, 1997: 65.

survival-level, people's choices are narrow: simply surviving takes most of their time and energy, and their culture tends to stress solidarity against dangerous outsiders and rigid conformity to group norms. But with rising prosperity, survival becomes more secure. People's values shift from Survival values to Self-expression values, bringing more tolerant, open worldviews that are more conducive to happiness and life satisfaction because they allow greater freedom to choose how to live one's life. This is particularly important for women and gays, whose life choices were very narrowly restricted until recently. But as we will see, rising tolerance and freedom of choice also tend to bring higher levels of life satisfaction and happiness for the society as a whole.

As people shift their emphasis from Survival values toward Self-expression values, they shift from pursuing happiness indirectly – maximizing the economic means to attain this goal – toward a more direct pursuit of happiness by maximizing free choice in all realms of life. The feeling that one has free choice and control over one's life is closely linked with happiness[11] and this link seems to be universal: happiness is linked with one's sense of freedom in all cultural zones.[12]

The fact that people change the way in which they pursue happiness does not necessarily mean that they will attain it. But in the years since 1981, Self-expression values became increasingly widespread, contributing to democratization, growing support for gender equality and growing acceptance of outgroups such as gays and lesbians – changes that are conducive to human happiness.[13]

People who live in democracies tend to be substantially happier than those who live in autocracies:[14] democracy provides a wider range of free choice, which is conducive to subjective well-being.[15] Social tolerance also broadens the range of choices available to people, enhancing their happiness. Accordingly, support for gender equality and tolerance of outgroups are strongly linked with happiness – not just because tolerant people are happier, but because living in a tolerant society makes life less stressful for everyone.[16]

Around 1990, dozens of societies experienced transitions to democracy that enhanced freedom of expression, freedom to travel and free choice in politics. Moreover, since 1981, support for both gender equality and tolerance of outgroups has increased substantially in most of the countries monitored by the Values Surveys.[17] And finally, during the past few decades, low-income countries containing fully half of the world's population experienced the highest rate of economic growth in history, allowing them to escape from subsistence-level poverty. By a fortuitous combination of circumstances, the societal changes of recent decades increased the economic resources of people in less-prosperous societies, and the political and social freedom of people in middle-income and high-income societies, enhancing the extent to which people in both types of societies have free choice in how to live their lives. I hypothesize that these changes were conducive to rising levels of happiness within entire societies.

Does Growing Freedom of Choice Increase Happiness and Life Satisfaction? Empirical Tests

The Values Surveys have carried out several waves of surveys since 1981 that included two widely used measures of subjective well-being, asking questions about (a) happiness and (b) overall life satisfaction.

Happiness and life satisfaction are shaped by somewhat different factors, but they tend to go together, showing a societal-level correlation of .81 Life satisfaction was measured by asking respondents how satisfied they were with their lives as a whole, using a scale ranging from 1 [*not at all satisfied*] to 10 [*very satisfied*]. Happiness was measured by asking respondents how happy they were, using four categories: *very happy*; *rather happy*; *not very happy*; *and not at all happy*. These items have been extensively validated as measures of subjective well-being.

From its inception, the World Values Survey group has been concerned with issues of cross-cultural equivalency, a serious but not insoluble problem. For many decades, researchers have been developing and refining techniques such as back-translation that help to produce equivalent translations – and also identifying questions that are so situation-specific as to have no meaningful equivalent, making them useless in comparative analysis. For example, asking whether it is acceptable for women to wear head scarves in public places would evoke negative responses from conservatives in France, positive responses from conservatives in Turkey, and puzzlement in countries where this is not an issue. It would be misleading to treat the responses as equivalent. But through analysis of an item's connotations and demographic correlates in pilot tests and successive waves of surveys, the WVS group has identified a number of key concepts that have comparable, though not identical, meanings around the world and the concepts of happiness and life satisfaction seem to be meaningful in every country we have surveyed. Virtually everyone answers these questions and their responses show consistent patterns of correlations with other indicators of subjective well-being, such as satisfaction with one's family or one's job,[18] and with external validating criteria such as the society's mean life expectancy or its level of democracy. The meaning of happiness is not *identical* everywhere – in low-income societies, it is more strongly correlated with income, while in high-income societies it is more strongly correlated with social tolerance – but there is a large component of shared meaning that makes valid comparisons possible. Although people often don't answer, or don't give logically consistent answers to questions about complex policy issues, they do know whether they are happy or unhappy, and virtually everyone can answer these questions, resulting in extremely low non-response levels.

We constructed a subjective well-being index based on reported happiness and life satisfaction, giving equal weight to each variable.[19]

This index provides a broader indicator of the subjective well-being levels of given societies than either of its two components. We examined the trends on this indicator and each of its components in 62 nations for which data are available from at least two surveys conducted at least ten years apart. On average, we analyze changes that took place over a period of 21 years, as measured by more than four surveys per country.

Since we hypothesize that having free choice and control over one's life is a major influence on happiness, we also measure changes on this variable.[20] To measure the impact of economic factors and democratization, we use the society's GDP/capita (using purchasing power parity estimates) and economic growth rate from the World Bank database; and a measure of democracy from the Polity IV project.[21]

Findings

As far back as the 1990s, cross-sectional evidence from the Values Surveys suggested that economic development is conducive to rising levels of subjective well-being,[22] but we did not yet have data examining changes over long periods of time – except from the USA, which showed very little change. Consequently, the claim that growing prosperity was conducive to rising happiness was not generally accepted. The following analyses test the hypothesis that economic development – along with other factors conducive to free choice, such as growing social tolerance and democratization – *does* bring rising levels of subjective well-being.

The last several decades brought unprecedented economic development in much of the world and a spread of democracy. At the same time, the people of rich democracies experienced major changes in social norms, with rising gender equality and growing tolerance of outgroups increasing freedom of choice for over half of the population and creating a more tolerant social environment for everyone. This suggests that subjective well-being levels should rise.

Before examining evidence that it does, let's examine the cross-sectional relationship between economic development and subjective well-being among most of the world's population. We will then examine actual changes over time in scores of countries, using a broader data base than has ever before been available, covering the years from 1981 to 2014.

Economic Development and Happiness: The Cross-sectional Relationship

Figure 8.2 shows the relationship between life satisfaction and per capita GDP in 95 countries containing 90 per cent of the world's population.[23] To maximize reliability, this figure is based on data from all of the Values Surveys carried out from 1981 to 2014. These countries' mean life satisfaction scores are plotted against per capita GDP in 2000. The curve on Figure 8.2 shows the logarithmic regression line for the relationship between per capita GDP and life satisfaction.[24] If each society's life satisfaction level were wholly determined by its level of economic development, all of the countries would fall on this line.

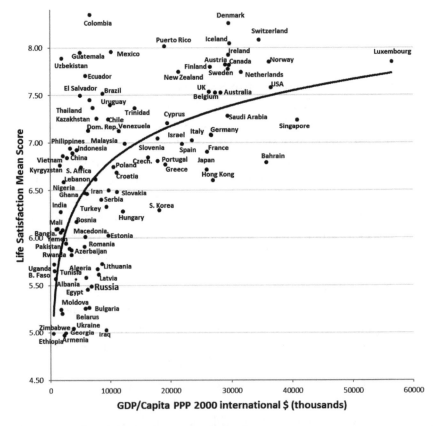

Figure 8.2 Life satisfaction by economic development.
Mean life satisfaction scores on all available WVS/EVS surveys from given country, 1981–2014, by World Bank 2000 GDP/capita purchasing power parity estimates. Logarithmic curve plotted (r = .60).

Most countries are fairly close to the regression line, but it shows a curve of diminishing returns. As hypothesized, at the low end of the scale even small economic gains bring relatively large gains in subjective well-being – but the curve then levels off among rich countries, and at the high end of the scale, further economic gains bring little or no further gains in subjective well-being. A country's GDP and its life satisfaction level correlate at r = .60, a fairly strong correlation but well short of a one-to-one relationship. It suggests that economic development has an important impact on subjective well-being, but that it is only part of the story. At the high end of the scale, different countries still show large differences in life satisfaction, but these differences seem to reflect the kind of society in which one lives, rather than economic factors. This suggests that, for an impoverished country, the most effective way to maximize well-being is to maximize economic growth – but that maximizing happiness in a high-income country requires a different strategy.

The cultural changes linked with modernization can be seen as a shift from maximizing one's chances of survival by striving for economic and physical security above all, to maximizing human happiness through cultural and societal changes. This shift in strategies seems to work: people who emphasize Self-expression values show higher levels of happiness and life satisfaction than those who emphasize Survival values; and people who live in democracies show higher levels of happiness than people who live in authoritarian societies.

A graph showing the relationship between economic development and self-reported happiness shows a similar curvilinear pattern: happiness rises steeply as one moves from extreme poverty to higher levels of economic development, and then levels off. Among the richest societies, further economic gains are only weakly linked with higher levels of happiness.

For desperately poor people, economic gains have a major impact on happiness: at the starvation level, happiness can almost be defined as getting enough to eat. As one moves from desperately poor countries like Zimbabwe or Ethiopia to other poor but less-impoverished countries, the curve rises sharply – but when one reaches the level of Cyprus or Slovenia, the curve levels off. Although Luxemburg is twice as rich as Denmark, the Danes are happier than the Luxemburgers. At this level, variation in life satisfaction reflects other factors than per capita GDP.

The people of high-income countries are both happier and more satisfied with their lives than the people of low-income countries, and the differences are substantial. In Denmark, 52 percent of the public said that they were highly satisfied with their lives (placing themselves at 9 or 10 on a ten-point scale), and 45 percent said they were very happy. In Armenia, only 5 percent were highly satisfied with their lives, and just 6 percent were very happy. In contrast with the modest differences found *within* most countries, the cross-national differences are huge.

Economic Development and Happiness in Two Types of Countries

Figure 8.3 again shows the relationship between economic development and subjective well-being – but this time the figure outlines the countries that fall into two distinctive groups (1) former communist countries and (2) Latin American societies. This makes it evident that, controlling for their level of economic development, some types of societies seem to do a better job of maximizing their citizens' subjective well-being than others. Although the two groups of countries have roughly similar income levels, the Latin American countries consistently show much higher levels of life satisfaction and happiness than the ex-communist countries. All 12 of the Latin American countries for which we have data fall above the regression line, showing show higher levels of subjective well-being than their economic levels would predict. Conversely, almost all of the ex-communist societies show lower levels of subjective well-being than their economic levels would predict. Indeed, Russia and several other ex-Soviet states show lower levels than much poorer countries such as India, Bangladesh, Nigeria, Mali, Uganda or Burkina Faso.

Life satisfaction and happiness show similar patterns, with the Latin American societies being over-achievers and the ex-communist societies being under-achievers on both indicators of subjective well-being. Among the Latin American countries, an average of 45 percent of the population described themselves as very happy, and 42 percent rated themselves as very satisfied with their lives as a whole – while in the ex-communist countries, only 12 percent described themselves as very happy, and only 14 percent were very satisfied with their lives.

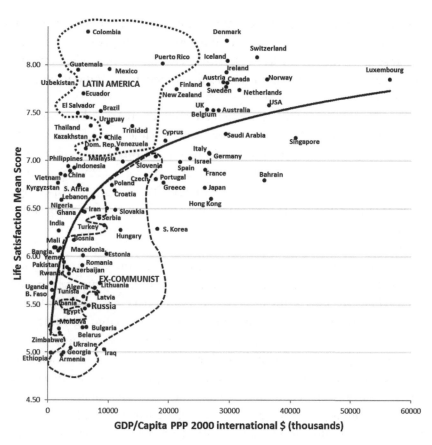

Figure 8.3 Life satisfaction by economic development, identifying two distinctive groups: (1) former communist countries and (2) Latin American societies.

Mean life satisfaction scores on all available WVS/EVS surveys from given country, 1981–2014, by World Bank 2000 GDP/capita purchasing power parity estimates. Logarithmic curve plotted (r = .60).

Communist rule is not necessarily linked with low levels of subjective well-being: China and Vietnam – still ruled by communist parties and currently enjoying high rates of economic growth – showed much higher levels of well-being than the Soviet successor states. But the collapse of their political, economic and belief systems seems to have sharply reduced the subjective well-being of the other ex-communist societies.

Belief systems play an important role. Although religion has long been weak in these countries, communist ideology once played a role comparable to that of religion. For many decades, communism seemed to be the wave of the future. The belief that they were build-ing a better society gave a sense of purpose to many people's lives. The collapse of communism left a spiritual vacuum in the ex-communist countries, but in Latin America, traditional beliefs in God and country remain strong.

Regression analyses of the factors conducive to subjective well-being show that high levels of religiosity at Time 1 predict relatively high levels of subjective well-being at a later time.[25] For, especially under conditions of low economic security, religion provides a sense of predictability and security.[26] Until recently, communist ideology filled this function for many people but its collapse left a void and a declining sense of well-being. Religiosity has been growing in most ex-communist countries to help fill this void.

These regression analyses indicate that the extent to which people live in a tolerant society *also* helps shape subjective well-being, even when we control for levels of economic development. Intolerant social norms rigidly restrict people's life choices, reducing subjective well-being. Tolerance of gender equality, gays and lesbians and people of other religions has a significant impact on subjective well-being. It is not just that being tolerant makes one happy – living in a tolerant social environment is conducive to happiness for everyone.[27]

Although national pride is strongly correlated with subjective well-being, it is also closely linked with strong emphasis on religion, so when religiosity is included in the analysis, national pride shows little impact. Both religion and national pride are stronger in less developed societies than in developed ones, partly compensating for low levels of development. Thus, the contrast between the Latin American societies and the ex-communist societies may partly reflect the fact that virtu-ally all of the Latin American publics are strongly religious and have a strong sense of national pride, while the publics of the ex-communist nations do not.

Democracy is also strongly linked with happiness: Our sub-jective well-being index showed a .74 correlation with democracy in 1987, just before a major wave of democratization: the people of democracies were substantially happier than the people of authoritar-ian countries.[28]

Evolutionary Modernization theory holds that the central reason why the changes of the past 30 years led to rising happiness is because they brought greater freedom of choice. Here, too, Latin

Americans rank much higher than the ex-communist countries: 45 percent of the Latin Americans said they had "a great deal of choice" (points 9 or 10 on a 10-point scale) as compared with a mean of 21 percent among the people of ex-communist countries.

Rising Happiness and Life Satisfaction: Time Series Evidence

The theory and cross-sectional evidence examined above imply that as a society becomes economically more secure, more democratic and more tolerant – increasing its people's freedom of choice in how to live their lives – its people's subjective well-being level should rise. In keeping with this expectation, during years from 1981 to 2014, both life satisfaction and happiness rose in an overwhelming majority of the 62 countries from which a substantial time series is available.

Thus, as Figure 8.4 shows, during this period happiness rose in 52 countries and fell in only ten; and as Figure 8.5 shows, life satisfaction rose in 40 countries and fell in only 19 (three showed no change). In short, happiness rose in 84 percent of these countries and life satisfaction rose in 65 percent of them: from 1981 to 2014, there was an overwhelming trend toward rising subjective well-being.

The trend toward rising happiness spans the spectrum from low-income to high-income countries and cuts across cultural zones. Many of the increases were sizeable: in the median country, the percentage of people saying they were "very happy" increased by eight points from the earliest to the latest available survey. The probability that these increases reflect random variation is negligible (one scholar claimed that this pervasive rise in happiness and life satisfaction was due to a change in the interviewer instructions used with the happiness question; empirical evidence refutes this claim, as Appendix 1 demonstrates).[29]

Happiness and life satisfaction are closely correlated, and increases in life satisfaction tend to accompany increases in happiness. But they reflect different aspects of subjective well-being. Life satisfaction is more closely linked with financial satisfaction and a society's economic level, while happiness is more closely linked with emotional factors. This helps explain why recent years brought a stronger trend toward rising happiness than toward rising life satisfaction. For

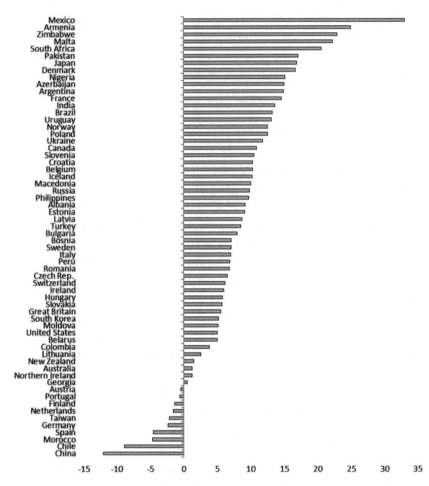

Figure 8.4 Change in percentage saying they are "very happy" taking all things together, from earliest to latest available survey.

Source: World Values Survey and European Values Study surveys carried out from 1981 to 2014, including all countries with at least a ten-year time series. The median time-span covered is 20 years.

while democratization brought a widespread expansion of freedom, it was not necessarily accompanied by rising prosperity. In most ex-communist countries, democratization was accompanied by economic collapse, leading life satisfaction to fall while happiness rose. Moreover (as Chapter 5 demonstrated) support for gender equality and tolerance of gays has been rising rapidly – but (as Chapter 9 will demonstrate) during the last three decades rich countries have experienced rising income inequality and declining real income. We would expect rising

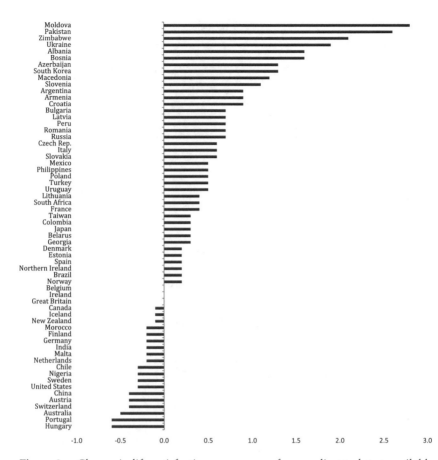

Figure 8.5 Change in life satisfaction mean score, from earliest to latest available survey.

Source: World Values Survey and European Values Study surveys carried out from 1981 to 2014, including all countries with at least a ten-year time series. The median time-span covered is 20 years.

gender equality and tolerance of gays to have a greater impact on happiness than on life satisfaction; conversely we would expect economic decline to have a greater impact on life satisfaction than on happiness. In keeping with these expectations, happiness has risen more consistently across the world than has life satisfaction.

Furthermore, we would expect the Great Recession to have had a negative impact on both happiness and life satisfaction.[30] Figure 8.6 tests this expectation, using data from all 12 countries for which data

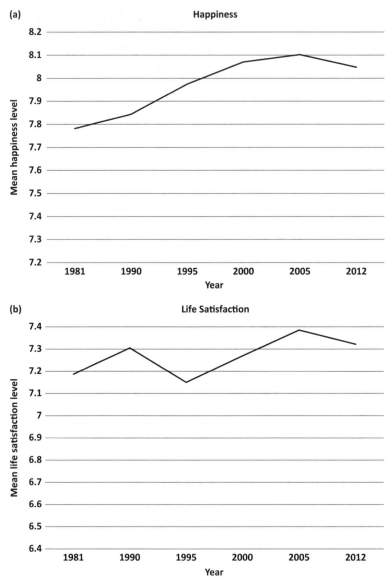

Figure 8.6 Life satisfaction and happiness trends in 12 countries, 1981–2012.
Source: Based on Values Survey data from all 12 countries from which data is available from both the first wave, carried out in 1981–1983 and from the sixth wave, carried out in 2010–2014, calculating the mean score in each year from surveys in Argentina, Australia, Finland, Germany, Japan, South Korea, Mexico, The Netherlands, South Africa, Spain, Sweden and the US. Life satisfaction was measured on a ten-point scale where 1 = very dissatisfied and 10 = very satisfied. Happiness was measured on a 4-point scale where 1 = very happy and 4 = very unhappy. To make the scales comparable, the polarity of the happiness scale was reversed and its scores were multiplied by 2.5.

are available from both the earliest Values survey and the most recent survey, carried out around 2012. As it demonstrates, both happiness and life satisfaction reached a peak in these countries around 2005 and then declined in the post-2008 surveys.

Why Did These Trends Escape Notice?

How did such an important phenomenon as this long-term rise in subjective well-being escape notice? We suggest three reasons. First, most of the earlier evidence came from rich countries that were already well past the point of diminishing returns from economic development, and showed relatively little change – supporting the interpretation that a society's happiness levels does not change. Second, the decisive social changes – global economic growth, widespread democratization, growing tolerance of diversity and a rising sense of freedom – are relatively recent and the earlier surveys, carried out in relatively few countries, did not reflect them. Finally, cross-national research on the determinants of happiness has tended to focus on life satisfaction rather than happiness, which shows the stronger trend.

The much-cited time series showing flat happiness levels in the USA began in 1946 – which may have been an historic high point. The USA had just emerged from World War II as the world's strongest and richest country. Moreover, the American public was probably experiencing a sense of euphoria linked with their historic victory of Good over Evil in World War II. If surveys had been taken during the Great Depression of the 1930s, they probably would have shown much lower levels of subjective well-being than those found in 1946. But even if one dismisses this possibility, the USA is not a typical country.

The conclusion that happiness has risen in most countries is supported by additional evidence from 26 countries from which the World Database of Happiness provides time series data on happiness going as far back as 1946,[31] supplemented by more recent data from the Values Surveys. Among these 26 countries, 19 show rising happiness levels. Several countries – India, Ireland, Mexico, Puerto Rico and South Korea – show *steeply* rising trends. Other countries with rising trends are Argentina, Canada, China, Denmark, Finland, France, Italy, Japan, Luxembourg, The Netherlands, Poland, South Africa, Spain and

Sweden. Three very rich countries – the USA, Switzerland and Norway – show flat trends from the earliest to latest available survey, but all three are at very high levels. Only four countries (Austria, Belgium, the UK and West Germany) show downward trends. In keeping with the hypothesis that the relationship between economic development and happiness follows a curve of diminishing returns, all but one of the countries that show steeply rising trends were low-income or middle-income countries when the time series started; and all of the countries showing flat or declining trends were high-income countries.

Under certain conditions, a society's happiness and life satisfaction can show massive and enduring changes that are incompatible with claims that subjective well-being is determined by fixed set-points or genetic factors. The collapse of the Soviet Union provides particularly dramatic evidence.[32]

Subjective Well-being and Societal Collapse: The Case of Russia

In 1982 the Russian people's happiness and life satisfaction ranked about where their level of economic development would predict. But with the subsequent collapse of their economic, political and belief systems, subjective well-being in Russia fell to levels never before seen – reaching a low point in 1995–99 at which most Russians described themselves as unhappy and dissatisfied with their lives as a whole. This was extraordinary. Before this was observed, articles had been published explaining why the publics of virtually every country always give positively skewed responses to questions about happiness and life satisfaction.[33]

Most of this decline occurred before the Soviet Union collapsed in 1991 – which suggests that a sharp decline in subjective well-being may be a leading indicator of political collapse. Considerable recovery occurred after 1999, but in 2011 life satisfaction in Russia was still below its 1982 level. Contrary to set-point theory, the collapse of communism was linked with a dramatic and enduring drop in subjective well-being.

Genetic factors may explain a large share of the variation in subjective well-being *within a given country, at a given point in time.* But genetic factors cannot possibly explain the massive and enduring changes in subjective well-being levels that occurred in Russia, where life satisfaction fell by almost two entire scale categories and the percentage describing themselves as "very happy" fell by fully 28 points. Moreover, these changes extended over a period of three decades, showing theoretically predictable shifts in both directions: first there was a massive downward movement in subjective well-being, accompanying Russia's economic, political, social and ideological collapse; seventeen years later, there was an upswing linked with economic and political recovery. It was also linked with growing religiosity and nationalism that seemed to be filling the void left by the abandonment of Marxist ideology. For Russia's dramatic decline of subjective well-being did not merely reflect economic and political collapse – it was also linked with the collapse of a Marxist belief system that once gave meaning to the lives of many Russians.

Throughout history there have been two strategies for reducing unhappiness: the first is to lower one's expectations and accept the inevitability of suffering – a strategy endorsed by virtually all of the world's major religions. The second is to expand one's range of material, political and social choices, a strategy called modernization. Both economic development and belief systems help shape people's subjective well-being. Humans have evolved to seek meaningful patterns, and a strong belief system, whether religious or secular, is linked with relatively high levels of subjective well-being.

Belief systems have probably always played an important role in subjective well-being, for religious people tend to be happier than non-believers.[34] Although religion was systematically discouraged in communist countries, Marxist ideology once played a role similar to that of religion. For many decades, communism seemed to be the wave of the future. The belief that they were building a better society seems to have given a sense of purpose to the lives of many people.

During the Brezhnev era, from 1964 to 1982, the Marxist belief system eroded in Russia. The once-vigorous Soviet economy fell into economic, technological and intellectual stagnation. It became evident that the revolutionary vision of an egalitarian classless society had given way to a society ruled by a privileged and self-perpetuating New Class, dominated by the Communist Party. The belief that the Soviet Union represented the wave of the future, gave way to demoralization, absenteeism and rising alcoholism. When Gorbachev took power in 1985, he attempted to halt this decline, but it became increasingly evident that the main barrier to reform was the Communist Party itself.

By the time that communist rule and the Soviet Union collapsed in 1991, it was evident that Marxist ideology was bankrupt in Russia.

Russian also emerged with a damaged national self-image. The Soviet Union once ranked with the USA as one of the world's two superpowers, which probably brought pride and satisfaction to many Russians. In 1991 the USSR splintered into 15 diminished successor states, damaging feelings of national pride. In Latin America, 72 percent of the public says they are very proud of their nationality, while in the ex-communist countries only 44 percent say so. In Latin America, traditional beliefs in God and country remain strong,[35] but in the ex-communist countries, the collapse of communism seems to have left a vacuum that nationalism and religion are beginning to fill.

The publics of most ex-communist societies show lower levels of subjective well-being than their economic level would predict. We argue that this has not always been the case – their distinctively low levels reflect the collapse of their economic, social and political systems and of the Marxist belief system.

To test this claim, let us examine the rise and fall of life satisfaction and happiness in Russia. To do so most effectively requires us to make an important assumption. Analyzing the impact of communism's collapse requires measures of subjective well-being from before and after the collapse. But as long as communist regimes were in power, they rarely permitted their country to take part in cross-national surveys. Hungary was exceptional, being the sole communist country included in the first Values survey in 1982. It was not possible to carry out a representative national survey in the Soviet Union at that time, but colleagues in the Soviet Academy of Science claimed that Tambov oblast – an administrative region of Russia – was representative of the Russian republic as a whole, and they carried out the Values survey there. The claim that Tambov is representative of Russia is crucial, since we will use the results from Tambov to estimate the first time point in our Russian time series. Though we also have a Russian survey from 1990, one year before the Soviet Union disintegrated, treating Tambov as a proxy for Russia as a whole enables us to examine a longer time series, from 1982 to 2011. To test whether Tambov is a reasonably good proxy for Russia as a whole, we carried out additional surveys of Tambov in 1995 and again in 2011. As we will see, in both years the results from Tambov closely approximate those from representative national surveys of Russia carried out at the same time. Our colleagues at the Soviet Academy of Science seem to have been correct in claiming that Tambov was representative of Russia as a whole.

Regression analyses designed to identify the factors conducive to subjective well-being indicate that having experienced communist rule has a significant negative impact on life satisfaction, even controlling for a country's prosperity and other factors. In part, this seems to reflect the vacuum left by the collapse of Marxist belief. As Figure 4.3 above demonstrated, religiosity is increasing more rapidly in the ex-communist world than anywhere else – as if it were filling such a vacuum. The extent to which people feel they have free choice in life has a major impact on a country's level of life satisfaction, and when we take free choice into account, the impact of both religiosity and communist experience drop sharply: this suggests that one reason why ex-communist societies score low is because their people have a relatively weak sense of control over their lives; and conversely, that religiosity is important because it helps people feel that their lives are safely in the hands of a higher power.

Figure 8.7 shows the trajectory of life satisfaction in Russia from 1982 to 2011 (using Tambov as a proxy for Russia in 1982). At the start of this period, the subjective well-being of the Russian people was about where its economic level would predict, and slightly higher than that of China and Vietnam – two societies where communism did not collapse. In the 1960s and 1970s, Russia's level of well-being was probably even higher, since by 1982 Russia already was experiencing rising alcoholism, absenteeism and declining male life expectancy. In subsequent years, with the collapse of the Soviet Union and the communist belief system, life satisfaction in Russia fell to levels never before seen.

The Russian people experienced profound social and economic shocks. Income per capita fell by 43 per cent, while unemployment rose from near zero to a peak of almost 14 per cent.[36] Along with this, Russia experienced an explosion of corruption, economic inequality and organized crime. Male life expectancy fell from a high of almost 65 years in the Soviet era, to less than 58 in 1995 – lower than in many countries of sub-Saharan Africa.[37]

In 1982 the Russian public showed a mean life satisfaction score of 7.13 on a ten-point scale. This fell to 5.37 in 1990 (just before the breakup of the Soviet Union), plummeting to an unprecedented low point of 4.45 in 1995, followed by a modest recovery to 4.65 in 1999, when a majority of the Russian public still placed themselves

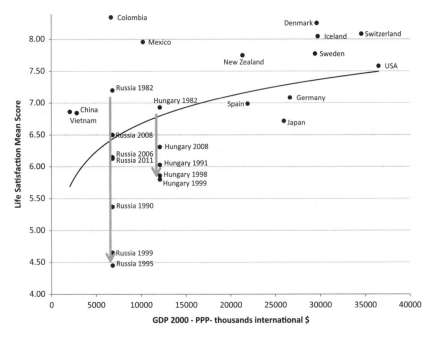

Figure 8.7 The collapse of communism and changing levels of life satisfaction, 1981–2011.

Mean life satisfaction scores from the World Values Surveys in years indicated, by World Bank 2000 GDP/capita purchasing power parity estimates.

well below the midpoint on the life satisfaction scale. When Putin took power in 2000, he restored order and a sharp rise in oil prices brought an economic boom. Life satisfaction rose to 6.15 in 2006, reached a high point of 6.50 in 2008 and then subsided to 6.13 in 2011 – still well below the 1982 level. The decline of life satisfaction in Russia was far from transient.

Hungary is the only other communist society in which it was possible to carry out the Values Surveys before communism collapsed. Hungary's transition to a market democracy was less severe than Russia's. Economic decline and the breakdown of civil order were milder, and Hungary retained its national identity while the Soviet Union disintegrated. By 2003, Hungary was sufficiently prosperous and democratic to be admitted to the European Union. Nevertheless, the collapse of communism was linked with a sharp decline of life satisfaction. In 1982 the Hungarians showed a mean life satisfaction score of 6.93 – close to Tambov's level at the time and slightly above China's level. But with the collapse of communism, Hungarian life satisfaction fell to 6.03 in 1991, dropped further to 5.69 in 1999 and then recovered to 6.3 in 2008, still well below its 1982 level.

We lack the before-and-after data from other ex-communist countries that would be needed to demonstrate that the collapse of communism led to declining life satisfaction there. But it is striking that ex-communist Armenia, Georgia, Ukraine, Belarus, Bulgaria, Albania, Latvia, Lithuania, Estonia, Macedonia, Romania and Azerbaijan all show much lower levels of subjective well-being than their economic levels would predict. It seems unlikely that this is due to some fixed cultural predisposition for people in this culturally diverse set of countries to say they are dissatisfied. We suspect that their low levels reflect the traumatic experiences linked with the disintegration of communism.

Similarly, we have no long-term time series data from Iraq, Ethiopia and Zimbabwe, so we cannot demonstrate that their publics have not *always* had the extremely low levels of subjective well-being shown on Figure 8.2 – but it is implausible. These societies are experiencing catastrophic economic, social and political conditions. Perhaps the Iraqis, Ethiopians and Zimbabweans are among the world's most dissatisfied people because they have unique cultural understandings of what life satisfaction means. But it seems much likelier that they are dissatisfied because life in their countries has become nasty, brutish and short.

Major events such as the collapse of communism can lastingly reshape the subjective well-being levels of entire societies. Such sharp declines in subjective well-being do not occur often, but when they occur they can have far-reaching consequences. The collapse of the Soviet Union in 1991 was *preceded* by sharply declining subjective well-being. Similarly, the breakup of the Belgian state in the 1980s and its reorganization into a federation based on ethnicity was *preceded* by a steep decline in subjective well-being.[38] A nation's level of subjective well-being is normally pretty stable – but a major decline of life satisfaction and happiness may be a leading indicator of political collapse.

Figure 8.8 puts Russia's changing life satisfaction into comparative context, showing mean levels in Russia and, for comparison, in two high-income stable democracies, Sweden and the USA. Throughout the 30-year period from 1981 to 2011, the Swedish and American publics showed stable high levels of life satisfaction, scoring about 7.5 on a 10-point scale. In 1982 the Russian public already

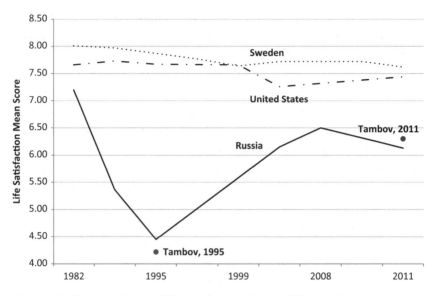

Figure 8.8 Changing levels of life satisfaction, Russia, USA, Sweden, 1982–2011. *Note*: Mean life satisfaction scores from the World Values Surveys.

showed a significantly lower score of 7.13 – which fell to a low point of 4.45 in 1995, followed by a recovery to 6.13 in 2011 – still well below the 1982 level.

As Figure 8.8 demonstrates, surveys of Tambov that were replicated in 1995 and 2011 show life satisfaction levels very similar to those of Russia in the same years – supporting the claim that Tambov's life satisfaction level in a given year provides a reasonably accurate estimate of Russia's. The stable high levels found in the USA and Sweden reflect the pattern typically found in high-income democracies, in which most previous research has been conducted. But the drastic swings observed in Russia and Hungary demonstrate that life satisfaction is not nearly as stable as set-point theory or social comparison theory imply.

The Role of Belief Systems: Religion vs. Free Choice as Sources of Happiness

There is extensive evidence that religious people are happier than non-believers, but the evidence comes mainly from developed democracies.[39] Is this true for the world as a whole? Figure 8.9 shows the relationship

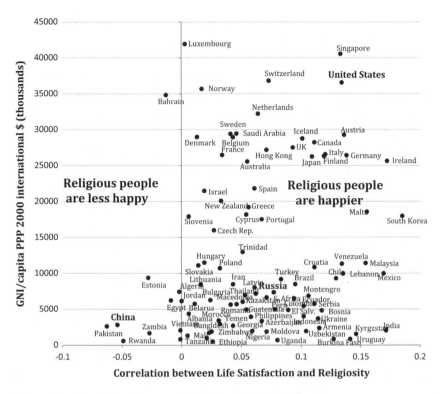

Figure 8.9 Correlation between religiosity and life satisfaction.
Life satisfaction and religiosity scores from the World Values Survey, 1981–2014; World Bank per capita GNI in 2000, purchasing power parity estimates.

between subjective well-being and religion in over 100 countries at various levels of economic development. The vertical axis shows the zero point where there is no correlation between religiosity and life satisfaction. Countries to the right of this line show positive correlations, while countries to the left show negative correlations. In an overwhelming majority of countries, we find positive correlations, indicating that religious people tend to be happier than non-religious people. Fully 79 countries show statistically significant positive correlations between religiosity and life satisfaction; six countries show significant negative correlations; and 23 countries show no significant correlation. Among the countries showing significant correlations, 93 percent show a positive relationship between religiosity and life satisfaction.

China, with 20 percent of the world's population, is the most important exception, showing a statistically significant negative correlation between religiosity and life satisfaction. We think this reflects the fact that most of China's religious people have turned to religion recently. In the first survey that measured religiosity in China, in 1990, only a tiny minority (1.2 percent) considered God to be very important in their lives, giving ratings of 9 or 10 on a 10-point scale. In 2012, 4.7 percent gave such ratings: Starting from an extremely low baseline, the proportion who were religious almost quadrupled. Religion may be conducive to subjective well-being in the long run – but in China, most religious people are recent converts, who probably turned to religion because they were unhappy. In the long run, religiosity may be conducive to subjective well-being, but it seems to recruit new followers among those who are dissatisfied with their lives. In keeping with this interpretation, most of the other cases showing negative correlations between religiosity and life satisfaction are low-income countries with low levels of life satisfaction.[40]

In Chapter 4, we examined changes in emphasis on religion from 1981 to 2014 in all countries for which a time series of at least 15 years was available (the median span being 23.5 years). Contrary to prominent claims, we did not find a global resurgence of religion.[41] Quite the opposite, the publics of most high-income countries show *declining* emphasis on religion. But the publics of some countries did show rising emphasis on religion, and all seven of the countries showing the greatest gains are ex-communist societies – Russia, Belarus, Bulgaria, China, Romania, Ukraine and Slovakia. Though Muslim-majority countries show the highest absolute *levels* of religiosity, the greatest *gains* in religiosity have occurred in ex-communist countries, where religion seems to be expanding to fill an ideological vacuum.

Does Rising Freedom of Choice Bring Rising Happiness? Analyzing the Causes of Changes in Subjective Well-being Levels

Evolutionary Modernization theory argues that a major reason why the changes of the past 30 years led to rising happiness is because they brought rising emphasis on Self-expression values, emphasizing freedom of choice.

Three key intervening factors predict the extent to which a country's sense of having free choice rose or fell during the years covered by the Values Surveys. First, people living in countries that experienced relatively strong economic growth felt a rising sense of free choice: economic scarcity severely limits free choice, while growing resources increase it. Democratization is equally important: the publics of countries that experienced rising levels of democracy also experienced a rising sense of free choice – in fact, *every* country that made a transition from authoritarian rule to democracy during this period showed a rising sense of free choice. But, surprising as it may seem, rising social tolerance has an even greater impact on people's sense of free choice than either economic growth or democratization.

As societies become wealthier, threats to survival recede and people become more tolerant of gender equality and social diversity. More open social norms concerning the role of women, ethnic diversity and alternative lifestyles give people a wider range of choice in how to live their lives, and during the past quarter century, tolerance of diversity has increased substantially. For example, the proportion of respondents claiming that homosexuality is never justifiable fell from 33 percent in 1981, to 15 percent around 2011, in the countries for which data are available from both time points. Discriminatory attitudes toward women showed similar downward trends in most countries.

As societies become wealthier, income has a diminishing impact on one's subjective well-being, but personal freedom has an increasing impact. When people are barely able to fill their basic needs, economic factors are a major determinant of their happiness and life satisfaction. But in more secure societies, people give higher priority to free choice and self-expression – which, accordingly, play an increasingly important role in shaping their well-being.

Evolutionary Modernization theory argues that the main reason why the changes of the past 30 years led to rising happiness is because they brought greater freedom of choice. And when we analyze *changes* in subjective well-being from the first available survey to the most recent one in each country, we find that a growing feeling that one has free choice was by far the most important influence on whether subjective well-being rose or fell. The feeling that one has free choice and control over one's life increased in 79 percent of the countries for which a substantial time series is available from the Values Surveys. And virtually every country that experienced a rising sense of freedom also experienced rising subjective well-being. This suggests that the changes of recent decades were conducive to happiness mainly by increasing free choice, as evolutionary moderni-zation theory argues.

Figure 8.10 summarizes the results of a path analysis, a statistical technique for analyzing causal sequences.[42] This is a dynamic model, indi-cating to what extent *changes* in one variable were followed by *changes* in another variable, controlling for the impact of the other variables in the model. This provides a much stronger test of causality than the cross-sectional analyses examined above. It analyzes the changes observed in all 56 countries[43] from which data are available covering a substantial time span (averaging more than 20 years before and after 1990). The width of the arrows indicates the relative impact of each factor.

As this figure indicates, both rising per capita GDP and rising levels of democracy were followed by statistically significant increases in the prevailing sense of free choice. But social liberalization (as indi-cated by rising levels of tolerance for outgroups) had an even stronger tendency to be linked with rising feelings of free choice. An increasing sense of free choice, in turn, had by far the strongest impact on ris-ing levels of subjective well-being, as measured by an index based on reported happiness and life satisfaction. The impact of economic devel-opment and democratization was almost entirely due to the fact that they tended to increase a sense of free choice, though growing social

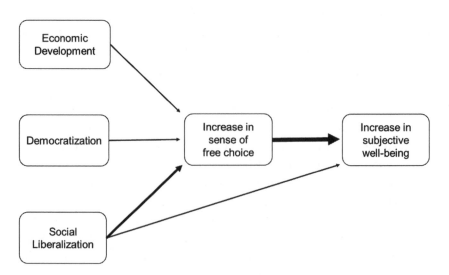

Figure 8.10 Factors contributing to *increase* in subjective well-being from earliest available survey to most recent survey, in 56 countries.
Based on graph in Inglehart et al., 2008: 280.

liberalization also had a modest direct impact on subjective well-being (as the arrow connecting them indicates).

The gains in economic development, democratization and social liberalization that a country experienced during this period explain 44 percent of a country's gains in a sense of freedom; and these gains, together with an increased sense of free choice, explain 62 percent of a country's increase in subjective well-being.

Though religiosity shows a significant cross-sectional linkage with subjective well-being, it does not show a significant impact on the *changes* in subjective well-being analyzed here: although religious people tend to be happier than non-religious people, *increasing* emphasis on religion was not associated with rising happiness. Indeed, evidence examined above suggests that rising religiosity tends to be found in relatively unhappy countries.

Our findings support the claim that research on happiness should not focus solely on economic growth.[44] Economic growth makes a substantial contribution to subjective well-being, but it is the weakest of the factors examined here.

A major reason why people living in high-income societies have relatively high levels of subjective well-being is that they have relatively great freedom of choice in how to live their lives. Since 1989, dozens of countries have become more democratic; and virtually all high-income and middle-income countries have become more supportive of gender equality and more tolerant of outgroups – all of which increased people's freedom of choice. In the great majority of countries from which time series data are available, the proportion of the public saying that they have free choice and control over their lives increased since 1981. The hedonic treadmill and social comparison models would dismiss these facts as irrelevant, claiming that the low-ranking countries have always been low and will remain so. But, as we have seen, the years from 1981 to 2014 saw rising levels of subjective well-being in an overwhelming majority of countries.

We would not expect subjective well-being to continue rising forever. Even apart from ceiling effects, the period we've been examining saw a remarkable conjunction of favorable circumstances. Many low-income and middle-income countries experienced exceptionally high rates of economic growth. Rich countries had less economic growth, but they experienced high rates of social liberalization, with hard-core opposition to gender equality and homosexuality becoming less than half as widespread as it was in 1981. And in this same period, dozens of countries experienced democratization, which tends to be a one-shot occurrence. It seems unlikely that such strong rates of economic growth and social liberalization as occurred from 1981 to 2007 will occur in the future.

Conclusion

The findings presented here indicate that the subjective well-being levels of entire societies are *not* immune to enduring change – as genetically determined, set-point and social comparison theories claim. We do not suggest that these factors have no impact – on the contrary, persuasive evidence indicates that they *do* have an effect, and within any given stable high-income country they may dominate what happens for substantial periods of time. But when mega-events occur, such as the collapse of a country's political, economic and belief systems, the happiness and life satisfaction levels of entire societies can experience massive changes.

Our findings suggest that the hedonic treadmill model should be revised but not abandoned. Recent research provides convincing evidence that genetic factors have an important impact on subjective well-being. And there is abundant and equally convincing evidence that people adapt to changes, so that subjective well-being levels tend to fluctuate around stable set-points. But these factors are not the full story, as earlier interpretations suggested. The hedonic treadmill model is a tendency that prevails only when other factors hold constant. It may be adequate to explain most of the variation in happiness that occurs during normal times, such as the prolonged period of prosperity and stable democracy that the USA experienced since World War II. It cannot account for the sharp decline of life satisfaction that accompanied the collapse of communism or the rise of happiness in most countries that was observed from 1981 to 2014.

Historical, cultural and institutional factors can have a major impact on subjective well-being. These factors have received relatively little attention in previous research because most of it has been carried out in single countries – where history, culture and national institutions are constants. Similarly, virtually all of the research on genetic influences on subjective well-being was carried out within single countries over relatively short periods of time – with subjective well-being vary-ing within a relatively narrow range. Within this range, genetic factors may explain most of the variance. But a society's economic and polit-ical institutions and its belief system help shape the subjective well-being of its people, and as one moves from one society to another or traces given societies over time, we find large amounts of variation that genetic factors can't explain.

Belief systems seem to play a major role in the subjective well-being of entire countries. Economic factors seem to have a strong impact on subjective well-being in low-income countries, but at higher levels of development, evolutionary cultural changes occur through which people place increasing emphasis on self-expression and free choice.[45] Successful modernization brings high levels of prosperity and a shift to Self-expression values that is conducive to social solidarity, tolerance, and democracy – which tend to pro-duce high levels of subjective well-being. In this sense, the shift from Survival values to Self-expression values is an example of successful cultural evolution.

Modernization does not necessarily increase a society's overall level of happiness. Subjective well-being is shaped by many factors, so economic development alone does not guarantee that happiness will rise. Nevertheless, the .60 correlation between life satisfaction and a society's per capita GDP suggests that development tends to bring rising happiness – but the relationship is probabilistic rather than deterministic and the payoff is greatest when one moves from starvation-level poverty to a modest level of economic security, with freedom and social tolerance becoming more important at higher lev-els of development. Historical evidence suggests that the transition from foraging to agricultural society did not do so: foragers tended to be taller, better-nourished, and had more autonomy than the people of early agrarian societies.

And the emergence of Artificial Intelligence Society brings sharply rising inequality that may eventually reduce overall happiness levels. But from 1980 to 2014, a fortunate combination of circum-stances linked with economic development and rising freedom brought rising happiness to the people of most countries.

Long before modernization became possible, traditional soci-eties evolved ways of coping with the stresses of human existence and the need for a sense of meaning. Thus, although religion today is strongest in poor countries – which have relatively low levels of happiness – it is conducive to happiness. Both faith and freedom can be conducive to happiness. To some extent they substitute for each other – but there is no reason why a society could not attain both high levels of autonomy and a belief system conducive to happiness.

This may explain why many Latin American countries have attained higher levels of subjective well-being than their economic level would predict. In recent decades, most Latin American countries have attained democratic institutions and experienced surprisingly rapid social liberalization in both gender equality and tolerance of homosexuality – while retaining relatively high levels of religious faith and national pride. This balancing act gains some of the benefits of both traditional and modern routes to happiness.

These findings have important implications for social scientists and policymakers: They indicate that human happiness is not fixed, but can be influenced by belief systems and social policies.

9 *THE SILENT REVOLUTION* IN REVERSE: THE RISE OF TRUMP AND THE AUTHORITARIAN POPULIST PARTIES*

Overview

Being able to take survival for granted makes people more open to new ideas and more tolerant of outgroups. Insecurity has the opposite effect, encouraging an Authoritarian Reflex in which people close ranks behind strong leaders, with strong in-group solidarity, rigid conformity to group norms and rejection of outsiders. The three decades of exceptional security experienced by developed democracies after World War II brought pervasive cultural changes, including the rise of Green parties and the spread of democracy. Economic growth has continued since 1975, but in high-income countries virtually all of the gains have gone to those at the top. Most of the population, especially the less-educated, have experienced sharply declining existential security, fueling support for xenophobic populist authoritarian movements such as British Exit from the European Union, France's National Front and Donald Trump's takeover of the Republican Party. This raises two questions: (1) "What motivates people to support xenophobic authoritarian movements in high-income countries?" And (2) "Why is the xenophobic vote in these countries much higher now than it was several decades ago?" The two questions have different answers.

---

* Much of this chapter appeared as Inglehart, 1997 and Inglehart and Norris, 2017.

Support for xenophobic populist authoritarian movements is motivated by a backlash against cultural change. From the start, the younger Postmaterialist birth cohorts disproportionately supported environmentalist parties, while older, less secure people supported xenophobic authoritarian parties, in an enduring intergenerational value clash. But during the past three decades, strong period effects have been working to increase support for xenophobic parties: a large share of the population experienced declining real income and job security, along with a massive influx of immigrants and refugees. Cultural backlash explains why given individuals support xenophobic populist authoritarian movements – but declining existential security explains why support for these movements is greater now than it was 30 years ago.

From the Silent Revolution to the Authoritarian Reflex

More than 40 years ago, *The Silent Revolution* argued that when people grow up taking survival for granted, they become more open to new ideas and more tolerant of outgroups. Accordingly, as we have seen, the unprecedentedly high level of existential security that developed democracies experienced after World War II gave rise to an intergenerational shift toward Postmaterialist values, bringing greater emphasis on freedom of expression, democratization, environmental protection, gender equality and tolerance of gays, handicapped people and foreigners.[1]

Insecurity has the opposite effect. For most its existence, humanity lived just above the starvation level and under extreme scarcity, xenophobia is realistic: when a tribe's territory produces just enough food to sustain it, and another tribe moves in, it can bring a struggle in which one tribe or the other survives. Such insecurity stimulates a xenophobic Authoritarian Reflex. Conversely, the high levels of existential security that emerged after World War II gave more room for individual free choice and openness to outsiders.

During the postwar era, the people of developed countries experienced peace, unprecedented prosperity and the emergence of advanced welfare states, making survival more secure than ever before. Postwar birth cohorts grew up taking survival for granted, bringing an intergenerational shift toward Postmaterialist values.[2] Survival is such a central goal that when it seems insecure, it dominates people's entire life strategy. Conversely, when survival can be taken for granted, it opens the way for new norms concerning everything from sexual orientation to democratic institutions. Compared with previous values, which emphasized economic and physical security above all, Postmaterialists are less conformist, more open to new ideas, less authoritarian and more tolerant of outgroups. But these values depend on high levels of economic and physical security. They did not emerge in low-income countries, and were most widespread among the younger and more secure strata of high-income countries.[3]

The three decades of rapid economic growth and high economic and physical security experienced by developed democracies after World War II brought pervasive cultural changes, contributing to the rise of Green parties and the spread of democracy.

These decades of exceptional security led to rising gender equality, growing tolerance of outgroups, and growing emphasis on environmental protection and individual autonomy. During the past few decades, these countries continued to have economic growth, but almost all of the gains went to the top ten percent; the less-educated experienced declining real income and an even more sharply declining relative position. At the same time, massive immigration also fueled support for populist authoritarian parties.

To some extent, Postmaterialism was its own gravedigger. From the start, the emergence of radical cultural changes provoked a reaction among older and less secure strata who felt threatened by the erosion of familiar values. Accordingly, Ignanzi has described the rise of extreme right parties in Europe as a "Silent Counter-revolution."[4] A Materialist reaction against these cultural changes led to the emergence of xenophobic parties like France's National Front. This brought declining social class voting, undermining the working-class-oriented Left parties that had implemented redistributive policies for most of the twentieth century. Moreover, the new non-economic issues introduced by Postmaterialists overshadowed the classic Left-Right economic issues, drawing attention away from redistribution to cultural issues, further paving the way for rising inequality.[5]

Forty years ago, the *Silent Revolution* explored the implications of the high prosperity and advanced welfare states that prevailed during the postwar era. The book you are reading explores the implications of a new phase that highly developed countries are entering – that of Artificial Intelligence Society. This new phase of development offers wonderful opportunities – but it has a winner-takes-all economy that brings steeply rising inequality. Unless offset by appropriate government policies, this undermines democracy and the cultural openness that emerged in the post-war era.

Cultural Backlash and the Rise of Xenophobic Populist Authoritarian Parties

The intergenerational shift toward Postmaterialist values generated support for movements advocating peace, environmental protection, human rights, democratization and gender equality. These developments first manifested themselves in the politics of high-income societies around 1968, when the postwar generation became old enough to have political impact, launching an era of student protest.[6] This cultural shift has been transforming postindustrial societies, as younger cohorts replace older ones in the population.

The Silent Revolution thesis predicted that as Postmaterialists became more numerous they would bring new non-economic issues into politics and declining social class conflict. Postmaterialists are concentrated among the more secure and better-educated strata, but they are relatively favorable to social change. Consequently, though recruited from the more secure strata that traditionally supported conservative parties, they have gravitated toward parties that support political and cultural change.

From the start, this triggered a cultural backlash among older and less secure people who felt threatened by the erosion of familiar values. Over twenty years ago, I described how this was stimulating support for xenophobic populist parties, presenting a picture that is strikingly relevant today:

> The Materialist/Postmaterialist dimension has become
> the basis of a major new axis of political polarization
> in Western Europe. During the 1980s, environmentalist
> parties emerged in West Germany, The Netherlands,
> Belgium, Austria and Switzerland. In the 1990s they
> made breakthroughs in Sweden and France, and are
> beginning to show significant levels of support in Great
> Britain. In every case, support for these parties comes
> from a disproportionately Postmaterialist constituency. As
> Figure 9.1 demonstrates, as we move from the Materialist
> to the Postmaterialist end of the continuum, the percentage
> intending to vote for the environmentalist party in their
> country rises steeply... Pure Postmaterialists are five to
> twelve times as likely to vote for environmentalist parties as
> are pure Materialists.

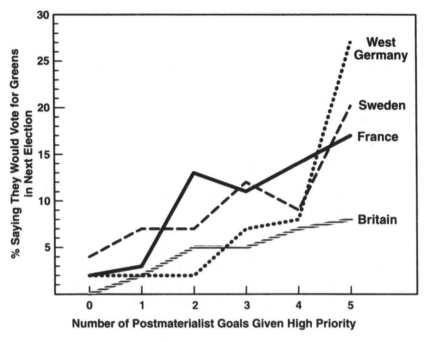

Figure 9.1 Intent to vote for environmentalist political parties, by Postmaterialist values in four countries having such parties.
Source: Inglehart, 1997: 243 (originally Figure 8.2).

West Germany was the scene of the first breakthrough by an environmentalist party in a major industrial nation. In 1983 the Greens were sufficiently strong to surmount Germany's 5 percent hurdle and enter the West German parliament. But more recently, the Greens have been pitted against a Republikaner party characterized by cultural conservatism and xenophobia. In the 1994 national elections, the Greens won 7 percent of the vote. The Republikaner, on the other hand, were stigmatized as the heirs of the Nazis and won only two percent of the vote, which was insufficient to win parliamentary representation. Nevertheless, xenophobic forces have already had a substantial impact on German politics, motivating the established parties to shift their policy positions in order to coopt the Republikaner electorate. These efforts included an amendment to the German constitution: to cut down the influx of foreigners, the clause guaranteeing free right of political asylum was eliminated in 1993, in a decision supported by a two-thirds majority of the German parliament.

The rise of the Green Party in Germany also had a major impact, for the Greens are much more than an ecological party. They seek to build a basically different kind of society from the prevailing industrial model. They have actively supported a wide range of Postmodern causes, from unilateral disarmament to women's emancipation, gay and lesbian rights, rights for the physically handicapped and citizenship rights for non-German immigrants.

Inglehart, 1997: 243–245.

The Greens and the Republikaner are located at opposite poles of a New Politics dimension, as Figure 9.2 indicates. The Republikaner did not call themselves the Anti-Environment Party and the Greens didn't call themselves the Pro-Immigrant Party, but they advocate opposite policies on these and other key issues. One pole reflects the Silent Revolution dynamic, while the opposite pole reflects the Authoritarian Reflex that motivates support for xenophobic authoritarian parties.

The older parties are arrayed on the traditional Left–Right axis that was established in an era when political cleavages were dominated

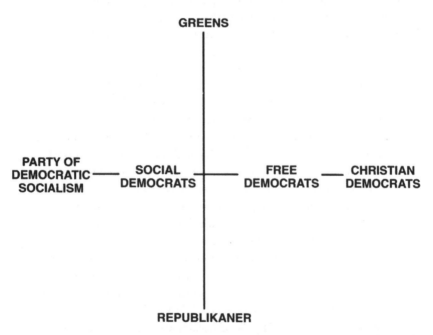

Figure 9.2 The social class-based Left–Right dimension and the Postmodern politics dimension in Germany.

Source: Inglehart, 1997: 245.

by social class conflict. On this axis (the horizontal dimension of Figure 9.2) the Party of Democratic Socialism (the ex-communists) was on the extreme Left, followed by the Social Democrats, with the Free Democrats and the Christian Democrats on the Right. Though most people think of the Greens as located on the Left, they actually fall on a new dimension. Traditionally, the Left parties were based on a working-class constituency, and advocated redistribution of income. In striking contrast, the Postmaterialist Left appeals primarily to a middle-class constituency and is only faintly interested in the classic program of the Left. But Postmaterialists *are* intensely favorable to major political and cultural changes, which frequently repel the Left's traditional working-class constituency, stimulating the rise of xenophobic authoritarian parties. Similarly, while prominent writers refer to the latter parties as Extreme Right or Radical Right parties, this suggests that they are like the traditional conservative parties only more so. This can be misleading because while the traditional right largely drew its support from the more prosperous segments of society and gave top priority to reducing taxes and government regulation, the Populist Authoritarian parties draw their support mainly from the less-educated strata, and are mainly motivated by xenophobia and rejection of rapid cultural change.

The vertical axis on Figure 9.2 reflects the polarization between Postmaterialist values and xenophobic authoritarian values. At one pole of this New Politics axis we find openness to ethnic diversity and gender equality; and at the opposite pole we find emphasis on authoritarian and xenophobic values.

As Figure 9.3 demonstrates, from the start, across five advanced industrial societies 70 percent of the pure Materialists supported a policy of reverse affirmative action – holding that "When jobs are scarce, employers should give priority to [one's own nationality] over immigrants." Among the pure Postmaterialist type, only 25 percent were in favor of giving preference to native-born citizens.[7] Similarly, in response to a question about whether they would like to have immigrants or foreign workers as neighbors, Materialists were six times as likely as the Postmaterialists to say they would not want foreigners as neighbors.

A New Politics axis also emerged in many other countries, including France, Denmark, Sweden, Switzerland, The Netherlands, Italy and Austria. The success of new parties partly depends on how skillfully they shape their appeal within their country's institutional

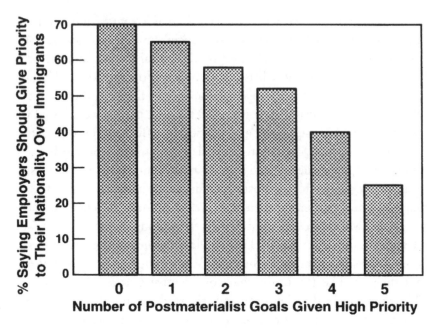

Figure 9.3 Support for giving preference to one's own nationality over immigrants, when jobs are scarce – in the USA, Britain, France, West Germany and Sweden. *Source*: Inglehart, 1997: 247.

constraints: a two-party system, for example, tends to stifle new parties.[8] But in 2016, New Politics movements broke through in the USA, despite its two-party system, stimulating major revolts *within* each of the two major parties – with Trump, backed by older, less-secure voters, capturing the Republican Presidential nomination and Sanders, backed by younger, better-educated voters, mounting a strong challenge for the Democratic nomination.

Why is xenophobic authoritarianism so much more powerful now than it was 30 years ago?

The backlash against Postmaterialism that motivates populist authoritarian parties is not new – it has been present for decades. What is new is the fact that, while these parties were once a fringe phenomenon, today they threaten to take over the governments of major countries.

The rise of xenophobic populist authoritarian parties raise two key questions: (1) "What motivates people to support these movements?" And (2) "Why is the xenophobic authoritarian vote so much higher now than it was several decades ago?" As we have suggested, the two questions have different answers.

Support for these parties is motivated by a backlash against the cultural changes linked with the rise of Postmaterialist and Self-expression values, more than by economic factors. The proximate cause of the populist vote is widespread anxiety that pervasive cultural changes and an influx of foreigners are eroding the way of life one knew since childhood. Though they are often called Radical Right parties,[9] the main common theme of these parties is a reaction against immigration and cultural change.[10] Indeed, several leading authorities argue that these parties should be called Anti-immigration parties instead of Radical Right parties, because this is their common denominator.[11] Other prominent writers suggest calling them Traditional–Authoritarian–Nationalist parties.[12] I prefer the label "authoritarian populist parties." A leading authority in the field, Herbert Kitschelt, concludes that: "We should look skeptically upon the idea that the radical right is purely a phenomenon of the politics of resentment among the 'new social cleavage' of low-skilled and low-qualified workers in inner-city areas, or that their rise can be attributed in any mechanical fashion to growing levels of unemployment and job insecurity in Europe."[13] Another leading expert, Cas Mudde is equally doubtful about purely economic explanations for the rise of these parties.[14]

Economic factors such as income and unemployment rates are surprisingly weak predictors of the populist authoritarian vote.[15] Exit polls from the US 2016 Presidential election show that those most concerned with economic problems disproportionately voted for Clinton, while those who considered immigration the most crucial problem voted for Trump.[16]

After he became President, support for Trump continued to be based on an intergenerational cultural cleavage far more than on economic factors. As Figure 9.4a demonstrates, in March 2017 only 20 percent of the American public less than 30 years old had favorable attitudes toward Trump – as compared with 52 percent of those who were 65 and older: members of the older group were more than twice as likely to support Trump as the younger group. Income was a much weaker predictor of support for Trump. As Figure 9.4b indicates, those with family incomes under $50,000 were only slightly less likely to support Trump than those with incomes over $100,000 and the relationship with income was curvilinear.

Analysis of European Social Survey data covering 32 countries finds that the strongest authoritarian populist support comes from

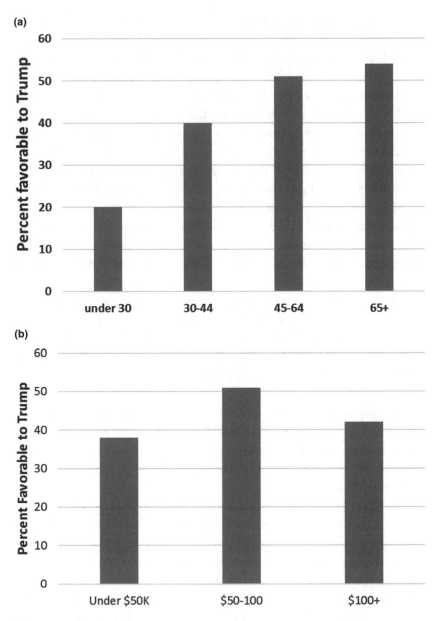

Figure 9.4 (a) Support for Trump by age in 2017 (b) Support for Trump by income in 2017.

Source: Economist/YOUGOV survey, March 13–14, 2017.

small proprietors, not from poorly paid manual workers.[17] Only one of five economic variables tested – employment status – was a significant predictor of support for xenophobic populist authoritarian parties. But when five cultural factors such as anti-immigrant attitudes and authoritarian values were tested, all five of them strongly predicted support for these parties. Authoritarian populist support is concentrated among the older generation, the less-educated, men, the religious and the ethnic majority – groups that hold traditional cultural values. Older voters are much likelier than younger voters to support these parties, although unemployment rates are higher among the young. And, although women tend to have lower-paying jobs, men are much likelier than women to support authoritarian populist parties.

For the last three decades, support for xenophobic authoritarian populist parties has come mainly from older, more Materialistic voters. But 30 years ago, the Republikaner and the National Front were relatively small. In the 2017 national elections, support for the Alternative for Germany (a successor to the Republikaner) had risen to almost 13 percent, making it Germany's third strongest party.[18] And in 2017, the leader of the National Front emerged as one of the two top candidates for the Presidency of France. Other things being equal, one would expect that, as younger, more Postmaterialist birth cohorts replaced older ones in the population, support for these parties would dwindle. But when dealing with intergenerational change, one must take current conditions or "period effects" into account as well as birth cohort effects. Let us see how this works.

One of the largest birth cohort analyses ever performed traced the shift from Materialist to Postmaterialist values among the publics of six West European countries, analyzing surveys carried out in almost every year from 1970 to 2009, interviewing several hundred thousand respondents (Chapter 2 presented this analysis in detail). Figure 9.5 shows a simplified model of the results. From the start, younger birth cohorts were substantially more Postmaterialist than older ones, and they remained so. Cohort analysis revealed that after almost 40 years, given birth cohorts were still about as Postmaterialist as they were at the start. They had not become more Materialist as they aged: there was no evidence of life-cycle effects. Consequently, intergenerational population replacement brought a major long-term shift from Materialist to Postmaterialist values. But strong period effects, reflecting current economic conditions, were also evident. From 1970 to 1980, the population as a whole became more Materialist in response to a major

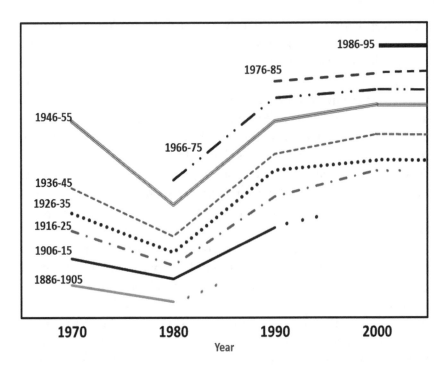

Figure 9.5 Model cohort analysis. Percentage of Postmaterialists minus percentage of Materialists in six West European countries, 1971–2009.

economic recession – but with subsequent economic recovery the proportion of Postmaterialists recovered. At every time point, the younger cohorts were more Postmaterialist (and more likely to support Green parties) than the older ones (who were likelier to support xenophobic parties). But at any time point, current socioeconomic conditions could make the population as a whole more (or less) Materialist – and more (or less) likely to support xenophobic parties.

We do not have the massive database that would be needed to carry out a cohort analysis of the vote for xenophobic authoritarian populist parties similar to this analysis of Materialist/Postmaterialist values, but it is clear that strong forces have been working to increase support for these parties. One of the most striking characteristics of the xenophobic authoritarian populist vote its strong linkage with age: older voters are consistently much likelier than younger voters to vote for these parties, reflecting an enduring pattern of intergenerational differences that was already evident in the 1990s.

Normally, this pattern of intergenerational differences would tend to gradually reduce the vote for Populist Authoritarian parties as younger, less xenophobic birth cohorts replace older ones in the adult population. But we find, instead, that the vote for these parties has increased substantially during the past 30 years. This implies the existence of a strong period effect – one strong enough to more than offset the effect of population replacement. What is driving this powerful period effect?

Two factors are immediately obvious. The first is the declining real income and rising economic inequality that many of the leading authorities in this field have emphasized.[19] This interpretation is consistent with a large body of evidence that economic insecurity is conducive to xenophobia. Indeed, it is so plausible that it comes as a surprise to find that economic factors are not the main predictor of the Populist Authoritarian vote: empirical evidence consistently indicates that this vote is driven by cultural backlash far more than by economic factors. Although rising economic insecurity is not the proximate cause of the Populist Authoritarian vote, the experts who emphasized its importance were not wrong: it plays a crucial role earlier in the causal process, helping explain why the Populist Authoritarian vote is much stronger today than it was 30 years ago.

The second factor driving the long-term shift toward Populist Authoritarian voting is equally obvious: it is the unprecedentedly high levels of immigration into high-income countries. Both factors are involved, and they complement each other. Massive immigration helps explain why it is that some of the most secure and (until recently) most tolerant countries such as Sweden, Denmark, Germany and The Netherlands now have strong xenophobic authoritarian populist parties: they have been the target of the largest immigration flows precisely *because* they are prosperous countries with strong social welfare nets, that (until recently) were relatively hospitable to refugees and immigrants. Though they may enter the European Union through Italy or Greece, few immigrants want to stay there, because conditions are much more attractive in Northern Europe.

In recent decades, much of the population of high-income countries has experienced declining real income, declining job security and rising income inequality, bringing growing existential insecurity. This has happened in context with a massive influx of immigrants and refugees. The first chapter of this book presented evidence from many sources indicating that insecurity triggers an Authoritarian Reflex linked with in-group conformity and xenophobia. Additional recent survey data confirms that xenophobia increases in times of insecurity.[20] Historical evidence points to the same conclusion. Under the relatively secure conditions of 1928, the German electorate viewed the Nazis as a lunatic fringe party, giving them less than 3 percent of the vote in national elections. But with the onset of the Great Depression, the Nazis won 44 percent of the vote in 1933, becoming the strongest party in the Reichstag and taking over the government. During the Great Depression a number of other countries, from Spain to Japan, also fell under Fascist rule.

Similarly, in 2005 the Danish public was remarkably tolerant when the publication of cartoons depicting Mohammed led to the burning of Danish consulates and angry demands that Muslim edicts against blasphemy take precedence over free speech. At the height of the cartoon crisis in 2005–2006, there was no backlash.[21] But after the Great Recession of 2007–2009, there was. In 2004, before the crisis erupted, the overtly anti-Muslim Danish People's Party won 7 percent of the vote; in 2014, it won 27 percent, becoming Denmark's largest party. Cultural backlash, rather than economic deprivation, was the strongest predictor of the vote for the Danish People's Party – but rising economic insecurity made people increasingly likely to vote for them.[22]

In high-income countries, at any given time, young Postmaterialist voters are much less likely than Materialists to support xenophobic parties – but the population as a whole has become increasingly likely to do so. Cultural backlash largely explains why given people vote for xenophobic parties – but declining economic and physical security helps explain why these parties are much stronger today than they were 30 years ago.

Decades of declining real income and rising inequality, together with unprecedented massive immigration, have produced a long-term period effect supporting the populist vote. Thus, although the proximate cause of the populist vote is cultural backlash, its high present level largely reflects the declining economic security, rising economic inequality and massive immigration that many writers have emphasized.

The fact that birth-cohort effects can coexist with period effects is not intuitively obvious and tends to be overlooked, but it explains the seeming paradox that economic factors do not explain why given individuals vote for populist parties – but *do* help explain why the populist vote is much stronger now than in the past. It also helps explains why, in the USA, the vote shifted most strongly from Obama (in 2012) to Trump (in 2016) in counties that experienced economic decline – even though at the *individual* level, the Trump vote was mainly motivated by cultural backlash.

The Distinctiveness of Attitudes toward Foreigners

As Chapter 5 demonstrated, favorable attitudes toward gender equality and gays have been spreading rapidly in high-income countries – but tolerance of immigrants has not. Why?

Like other aspects of intergenerational change, xenophobia shows both cohort effects and period effects, but attitudes toward foreigners are distinctive. They have been influenced by an unprecedentedly large influx of immigrants and refugees. This has happened in context with massive media coverage of terrorist attacks (usually by foreigners) conveying the perception that foreigners are dangerous. In recent decades, Western mass media have intentionally presented positive images of gays and emancipated women – almost certainly contributing to increasingly favorable public attitudes toward them. Although the mass media have not intentionally conveyed negative images of foreigners, their extensive coverage of terrorism has had that effect. Terrorist acts are designed to attract maximum media exposure, and they get it. To an immense degree. The World Values Survey has covered nine Arabic-speaking countries, and I've become friends with a number of Arabs. It's only a slight exaggeration to say that virtually all the Arabs I know personally are engaging, interesting, friendly people – and all the Arabs I hear about on television are terrorists.

In high-income countries, the objective danger of dying from smoking (or even from riding a bicycle) is much greater than the danger of being killed by a terrorist – yet the media (especially TV) rarely mention the dangers of smoking (or bicycles), but provide massive coverage of terrorist incidents. This is reinforced by the fact that before any airline flight, the process of taking off your coat and shoes, opening your luggage and taking out your computer in order to be searched, subtly conveys the message that terrorists are lurking in every airport.

Women and gays have always been present – but foreigners have become much more visible through massive immigration. From 1970 to 2015, the Hispanic population of the USA rose from 5 percent to more than 20 percent. Sweden, which in 1970 was inhabited almost entirely by ethnic Swedes, now has a foreign-born population of 16 percent; in Switzerland, the foreign-born population has risen to over 28 percent. In 2013, 20 percent of the German population had a migrant background. The influx of large numbers of visibly different strangers tends to trigger a deep-rooted Authoritarian Reflex that may have evolved during humanity's prehistoric hunting and gathering phase, when it was linked with survival. That reflex is still with us today (and the tendency to respond to it may even have a genetic component, as Chapter 1 suggests).[23] Rapid cultural change, coupled with large-scale immigration, tends to make older people feel that they are no longer living in the country in which they grew up – making them feel uprooted and evoking their support for xenophobic authoritarian populist parties that promise to stop immigration.

The period effects based on immigration and rising income inequality did not wipe out the birth cohort differences in developed societies: younger and better-educated respondents (who tend to be Postmaterialists) continue to be substantially less likely to support authoritarian populist parties than the rest of the population. Many members of the younger birth cohorts in these societies grew up under secure conditions in multi-ethnic settings and find diversity less threatening than older people do. And in virtually all high-income countries, younger respondents are significantly less xenophobic than older ones, as Figure A4.1 in Appendix 4 demonstrates.[24] Consequently, although declining economic and physical security encourage growing support for xenophobic authoritarianism, age-linked cultural differences continue to be the strongest predictors of who votes for populist parties.

Its Own Gravedigger: The Shift from Class-Based Politics to Values Politics

For most of the twentieth century, working-class voters in developed countries mainly supported Left-oriented parties, while middle-class and upper-class voters supported Right-oriented economically conservative parties.[25] Governments of the Left brought redistribution and rising income equality, largely through their influence on the size of the welfare state.[26] Parties of the class-based Left successfully fought for greater economic equality.

As the century continued, however, postwar generations emerged with a Postmaterialist outlook, bringing declining emphasis on economic redistribution and growing emphasis on non-economic issues. This, plus large immigration flows from low-income countries with different cultures and religions, stimulated a reaction in which much of the working class moved to the Right, in defense of traditional values.

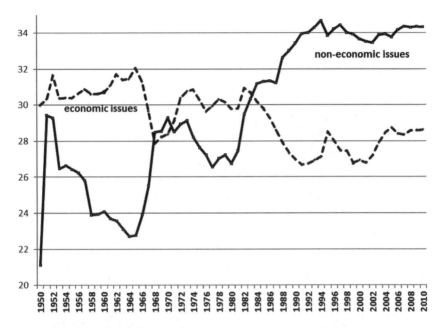

Figure 9.6 Changing salience of economic vs. non-economic issues in the party manifestos of 13 Western Democracies, 1950–2010.

Source: Party Manifestos data from Austria, Belgium, Canada, Denmark, France, Germany, Ireland, Italy, Netherlands, Norway, Sweden and Switzerland, in Zakharov (2016). Note: Table A.1 in the appendix shows how Zakharov coded issues as economic or non-economic.

The classic economic issues did not disappear. But their relative salience declined to such an extent that non-economic issues became more prominent than economic ones in Western political parties' campaign platforms. Figure 9.6 shows how the issues emphasized in 13 Western democracies evolved from 1950 to 2010. Economic issues were almost always more prominent than non-economic ones from 1950 to about 1983, when non-economic issues became more prominent. Since then, non-economic issues have dominated the stage.

Moreover, the rise of Postmaterialist issues tended to neutralize class-based political polarization. The social basis of support for the left increasingly has come from the middle class, while a substantial share of the working class has shifted to the right. Consequently, as Figure 9.7 demonstrates, social class voting declined markedly. If 75 per cent of the working class voted for the Left while only 25 per cent of the middle class did so, one would obtain a class voting index of 50.

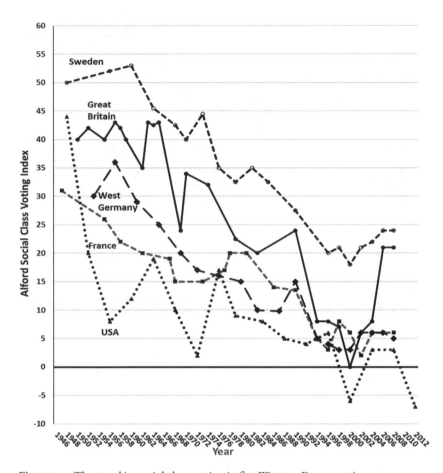

Figure 9.7 The trend in social class voting in five Western Democracies, 1947–2012. *Source:* 1947–1992 data from Inglehart, 1997: 255. More recent data for USA from ANES surveys; for other countries, from Euro Barometer surveys, taking rolling average of social class voting indices from the most recent survey before, after and during given year, supplemented with data from national election surveys (British Election Survey, 1992, 1997, 2001, 2005, 2010; German Election Study 1998, 2002, 2005, 2009; Politbarometer. 2012). US data from 1948 through 2008 are from Paul Abramson et al., 2015: 128–129. Because of inconsistent sampling of the non-white population across surveys, they reflect social-class voting among the white population. A similar index, based on exit poll data from the 2016 election, yields a social class voting index of –8.

This is about where the Swedish electorate was located in 1948 – but by 2008, Sweden's index had fallen to 24. But Swedish class voting was still relatively high: in France and Germany the social-class voting indices had dropped from about 30 to about 5 and in the United

States, they fell to zero and even lower. Class and income became much weaker indicators of political preferences than cultural issues: by wide margins, those who opposed abortion and same-sex marriage supported Republican Presidential candidates over Democrats. The 2016 US Presidential elections actually showed a negative social-class voting index, with white working-class voters being more likely to vote for Trump than for the Clinton. The electorate had shifted from class-based polarization toward value-based polarization, unraveling a coalition that once brought economic redistribution.

Declining Real Income and Rising Income Inequality

During the past 40 years, the real income and existential security of the less-educated half of the population of many high-income societies has been declining. Economic inequality declined in advanced industrial societies for most of the twentieth century, but since about 1970 it has been rising steeply, as Piketty has demonstrated.[27] To take one example, in 1915 the richest 1 percent of Americans earned about 18 percent of the national income. From the 1930s to the 1970s, their share

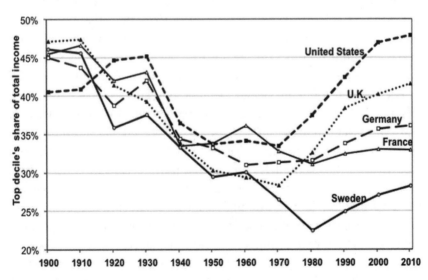

Figure 9.8 The top decile's share of total income in Europe and the USA, 1900–2010.

Source: Based on data from Piketty, 2014: 323; his data sources are shown in http://piketty.pse.ens.fr/capital21c.

fell below 10 percent – but by 2007, it had risen to 24 percent. The US case is far from unique: all but one of the OECD countries for which data are available experienced rising income inequality before taxes and transfers from 1980 to 2009.[28]

Piketty's work has been corrected on some points, but his claim that economic inequality is rising in developed countries is clearly accurate. He analyzes the evolution of income inequality in the US, Britain, Germany, France and Sweden from 1900 to 2010. His evidence shows that at the start of the twentieth century all four European countries had higher levels of income inequality than the USA, with the top tenth of the population taking from 40 percent to 47 percent of the total income. Inequality declined substantially from then on, so that from 1950 to 1970 the top decile's share ranged from 25 to 35 percent of the total income. Since 1980, income inequality has been rising – so much so that in the US, the top decile is now taking about 48 percent of the total income.

Though all five countries in Figure 9.8 show a U-shaped pattern, there is striking cross-national variation that reflects the country's political system – for economic inequality is ultimately a political question. Sweden stands out: though it had substantially higher levels of inequality than the USA in the early twentieth century, by the 1920s Sweden had attained lower levels than the other four countries – and has maintained them to the present. In the USA, the top decile got almost half of the total income in 2010, while in Sweden it got only 28 percent. The advanced welfare state culture introduced by Sweden's long-dominant Social Democrats seems to have had lasting effects. Conversely, neo-conservative regimes led by Ronald Reagan and Margaret Thatcher in the 1980s weakened labor unions and sharply cut back state regulation. They left a heritage in which conservatives in those countries seek to reduce government expenditures with almost religious zeal – and the USA (and to a lesser extent the United Kingdom) now show higher levels of income inequality than other developed capitalist societies. It seems more than sheer coincidence that these two countries recently displayed the most powerful xenophobic reactions to be found among highly developed societies, producing Trump's election to the Presidency and British withdrawal from the European Union.

The dramatic changes that occurred when former communist countries abandoned their state-run economies is further evidence that income inequality reflects a country's political system. The collapse of communism brought even larger increases in income inequality than in the West.[29] Around 1980, most communist regimes had relatively low economic inequality but, as Figure A5.1 in the appendix indicates, both China and Russia now have even higher Gini indices of inequality than the USA or the UK.

Piketty holds that rising inequality is the normal state of affairs, which was temporarily offset by exogenous shocks (the two World Wars and the Great Depression). But historical evidence doesn't support this claim. Inequality began falling in many capitalist countries before World War I, and major welfare state legislation continued to be adopted long after World War II. Indeed, Sweden established one of the world's most advanced welfare states without participating in either world war.

Political factors are outside Piketty's model so he treats them as random shocks. But they are far from random. Economic equality or inequality ultimately depends on the balance of political power between owners and workers, which varies at different stages of economic development. The transition from agrarian society to industrial society created rising demand for industrial workers. Initially they were exploited, but when they became organized in labor unions and working-class-oriented political parties, they were able to elect governments that redistributed income, regulated finance and industry and established welfare states that brought growing income equality throughout most of the twentieth century. Since about 1970, organized labor has dwindled to a small minority of the workforce, weakening its political influence. Government redistribution and regulation of the economy were cut back during the Reagan–Thatcher era; and the rise of the knowledge society tends to establish a winner-takes-all economy in which the rewards go mainly to those at the very top.

The Elephant Curve

A brilliant book by Branko Milanovic puts Piketty's findings in global context, demonstrating that rising inequality is not an inherent feature of capitalist economies: it depends on their stage of development.[30] As Milanovic demonstrates, the world as a whole is getting richer, but it is doing so on a very uneven trajectory that he describes

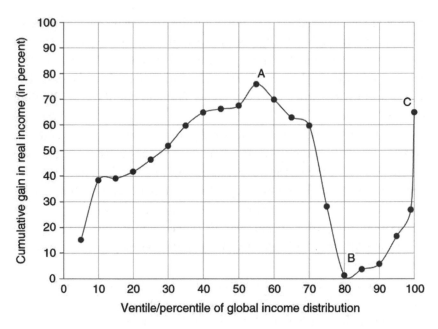

Figure 9.9 Relative gain in real per capita income by global income level, 1988–2008.
Source: Milanovic, 2016: 11.

as an "elephant curve." This curve is depicted by Figure 9.9, which shows the world-wide gains in real per capita income that were made from 1988 to 2008. The poorest tenth of the world's population (the elephant's tail at the left end of the curve) made modest progress, with real incomes increasing by 15 percent. But most of the world's population experienced large gains in real income. The largest gains were made by the 40 percent near point A (mostly living in China, India, Thailand, Vietnam and Indonesia) – whose real incomes increased by 80 percent during this 20-year period. In sharp contrast, the decile near point B (mostly living in the high-income societies of Western Europe, the USA, Canada, Australia and Japan) started from a much higher base, but they made no gains during these 20 years – and for a large share of the population, real income declined. This is the exact opposite of what people were led to expect by politicians who pushed for deregulation, lower taxes and greater reliance on markets during the Reagan–Thatcher revolution.

The winners in recent decades have been the people of China, India and Southeast Asia, while the losers have been almost everyone living in high-income countries. But the greatest absolute gains by far were made by the global top one percent at point C – the very rich in high-income countries – who started out with very high incomes *and* made massive gains, sharply increasing inequality.

Rising inequality and impoverishment of the poor is not an inevitable aspect of capitalism. It reflects a society's stage of development. Though inequality has been increasing in high-income countries, real income has been rising for most of the people in China, India and other developing countries. For the transition from agrarian to industrial economies creates a demand for large numbers of industrial workers, increasing their bargaining power. The transition from industrial to service economies has the opposite effect, undermining the power of organized labor, as automation replaces humans – first undermining the bargaining power of industrial workers and then, as a later stage, undermining that of highly educated professionals.

High-income countries are now moving into an advanced phase of the Knowledge Society – that of Artificial Intelligence Society. This tends to produce increasingly high levels of inequality. In industrial society the cost of producing and distributing material products is substantial, so there are niches for a wide range of products ranging from the very cheap to the very expensive. But once you have produced a knowledge product such as Microsoft, it costs almost nothing to produce and distribute additional copies. There is no need to buy anything but the top product, which can take over the entire market, producing enormous rewards for those who produce the top product, but nothing for any other producers. Inequality becomes still worse with the transition to Artificial Intelligence Society – a phase of development in which virtually anyone's job can be replaced by computer programs, making it possible to squeeze the entire workforce and funnel economic gains to the very top. Outsourcing is only a transitional problem: even China is now starting to automate its factories. The long-term problem is automation, and erecting walls and trade barriers won't solve it.

One might attribute the fact that most of the world's population made major economic gains during the past 20 years to some random shock that somehow did not affect high-income countries. But it seems much likelier that the contrasting performance of China–India–Indonesia–Thailand–Vietnam versus that of the high-income countries reflects the fact that the two groups of countries are at different phases of modernization. China–India–Indonesia–Thailand–Vietnam have been making the transition from agricultural society to industrial society, in which the average person's bargaining power is inherently greater than in knowledge economies. High-income countries have been making the transition from industrial society to knowledge economies, in which jobs are highly differentiated according to educational levels, giving the less educated little or no bargaining power. Moreover, even the highly educated lose their bargaining power as these countries become artificial intelligence societies, where almost everyone's job can be automated, leaving them at the mercy of those who control large corporations.

Pay No Attention to That Man behind the Curtain

Conservatives argue that rising inequality doesn't really matter. As long as the economy as a whole is growing, everyone will get richer, and we should pay no attention to rising inequality.

But everyone *isn't* getting richer. For decades, the real income of the developed world's working class has been declining, while the material basis of what counts as an acceptable standard of living has been rising. In the nineteenth century, having enough to eat counted as doing well and "A chicken in every pot" was an inspiring political slogan. Later, the slogan "A car in every garage" was an ambitious goal. Today, having an automobile and enough to eat are part of a minimal living standard in high-income countries, but the working class has precarious job prospects and an awareness of the vast economic gains made by those above them – and they feel shut out from the benefits of growth. A growing awareness of their declining relative position is shaping how they see their social position: in 2000, 33 percent of the US public described themselves as "working class"; by 2015, that figure had risen to 48 percent.[31]

Conservative economists used to argue that even very steep taxes on the top earners wouldn't raise enough money to change things substantially. That is no longer true. Inequality has risen so rapidly that by 2007, the top 1 percent took home 24 percent of the US total income[32] and in 2011 the top 1 percent of households controlled 40 percent of the nation's wealth.[33] In 2014, Wall Street paid out in bonuses roughly twice as much as the total earnings of all Americans who work full time at the federal minimum wage.[34] And in 2015, 25 hedge fund managers were paid more than all the kindergarten teachers in the USA.[35]

Since the start of the twentieth century, it seemed to be a law of nature that modernization brought rising life expectancy. But since 2000 the life expectancy of middle-aged non-Hispanic whites in the USA has been falling.[36] The decline is concentrated among those with less than a college education, and is largely attributable to drug abuse, alcohol abuse and suicide. This is a sign of severe malaise. The only comparable phenomenon in modern times was the sharp decline in male life expectancy that accompanied the collapse of the Soviet Union. In knowledge economies, economic growth no longer raises everyone's standard of living – or even their life expectancy.

Political Mobilization Shapes the Rise and Fall of Inequality

Inequality reflects the balance of political power between elites and mass – which is shaped by modernization. Early industrialization brought ruthless exploitation of workers, low wages, long working days, and suppression of unions. But eventually, cognitive mobilization narrowed the gap between elites and masses by redressing the balance of political skills. Urbanization brought people into closer proximity; workers were concentrated in factories, facilitating communication among them, and the spread of mass literacy put them in touch with national politics, enabling workers to organize for effective action. In the late nineteenth century and early twentieth century, unions won the right to organize, enabling workers to bargain collectively. The expansion of the franchise gave workers the vote, and left-oriented political parties mobilized them. These newly mobilized voters eventually elected governments that implemented redistributive policies such as progressive taxation, social insurance and extensive welfare states, causing inequality to decline for most of the twentieth century.

But that was when strong parties of the redistributive Left existed. Under current conditions, the rich are able to shape government policies in ways that increase the concentration of wealth. In 2012, the American public discovered that billionaire Presidential candidate Mitt Romney was being taxed at a lower rate than his secretary. And in 2016, despite repeated requests, billionaire Presidential candidate Donald Trump refused to release his income tax returns, evoking widespread belief that he wasn't paying his share. Gilens presents evidence that the US government responds so faithfully to the preferences of the most affluent ten percent of the country's citizens that "under most circumstances, the preferences of the vast majority of Americans appear to have essentially no impact on which policies the government does or doesn't adopt."[37]

The safety net that once protected the American public is unraveling, as politicians and corporations cut back on health care, income security and retirement pensions.[38] In the USA, financial institutions employ two to three lobbyists for every representative in Congress – largely to dissuade them from regulating banks more closely.[39] The fact that Congress has been so reluctant to regulate banks, even after inadequate regulation of the financial sector, led to a Great Recession that cost millions of people their jobs and homes, suggests that this investment is paying off.

Stiglitz argues convincingly that a tiny minority of extremely rich individuals has attained tremendous political influence in the USA, which they are using to shape policies that systematically increase the concentration of wealth, undermining economic growth and diminishing investment in education, research and infrastructure.[40] Hacker and Pierson argue that winner-take-all politics in the USA is based on an alliance between big business and conservative politicians that has cut taxes for the rich from 75 percent in 1970 to less than 35 percent in 2004 and sharply reduced regulation of the economy and financial markets.[41] This is indeed the proximate cause. But the ability of USA politicians to adopt one-sidedly pro-business policies was enhanced by the weakening of organized labor, globalization and the trend toward a winner-takes-all economy. Fifty years ago, capitalists and conservative politicians were probably just as greedy and as clever as they are today – but they were restrained by an alliance of strong labor unions and left-oriented political parties that was able to offset the power of the rich, and establish redistributive policies. The decline of labor-based parties and the rise of a winner-takes-all economy has undermined this political alignment, and inequality is rising in virtually all highly developed countries.

Rising inequality and economic insecurity are already generating powerful political dissatisfaction. As the following chapter argues, inequality and insecurity are likely to become even more severe as these societies move into a mature phase of the Knowledge Society – that of Artificial Intelligence Society.

10 THE COMING OF ARTIFICIAL INTELLIGENCE SOCIETY

Overview

High-income countries are now entering the stage of Artificial Intelligence Society – an advanced phase of the Knowledge Society, in which virtually anyone's job can be automated. Artificial intelligence has a huge potential to improve our prosperity and health if used on behalf of society as a whole. But if left to market forces, it brings a winner-takes-all society in which the gains go almost entirely to the top.

Artificial Intelligence Society produces increasingly high levels of inequality for two reasons:

(1) Industrial society produces material products that are expensive to produce and distribute, creating niches for a wide range of products ranging from very cheap to very expensive. But once you have produced a knowledge product, it costs almost nothing to duplicate and distribute. There is no reason to buy anything but the top product, which tends to take over the entire market, generating huge profits – but only for the top product.

(2) Inequality becomes even more extreme with the transition to Artificial Intelligence Society – a phase of development in which virtually anyone's job can be replaced by computer programs, making it possible to squeeze the workforce and funnel economic gains even more narrowly to the very top.

The Impact of Artificial Intelligence Society

In manufacturing material objects, there is room for a wide range of products – from very small cars that cost very little to produce, to mid-size cars, to large cars, to extremely expensive luxury cars. A wide range of products compete on price. But in the knowledge economy, the cost of reproduction approaches zero: once you have produced Microsoft software, it costs almost nothing to produce and distribute additional copies – which means that there is no reason to buy anything but Microsoft. In this winner-takes-all economy, Bill Gates became a billionaire before he was 40, and Mark Zuckerberg became a billionaire before he was 30. The rewards to those at the top are immense – but they are largely limited to those at the top.

This trend is exacerbated by the fact that in Artificial Intelligence Society, virtually anyone's job can be automated. In the early stages of the Knowledge Society, there is growing demand for people with high levels of education and skills and they can get secure, well-paid jobs. But the transition to Artificial Intelligence Society changes this: computers begin to replace even highly educated professionals. If left to market forces, secure well-paid jobs will continue to disappear – even for the highly educated. In Artificial Intelligence Society, the key economic conflict is no longer between a working class and a middle class, but between the top one percent and the remaining 99 percent, as Stiglitz puts it.[1]

For the past 50 years the real income and existential security of the less-educated people of high-income societies have been declining. Fifty years ago, the largest US employer was General Motors, where workers earned an equivalent of $50 per hour in 2016 dollars. Today, the largest employer – Walmart – pays around $8 per hour. More recently, artificial intelligence has been undermining the economic position of the more educated strata, with computer programs taking over the jobs of the college educated and those with graduate degrees. Initially, the knowledge society brought them greater opportunities and rising living standards but as Figure 10.1 shows, this is no longer true. From 1991 to 2015, median real incomes in the USA were flat across the entire educational spectrum. This applies to college graduates, those with PhDs, and to lawyers, physicians and others with professional degrees. The median real income of even these highly educated groups

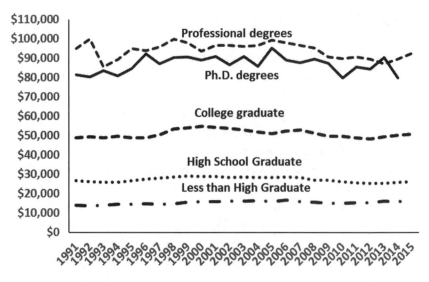

Figure 10.1 Median real income of US employed people in 2013 dollars, by educational level, 1991–2015.
Source: United Census Bureau (available at www.census.gov/data/tables/time-series/demo/income-poverty/historical-income-people.html).
The income for each year is the mean of the median male and female incomes.

have been stagnant since 1991 – and has actually *declined* since 1999. This figure shows the mean incomes of men and women combined. This masks the fact that, while women's real incomes were rising, men's real incomes were falling by more than enough to offset it – contributing to the fact that men were much likelier than women to support xenophobic populists like Trump.

The highly educated still make substantially higher salaries than the less educated, but since 1991, the real incomes of not only the less educated, but also those of the highly educated have been stagnant in the USA. The problem is not lack of economic growth. Gross domestic product has increased substantially since 1991. So where did the money go? To the elite of the elite, such as the Chief Executive Officers (CEOs) of the country's largest corporations. During a period in which the real incomes of highly educated professionals including doctors, lawyers, scientists, university professors, journalists and engineers were flat, the real incomes of the CEOs rose immensely. In 1965, the average CEO at the 350 largest US companies was paid 20 times as much as the company's average worker; in 1989, they were paid 58 times as much; and in 2012 the CEOs were paid 354 times as much as the average worker.[2] This vastly increased disparity doesn't reflect improved CEO performance: economic growth was higher in the 1960s than it is today. The CEOs are not 17 times as productive as they were in 1965. Instead, we are living in a world where the people who drove General Motors into bankruptcy were able to retire with huge bonuses, while the workers lost their jobs and benefits.

In 1860, most of the US workforce was employed in agriculture. By 1950, most jobs in the agricultural sector had disappeared but this didn't bring widespread unemployment and poverty because there was a massive rise in industrial employment. But by 2017, automation and outsourcing had reduced the ranks of industrial workers to less than 9 percent of the workforce. The loss of industrial jobs was offset by a dramatic rise in service-sector jobs, which now employ most of the US workforce.

A key part of the service sector is the high-technology sector, consisting of those employed in the information, professional, scientific and technical services, and finance and insurance categories. It is often assumed that the high-tech sector will produce large numbers of high-paying jobs. But – surprising as it may seem – high-tech employment is not increasing. As Figure 10.2 shows, the high-tech sector's share of total employment in the USA has been flat since statistics first became available about three decades ago. As Figure A5.2 in the appendix indicates, this also holds true of high-technology employment in other countries from which data are available, including Canada, Germany, France, Sweden and the United Kingdom. Unlike the transition from agricultural to industrial society, Artificial Intelligence Society is not generating large numbers of secure, well-paid jobs. For example, at peak employment in 1979, General Motors alone employed nearly 840,000 workers and earned about $11 billion in 2010 dollars. By contrast, in 2010 Google generated a profit of nearly $14 billion while employing only 38,000 people – less than one twentieth as many as General Motors once employed.[3] In 2005, YouTube was founded by three people. Two years later, still employing only 65 people, it was bought by Google for $1.65 billion. Artificial intelligence-based companies can monopolize markets that serve millions, generating huge profits with relatively few employees. For artificial intelligence is like a self-devouring snake: it is getting better and better at doing anything that humans can do – including writing computer programs.

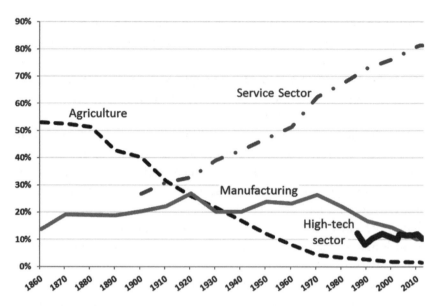

Figure 10.2 Percentage of US workforce employed in agriculture and industry, 1860–2012, in service sector, 1900–2012 and high-technology sector since 1986 (data not available for service sector before 1900 and for high-technology sector before 1986).

Sources: Federal Reserve Bank of St. Louis, 2014; Hadlock, 1991; Hecker, 1999; Hecker, 2005; Kutscher and Mark, 1983; Lebergott, 1966; National Science Board, 2012; National Science Board, 2014; Powell and Snellman, 2004; United States Bureau of Labor Statistics, 2013; United States Bureau of Labor Statistics, 2014; United States Bureau of the Census, 1977.

The number of industrial workers has already declined drastically, weakening the electoral base of the labor-oriented political parties that once were able to implement the welfare state. Automation and outsourcing have long since eroded the bargaining position of industrial workers – and with the rise of the artificial intelligence economy, the entire human workforce is losing its bargaining power. Until recently, law was considered a secure profession. Law firms used to hire large numbers of newly minted lawyers who were put to work sifting through thousands of pages of documents to determine the basic facts of a case. Today computers can do this process of discovery much faster, more cheaply and more accurately than lawyers. A law degree once meant a good salary and a low risk of unemployment. In recent years, 40 percent of those who graduated from law school in the USA didn't get jobs requiring law degrees. Many young lawyers are unemployed or underemployed, bringing a 30 percent drop in law school enrollment from 2010 to 2015.

The medical profession is better off because developed societies have aging populations, creating a rising demand for medical care. But most doctors are now employed by large corporations that can dictate their salaries and working conditions. The bargaining power of physicians is being further undermined by outsourcing. When you get an X-ray in the USA it is likely to be transmitted to India, where it will be interpreted by a physician who is paid a fraction of an American doctor's salary. But this is only the first stage of the squeeze. Synthetic intellects are being developed that learn independently and can do medical diagnoses based on millions of cases more accurately and faster than physicians – and far more cheaply. They are starting to replace the Indian radiologists. Outsourcing jobs to other countries is an interim phenomenon, not the long-term problem. The transfer of jobs from humans to artificial intelligence is a far more serious long-term challenge.

The profession of print journalism is disappearing – giving way to internet news sources on which it's difficult to distinguish fake news from genuine news, weakening a crucial safeguard of democracy. And the intellectual integrity of academic life is being undermined. Fifty years ago, when people went into teaching at the university level, they assumed that they would eventually get tenure and be free to investigate any topic that interested them. In 1970, most of the university-level teaching in the USA was done by people with tenure track jobs. In the last few decades, the percentage of university educators with full-time tenure track jobs has fallen from 45 percent to 25 percent.[4] University presidents are behaving exactly like the other CEOs, abolishing secure jobs and replacing them with adjunct and part-time instructors with low salaries and insecure jobs. Most academics now spend their careers seeking one temporary job after another.

And increasingly, computer programs themselves are being written by computer programs – a major reason why the number of jobs in the high-technology sector is not increasing.

Building walls and denying visas will not stop this process. Although politicians and voters blame global trade and offshoring for their countries' economic difficulties, between 2000 and 2010 only 13 percent of American manufacturing jobs were lost to trade, while over 85 percent were eliminated due to productivity gains from technological advances.[5] Automation eliminates far more jobs than international trade, for computers are less expensive than even the most poorly paid humans. Computers will work very fast and accurately for 24 hours a day without demanding salaries, pensions or health benefits – and their costs are declining rapidly.

Artificial intelligence has great promise. Properly harnessed, it could make life safer, longer and better for everyone. But it is rapidly replacing large numbers of jobs – including highly skilled middle-class jobs.[6] If this is true, why don't we see widespread unemployment? Superficially, the US economy seems to be flourishing. In 2016 the economy was growing, the stock market hit record highs and unemployment seemed low. By normal standards, the 2016 Presidential election should have brought a resounding vote of confidence for the incumbent party. Instead, there were massive rebellions against the leadership of both major parties. Why?

One reason why artificial intelligence does not seem to be producing unemployment is because dismal employment prospects have caused large numbers of people to drop out of the workforce. The civilian unemployment rate in December 2016 was down to 4.7 percent, which seems like full employment. But this doesn't take workforce dropouts into account – and the adult work rate in America was at its lowest level in more than 30 years. From 1970 to 2016, the jobs-to-population ratio for civilian men and women for Americans aged 20 and older fell from 64.6 to 59.7.[7] The sharp drop in work rates for US adults between 2008 and 2010 was roughly twice as large as that experienced during the country's worst previous postwar recession. In 2017, for every unemployed American man between 25 and 55 years of age, there were another three who were neither working nor looking for work. Work rates for women had been rising steadily ever since World War II – until the year 2000. Since then, they too have declined.[8]

An impressive book by Martin Ford provides a detailed account of how artificial intelligence is rapidly developing the ability to replace almost any job; he makes a strong argument for establishing a universal basic income.[9] This would be better than doing nothing but it is not the optimal solution.

Being unemployed or a labor-force dropout is not a happy experience. Prime age men who are out of the labor force report very low levels of emotional well-being and derive little meaning from their daily activities.[10] Being out of the labor force can even lead to premature death. From 1999 to 2013, US death rates rose slightly for all non-Hispanic white men and women 45–54 years of age – but they rose sharply for those with high school degrees or less, and for this less-educated group, most of the rise in death rates was accounted for by suicides, liver cirrhosis and drug overdoses.[11] A 2016 study examined the opioid epidemic in America, demonstrating that nearly half of all working-age male labor-force dropouts – now comprising roughly 7 million men – currently take addictive pain medication on a daily basis.[12] They are dying, not from starvation but from leading pointless lives. In 2016 US deaths from drug overdoses had risen to almost ten times their 1980 level. They are now the leading cause of death among Americans under 50.[13] This is one reason why simply providing a universal basic income is not an adequate solution. The rising death rates of labor-force dropouts have helped bring down the country's overall life expectancy. In December 2016, the Centers for Disease Control and Prevention reported that for the first time in decades, life expectancy at birth *for the American population as a whole* had dropped slightly.[14]

Artificial intelligence is hollowing out the economy – replacing secure, well-paid jobs with insecure, poorly paid ones. At first, industrial workers with strong unions were replaced by non-unionized workers with weaker bargaining power and job security; now, lawyers are being replaced by computers and tenured professors are being replaced by poorly paid part-time instructors. Figure 10.3 illustrates this process, comparing the changes in the structure of the US workforce from 1979 to 1999, with the changes that occurred from 1999 to 2012.

From 1979 to 1999, the overall skill-level of the workforce was still rising, as poorly paid jobs were replaced by well-paid jobs requiring higher skill levels – continuing a long-standing trend in which each generation expected to do better than their parents. After 1999, a hollowing-out of the economy set in. From 1999 to 2012, the proportion of middle-class jobs declined and there was a massive increase in poorly paid and insecure jobs. The growth of highly skilled, well-paid jobs was tiny in comparison with previous growth. A December 2016 report calculated that the odds of a 30-year-old's earning more than his parents at the same age was now just 51 percent – down from 86 percent 40 years ago.[15] The odds of doing better than one's parents have fallen to about 50:50 and are declining sharply.

In the twenty-first century, many lawyers were unable to get jobs requiring law degrees. Most of them did not become unemployed,

Smoothed Employment Changes:

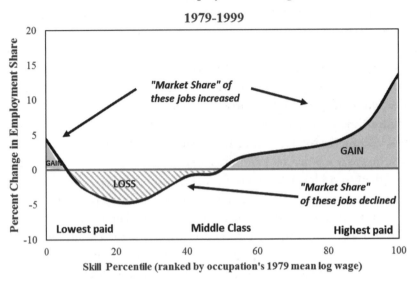

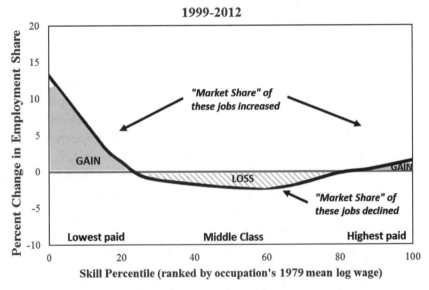

Figure 10.3 Changes in structure of US workforce: 1979–1999 vs. 1999–2012. *Source*: Based on data in McAfee, 2017 and Autor and Dorn, 2013.

but took jobs below their expected level. Similarly, because of across-the-board cuts in government spending, many medical doctors were unable to get internships and consequently couldn't practice as physicians – despite a shortage of doctors. Most of them did not become unemployed, but they worked at levels far below their expectations. Superficially, the economy seemed to be doing well, but the workforce was not. This pattern is not unique to the USA. From 1993 to 2010, 16 high-income West European countries also experienced a hollowing-out of their economies, losing large numbers of middle-class jobs.[16]

Will this trend continue? The future is inherently unpredictable, but market forces create a powerful incentive for it to do so. From a CEO's viewpoint, replacing your workforce with unorganized workers, poorly paid foreigners or robots maximizes your corporation's profits and strengthens its position against competitors. Ideally, one would dispense with the human workforce entirely. If every corporation did so, the country would be in a far deeper depression than that of the 1930s – but from the viewpoint of each corporation, squeezing the workforce in this way is almost irresistible and it's the prevailing strategy.

These problems are soluble. High-income societies are not becoming poorer. They are becoming more productive. The US economy has grown substantially since 1970. Wealth is increasing and top salaries are soaring. What has changed is the relationship between the bargaining power of the people who control corporations, and that of their employees. Even highly educated workers are no longer moving ahead, with the gains from the growing gross domestic product going almost entirely to a thin stratum of financiers, entrepreneurs and managers at the very top. As artificial intelligence replaces people, unregulated market forces bring a situation in which a tiny minority controls the economy, while the majority have precarious jobs, serving them as gardeners, waiters, nannies and hairdressers – a future foreshadowed by the social structure of Silicon Valley today.

The key political conflict today is no longer between the working class and the middle class. It is between the 1 percent and the 99 percent. Until a new political coalition emerges that represents the interests of the 99 percent – including less-educated whites – the economy will continue to be hollowed out and most people's existential security will continue to decline.

Government intervention is the only feasible way to overcome the growing concentration of income at the top in technologically advanced societies. A universal basic income has serious economic and psychological drawbacks. A more effective solution would be for government to create jobs that put people to work doing useful things that improve the society's quality of life and give people a sense of purpose and self-esteem. During the New Deal era in the USA, government-sponsored programs built highways and post offices, protected the environment and contributed to education and cultural life. Today, people are as imaginative and as capable of designing effective programs that require humans as they were then – but they are not yet organized to do so.

The Need for a New Political Coalition

There are indications that the 99 percent are becoming increasingly dissatisfied. Historically, being a socialist was fatal to a career in American politics. But in the 2016 US Presidential primary elections, Hillary Clinton, despite being strongly favored by the Democratic Party establishment, lost a number of primary elections to Bernie Sanders, a relative unknown who was an openly acknowledged socialist – in a country famous for having no socialism. There is growing awareness among younger voters that we need to change our political system. If only people under 35 could vote, Sanders would probably have won the Presidency. There was also an open rebellion within the Republican Party, with Donald Trump winning the nomination despite being disavowed by virtually all of the party's top leaders. There is a widespread feeling that neither major party is effectively representing the interests of most people – and it is well-founded. The American economy is being hollowed out and job security is fading.

In 2012, the gap between the richest one percent and the remaining 99 percent in the USA was the widest it has been since the 1920s.[17] In the long run, growing economic inequality is likely to bring a resurgence of mass support for government intervention – but for now, it is held in check by emotionally hot cultural issues such as immigration and same-sex marriage that enable conservative politicians to win the support of low-income voters.

Effective politics is always a difficult balancing act. You can get too much government intervention and you can get too little. Today, the political stability and economic health of high-income societies requires greater emphasis on the redistributive policies that were operating for most of the twentieth century. The social base of the New Deal coalition and its European counterparts is gone, but the conflicting interests of the 99 percent and the dominant one percent have created the potential for a new coalition. A punitive attitude toward the top one percent would be counter-productive – it includes many of the country's most valuable people. But moving toward a more progressive income tax would be perfectly reasonable. From 1950 to 1970, the US top one percent paid a much higher share of their income in taxes than they do today. This did not strangle economic growth – it was stronger then than now. Two of the richest Americans, Warren Buffet and Bill Gates, advocate higher taxes for the very rich. They also argue that the inheritance tax is a relatively painless way to raise funding that is badly needed for investment in education, medical care, research and development, and infrastructure. But powerful conservative interests have moved the USA in the opposite direction, sharply reducing the inheritance tax and cutting government expenditures.

Trump promised to make America great again. But Trump's policies of deregulating the financial sector, cutting medical coverage and reducing taxes on the very rich are the opposite of what is needed by the people who have been left behind. They will make America great for billionaires who pay no income tax.[18]

Hochschild argues that the paradox of low-income Americans voting against their own economic interests by supporting conservative Republicans reflects a powerful emotional reaction.[19] It is not just that right-wing politicians are duping them by directing their anger to cultural issues, away from possible solutions to their status as a permanent under-class. Less-educated white Americans feel that they have become "strangers in their own land." They see themselves as victims of affirmative action and betrayed by "line-cutters" – African-Americans, immigrants, refugees and women – who cut in ahead of them in the waiting-line for the American Dream. They resent liberal intellectuals who tell them they should feel sorry for the line-cutters, and dismiss them as bigots or deplorables when they don't. Donald Trump provides emotional support when he openly expresses racist and xenophobic feelings.

A prominent Swedish social democrat asks:

> In a country with staggering and increasing economic inequality, why would people who will undoubtedly lose economically from [Trump's] policies support him? Why did his anti-government policies such as cutting taxes for the super-rich and slashing the

newly established health care insurance system succeed to such a large extent? Moreover, why were these policies especially effective in securing votes from the white working class? ... Instead of focusing on universal programs for all or very broad segments of the population, the Democrats and Clinton came to represent policies seen by the white male working class as favoritism towards minority groups.[20]

We are witnessing a shift in political cleavages comparable to that of the 1930s, which saw the rise of Fascism on one hand, and the emergence of the New Deal and its European counterparts on the other hand. The reaction against rapid cultural change and immigration has brought a surge of support for xenophobic populist parties. But rising inequality has also produced an insurgency on the Left by people who see the need for redistributive policies. So far this movement has been supported mainly by younger and more educated voters. Cultural politics continues to dominate electoral behavior – but demands for political realignment are emerging.

Increasingly, high-income societies have winner-takes-all economies that lead to societies dominated by a small minority, while the overwhelming majority have precarious jobs. If left to market forces, this tendency will prevail. But government can be a countervailing force that reallocates resources for the benefit of society as a whole. In recent decades, government has mainly had the opposite effect, but a huge majority of the population now has an incentive to elect governments committed to reallocation. If a large share of the 99 percent becomes aware of this fact, it can form a new winning coalition. There are signs that this is happening.

In surveys carried out from 1989 to 2014, respondents around the world were asked whether their views came closer to the statement "Incomes should be made more equal" or that "Income differences should be larger to provide incentives for individual effort." In the earliest surveys, majorities in four-fifths of the 65 countries surveyed at least twice (over a median span of almost 18 years) believed that greater incentives for individual effort were needed. But the situation reversed itself during the next 25 years, as Figure 10.4 demonstrates, and in the most recent available survey, the publics in four-fifths of the 65 countries had become more favorable to making income more equal. The American public was among those that shifted in favor of greater income equality.

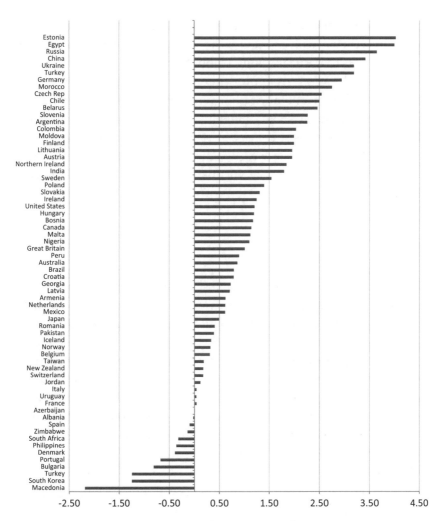

Figure 10.4 Changing attitudes toward income inequality.
Source: World Values Survey and European Values Study surveys carried out from 1989 to 2014, including all countries with at least a ten-year time series. The median change is a shift of .86 scale-points toward greater support for income equality; the median time-span is 17.6 years.

So far, emotionally charged cultural issues have hindered the emergence of a new coalition. But both the rise of populist movements and the growing concern for inequality reflect widespread dissatisfaction with existing political alignments. A large share of the public is angry – and it should be. Government is not working on their behalf.

Artificial intelligence is making greater resources available, but government intervention will be required to reallocate a significant part of these resources to create meaningful jobs that require a human touch, in health care, education (from pre-school to post-graduate levels), infrastructure, environmental protection, research and development, care of the elderly, and the arts and humanities – with the goal of improving the quality of life for society as a whole, rather than maximizing corporate profits. Developing well-designed programs to attain this goal will be a crucial task for social scientists and policy-makers during the next 20 years.

Conclusion

Whether survival seems secure or insecure shapes a society's worldview. One of the great achievements of the nineteenth and twentieth centuries was the emergence of political movements that represented the interests of the industrial working class. In the course of a long struggle, they helped elect governments that brought higher salaries, greater job security, retirement security, education and health care to most people. This eventually brought high levels of existential security that led to another great achievement – the cultural and political changes of the Silent Revolution era. High-income societies became more open, trusting and tolerant, emancipating women, ethnic minorities and gays, giving people more freedom of choice in how to live their lives – encouraging the spread of democracy and producing higher levels of happiness.

But history rarely moves in a straight line. The working-class base of the classic Left melted away, and the coming of Artificial Intelligence Society brought a winner-takes-all economy that is concentrating wealth and political power in the hands of a small minority – undermining existential security for most of the population. High-income societies are currently regressing toward the xenophobic authoritarian politics linked with insecurity. But – unlike the xenophobic authoritarianism that surged during the Great Depression – this does not result from objective scarcity. These societies possess abundant and growing resources, but they are increasingly misallocated from the standpoint of maximizing human well-being. Insecurity today results not from inadequate resources but from growing inequality – which is ultimately a political question. With appropriate political realignment, governments could emerge that play the role the classic Left once performed.

Developed societies could become dystopias controlled by a small minority. Or their growing resources could be used to produce confident and tolerant societies with high levels of existential security. There is no objective reason why support for xenophobic authoritarianism should continue to increase. The world is not in the depths of another Great Depression. Resources are plentiful and increasing. Between early 2000 and late 2016, the estimated net worth of American households and nonprofit institutions more than doubled, from $44 trillion to $90 trillion – an average of over a million dollars for every family of four.[21] This upsurge of wealth took place despite the crash of 2008. Widespread insecurity in high-income societies does not stem from inadequate resources – it reflects the fact that economic gains are going almost entirely to those at the top, and secure, well-paid jobs are disappearing. Whether they continue to do so is a political question. It depends on whether a new coalition emerges that restores political power to the majority.

It took decades for the industrial working class to become literate, cognitively mobilized and organized as an effective political force. But today's knowledge societies already have highly educated publics who are accustomed to thinking for themselves. A large share of the 99 percent are articulate and have political skills. All that is needed is an awareness that the key economic conflict today is between them and the one percent.

Constructing a new political coalition will not be easy. The abstraction of "inequality" doesn't mean much to most voters. Inequality is hard to visualize and hard to measure. It's unlikely that one citizen in a thousand could calculate or explain a Gini index of inequality. It's much easier to blame foreigners for the fact that life has become insecure. Foreigners are easy to visualize – we see them every day (especially on television) in ways that reinforce a deep-rooted tendency to view them as dangerous. Doing so obscures the fact that the key conflict in contemporary high-income societies is between the majority and the one percent.

Foreigners are not the main threat. If developed societies excluded all foreigners and all imports, secure jobs would continue to disappear, since the leading cause – overwhelmingly – is automation.

Once artificial intelligence starts learning independently, it moves at a pace that vastly outstrips human intelligence. Humanity needs to devise the means to stay in control of artificial intelligence. I suspect that unless we do so within the next 20 years or so, we will no longer have the option. Developing successful strategies to cope with artificial intelligence is a crucial task that will require imagination, persistence and experimentation.

And building a political coalition that represents the 99 percent will not occur automatically. But in democracies it reflects the interests of the overwhelming majority, and it is likely to emerge.

During the first half of the twentieth century a major component of cultural evolution consisted of learning the benefits of government intervention, as industrialized societies adopted universal compulsory education, child labor laws, public health programs, pure food and drug laws, old age pensions and social security systems. During the Great Depression capitalism collapsed, giving way to fascism or communism in many countries and probably would not have survived in the remaining ones without the evolution of New Deals and postwar welfare states. During the second half of the twentieth century, the world learned that state-run economies don't function well. Communist regimes from East Berlin to Beijing collapsed or moved toward market economies because successful politics is a balancing act between too much and too little government intervention. In the twenty-first century, we are in the process of learning that artificial intelligence society has strong, inherent winner-takes-all tendencies that can only be offset by government intervention. Developing the right balance between market and state will also require experimentation and insightful innovation, but when survival is at stake, humans usually rise to the occasion.

APPENDICES

APPENDIX 1
THE EASTERLIN PARADOX

The original Easterlin paradox held that the people of rich countries do not have higher levels of life satisfaction than the people of poor countries. Analyzing a sample of data from 14 countries surveyed in the 1950s, Easterlin (1974)[1] found almost no correlation between per capita gross national product and life satisfaction: though West Germany was twice as wealthy as Ireland, the Irish showed higher levels of life satisfaction. He concluded that the absence of a correlation between GNP/capita and subjective well-being meant that economic development did not improve the human lot – a finding that was widely cited as the "Easterlin Paradox."

But Easterlin's finding was based on a relatively small sample consisting mainly of rich countries. Inglehart (1990)[2] analyzed data from a broader sample of countries and found a .67 correlation between GNP and life satisfaction. Subsequent studies based on broad ranges of countries confirmed this finding: contrary to the original Easterlin Paradox, rich countries do have higher levels of subjective well-being than poor ones.

After these findings were published, Easterlin reformulated the paradox to hold that economic development does not bring *increases* over time in subjective well-being (which implies that the strong cross-sectional correlation must be due to sheer coincidence). Since the longest time series of happiness measures (by far) came from the USA and it showed no increase from 1946 to the latest measurement, this claim seemed plausible.

But Inglehart, Foa, Peterson and Welzel (2008) analyzed data from scores of countries covering the full range of development, gathered from 1981 to 2008 – finding that both happiness and life satisfaction increased in the overwhelming majority of countries. As Figure 8.2 demonstrates, life satisfaction rises sharply as we move from very poor countries to moderately prosperous ones and then levels off.

Easterlin (2009) claimed that the pervasive increase in happiness and life satisfaction from 1981 to 2008 was due to a change in the interviewer instructions used with the happiness question:

> Between wave 2 and wave 3 of the WVS (from 1990 to 1995) the instruction to interviewers to alternate the order of response choice from one respondent to the next was dropped. Consequently a primacy effect kicked in: a tendency for respondents to favor early over later choices – making more people choose "very happy" and fewer "not at all happy." This biased happiness choices upward so happiness rose though life satisfaction declined in ex-communist countries.[3]

If the rise in happiness were due to this change in interviewer instructions, the data would show a huge one-time increase in happiness in the 1995 survey, and no increases in the earlier and later waves of surveys. But the data show no such pattern: as Figure 8.6 demonstrates, happiness rose steadily from 1981 to 2005 with no perceptible surge in 1995.

Moreover, the change in interviewer instructions for the happiness question could not possibly explain the rise in life satisfaction. Easterlin does not acknowledge this fact. Instead he comments that life satisfaction declined in ex-communist countries, as if this were the prevailing pattern (which it clearly is not).

Easterlin is attempting to explain away a massive increase in happiness by attributing it to primacy effects, which normally have little impact unless one is dealing with topics on which the respondent has no real opinion – in which case, one also tends to get large amounts of non-response. Questions about one's happiness and life satisfaction are topics on which nearly everyone has an opinion, and they produce extremely low levels of non-response: instead of the 30–40 percent non-response found in response to unclear or confusing questions, non-response to the happiness question is about one percent. The average citizen may have no clear opinion about the causes of global warming – but is well aware of whether he or she is happy or unhappy. The interviewer instruction was dropped because it was expected to have no effect. The empirical results in Figure 8.6 support this expectation: dropping it in 1995 had no perceptible impact.

The Easterlin Paradox is unsustainable. Economic development *does* seem to improve the human lot – though it does so on a curve of diminishing returns, and (as Chapter 8 demonstrates) is only one of several factors influencing happiness and life satisfaction.

APPENDIX 2

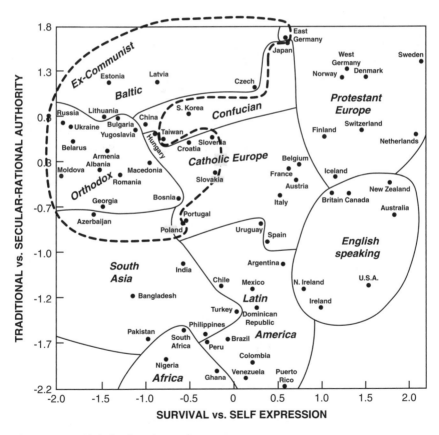

Figure A2.1 Global cultural map from 1995.

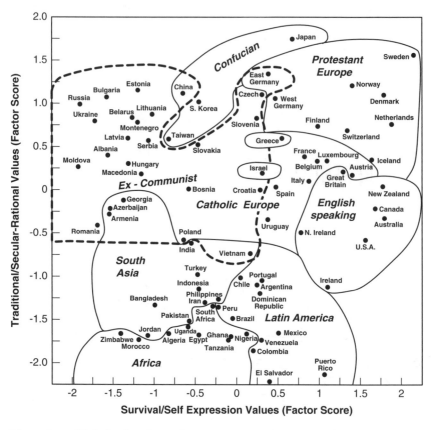

Figure A2.2 Global cultural map from 2000.

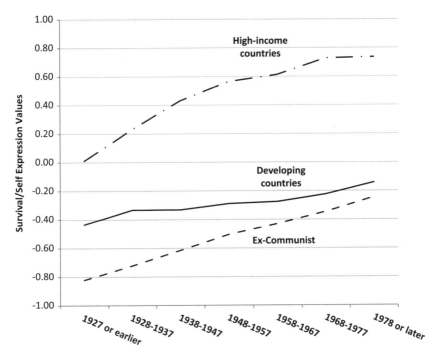

Figure A2.3 Age-related differences on Survival/Self-expression values, in three types of societies.
Data from the following countries were used:

High Income countries (as of 1992): Andorra, Australia, Austria, Belgium, Canada, Cyprus, Denmark, Finland, France, Germany, Great Britain, Iceland, Ireland, Israel, Italy, Japan, Luxembourg, Netherlands, New Zealand, Northern Ireland, Norway, Singapore, Spain, Sweden, Switzerland, Taiwan, United States.

Developing countries (as of 1992): Algeria, Argentina, Bangladesh, Brazil, Burkina Faso, Chile, China, Colombia, Dominican Republic, Ecuador, Egypt, Ethiopia, Ghana, Greece, Guatemala, India, Indonesia, Jordan, Malaysia, Mali, Malta, Mexico, Morocco, Nigeria, Pakistan, Peru, Philippines, Portugal, Rwanda, South Africa, South Korea, Tanzania, Thailand, Trinidad and Tobago, Turkey, Uganda, Uruguay, Venezuela, Vietnam, Zambia, Zimbabwe.

Ex-Communist countries: Albania, Azerbaijan, Armenia, Bosnia, Bulgaria, Croatia, Czech Republic, Estonia, Georgia, Hungary, Kazakhstan, Kosovo, Kyrgyzstan, Latvia, Lithuania, Macedonia, Moldova, Montenegro, Poland, Romania, Russia, Serbia, Slovakia, Slovenia, Ukraine.

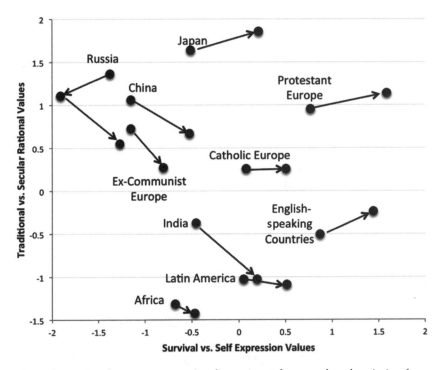

Figure A2.4 Net change on two major dimensions of cross-cultural variation from earliest to latest available survey (1981–2014) in ten types of societies.

The countries included in each of the ten types of societies are:

Ex-Communist countries: Albania (1998–2008), Azerbaijan (1997–2011), Armenia (1997–2011), Bosnia (1998–2008), Bulgaria (1991–2008), Belarus (1990–2008), Croatia (1996–2008), Czech Republic (1991–2008), Estonia (1996–2011), Georgia (1996–2009), Hungary (1991–2008), Kyrgyzstan (2003–2011), Latvia (1996–2008), Lithuania (1997–2008), Moldova (1996–2008), Poland (1990–2012), Romania (1998–2012), Serbia (1996–2008), Slovakia (1991–2008), Slovenia (1992–2011), Ukraine (1996–2011).

Latin American countries: Argentina (1984–2006), Brazil (1991–2006), Chile (1990–2011), Colombia (2005–2011), Mexico (1981–2012), Peru (1996–2012), Uruguay (1996–2011), Venezuela (1996–2000).

African countries: Ghana (2007–2012), Morocco (2007–2011), Nigeria (1990–2011), Rwanda (2007–2012), South Africa (1982–2006), Zimbabwe (2001–2012).

Catholic European countries: Austria (1990–2008), Belgium (1981–2009), France (1981–2008), Greece (1999–2008), Italy (1981–2005), Luxembourg (1999–2008), Portugal (1990–2008), Spain (1981–2011).

Protestant European countries: Denmark (1981–2008), Finland (1990–2009), Germany (1981–2008), Iceland (1990–2009), Netherlands (1981–2012), Norway (1982–2008), Sweden (1982–2011), Switzerland (1996–2008).

English-speaking countries: Australia (1981–2012), Canada (1982–2006), Great Britain (1981–2009), Ireland (1981–2008), New Zealand (1998–2011), Northern Ireland (1981–2008), United States (1982–2011).

Russia (1990, 1995–2011), China (2007–2012), Japan (1981–2010), India (1990–2012).

APPENDIX 3

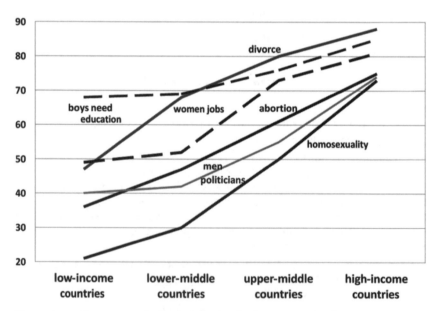

Figure A3.1 Six aspects of tolerance, by level of economic development. Percentage expressing tolerant views on given topic.

The countries included in each category are:

Low-income countries (as classified by World Bank in 2000): Azerbaijan, Bangladesh, Burkina Faso, Armenia, Ethiopia, Georgia, Ghana, India, Indonesia,

Kyrgyzstan, Mali, Moldova, Nigeria, Pakistan, Rwanda, Tanzania, Uganda, Ukraine, Uzbekistan, Viet Nam, Zambia, Zimbabwe; **Lower-middle income:** Albania, Algeria, Bosnia, Bulgaria, Belarus, China, Colombia, Dominican Rep., Ecuador, Egypt, El Salvador, Guatemala, Iran, Iraq Kazakhstan, Jordan, Latvia, Lithuania, Macedonia, Montenegro, Morocco, Peru, Philippines, Romania, Russia, Serbia, Thailand, Tunisia, Turkey; **Upper-middle income:** Argentina, Brazil, Chile, Croatia, Czech Rep., Estonia, Hungary, South Korea, Malaysia, Malta, Mexico, Poland, Puerto Rico, Saudi Arabia, Slovakia, South Africa, Taiwan, Trinidad, Uruguay, Venezuela; **High-income:** Australia, Austria, Belgium, Canada, Cyprus, Denmark, Finland, France, Germany, Greece, Hong Kong, Iceland, Ireland, Israel, Italy, Japan, Luxembourg, Netherlands, New Zealand, Norway, Portugal, Singapore, Slovenia, Spain, Sweden, Switzerland, United Kingdom, United States.

APPENDIX 4

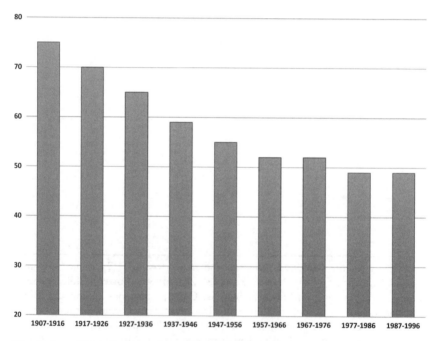

Figure A4.1 Xenophobia and intergenerational change.
"When jobs are scarce, employers should give priority to people of this country over immigrants" (percent agreeing by year of birth in 26 high-income countries)

Source: Based on all available Values Survey data from all available countries that the World Bank classified as "high-income" countries in 1990 (we use the 1990 classification because of the intergenerational time-lags involved here). The countries are Andorra, Australia, Austria, Belgium, Canada, Cyprus (Greek), Denmark, Finland, France, Germany, Great Britain, Hong Kong, Iceland, Ireland, Israel, Italy, Japan, Luxembourg, Netherlands, New Zealand, Qatar, Singapore, Spain, Sweden, Taiwan and United States. Total number of respondents is 122,008.

APPENDIX 5

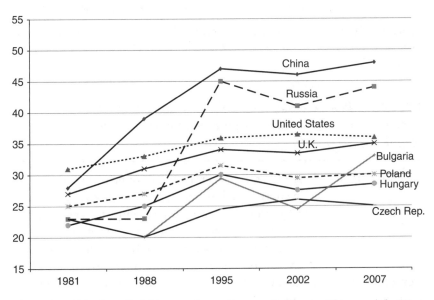

Figure A5.1 Net household income inequality trends: Russia, China and the West, 1981–2007. Vertical axis shows Gini indices.

Source: data from Whyte, 2014.

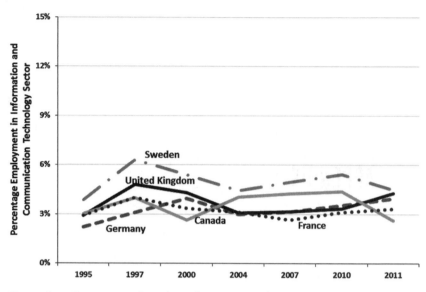

Figure A5.2 Percentage of total employment in information and communication technology sector in five advanced economies, 1995–2011.
Source: OECD (2014).

Table A5.1 *How Zakharov (2016) coded given issues as economic or non-economic from the categories used in the Comparative Party Manifestos dataset*

Economic right:	Free enterprise, incentives, economic orthodoxy, welfare state limitation, labor groups (negative)
Economic left:	Market regulation, economic planning, Keynesian demand management, controlled economy, nationalization, Marxist analysis, welfare state expansion, social justice, labor groups (positive)
Non-economic right:	National way of life (positive), traditional morality (positive), law and order, multiculturalism (negative), political authority, military (positive), internationalism (negative)
Non-economic left	National way of life (negative), traditional morality (negative), multiculturalism (positive), underprivileged minority groups, freedom and human rights, democracy, internationalism (positive), peace, anti-imperialism, military (negative), environmental protection.

NOTES

Introduction: An Overview of This Book

1 Stiglitz, Joseph E., 2011. "Of the 1 Percent, by the 1 percent, for the 1 Percent," *Vanity Fair*, May.
2 They also launched a new wave of surveys in 2017.
3 Inglehart, Ronald and Christian Welzel, 2010. "Changing Mass Priorities: The Link between Modernization and Democracy," *Perspectives on Politics* 8, 2: 551–567.

Chapter 1 Evolutionary Modernization and Cultural Change

1 Adorno, Theodor W., Else Frenkel-Brunswik, Daniel J. Levinson and R. Nevitt Sanford, 1950. *The Authoritarian Personality*. New York: Harper & Row.
2 Christie, R. E. and M. E. Jahoda, 1954. *Studies in the Scope and Method of "The authoritarian personality*," Glencoe: The Free Press.
3 Stenner, Karen, 2005. *The Authoritarian Dynamic*. Cambridge: Cambridge University Press.
4 Survival–Self-expression values are described in detail in Table 3.1 and the related discussion.
5 Inglehart, Ronald and Wayne E. Baker, 2000. "Modernization and Cultural Change and the Persistence of Traditional Values," *American Sociological Review* 65, 1: 19–51; Inglehart, Ronald and Pippa Norris, 2004. *Rising Tide: Gender Equality in Global Perspective*.

Cambridge: Cambridge University Press; Inglehart, Ronald and Christian Welzel, 2005. *Modernization, Cultural Change and Democracy: The Human Development Sequence.* New York: Cambridge University Press; Welzel, Christian, 2013. *Freedom Rising: Human Empowerment and the Quest for Emancipation.* New York: Cambridge University Press.

6 Inglehart, Ronald, 1971. "The Silent Revolution in Europe: Intergenerational Change in Post-Industrial Societies," *American Political Science Review* 65, 4: 991–1017; Inglehart, Ronald, 1977. *The Silent Revolution: Changing Values and Political Styles among Western Publics.* Princeton: Princeton University Press; Inglehart, Ronald, 1990. *Cultural Shift in Advanced Industrial Society.* Princeton: Princeton University Press; Inglehart, Ronald, 1997. *Modernization and Postmodernization: Cultural, Economic and Political Change in 43 Societies.* Princeton: Princeton University Press; Abramson, Paul and Ronald F. Inglehart, 1995. *Value Change in Global Perspective.* Ann Arbor: University of Michigan Press; Inglehart, Ronald and Wayne E. Baker, 2000. "Modernization and Cultural Change and the Persistence of Traditional Values," *American Sociological Review* 65, 1: 19–51; Inglehart, Ronald and Pippa Norris, 2004. *Rising Tide: Gender Equality in Global Perspective.* Cambridge: Cambridge University Press; Norris, Pippa and Ronald F. Inglehart, 2004. *Sacred and Secular: Religion and Politics Worldwide.* New York: Cambridge University Press; Inglehart, Ronald and Christian Welzel, 2005. *Modernization, Cultural Change and Democracy: The Human Development Sequence.* New York: Cambridge University Press; Welzel, Christian, 2013. *Freedom Rising: Human Empowerment and the Quest for Emancipation.* New York: Cambridge University Press.

7 Gelfand, Michele J. et al., 2011. "Differences between Tight and Loose Cultures: A 33-Nation Study," *Science* 332, 6033: 1100–1104.

8 Thornhill, Randy, Corey L. Fincher and Devaraj Aran, 2009. "Parasites, Democratization, and the Liberalization of Values across Contemporary Countries," *Biological Reviews* 84, 1: 113–131; Thornhill, Randy, Corey L. Fincher, Damian R. Murray and Mark Schaller, 2010. "Zoonotic and Non-zoonotic Diseases in Relation to Human Personality and Societal Values," *Evolutionary Psychology* 8:151–155; Fincher, Corey L. and Randy Thornhill, 2008. "Assortative Sociality, Limited Dispersal, Infectious Disease and the Genesis of the Global Pattern of Religion Diversity," *Proceedings of the Royal Society* 275, 1651: 2587–2594; Fincher, Corey L., Randy Thornhill, Damian R. Murray and Mark Schaller, 2008. "Pathogen Prevalence Predicts Human Cross-cultural Variability in Individualism/ Collectivism," *Proceedings of the Royal Society B* 275, 1640: 1279–1285.

9 Barber, Nigel, 2011. "A Cross-national Test of the Uncertainty Hypothesis of Religious Belief," *Cross-Cultural Research* 45, 3: 318–333.

10 Morris, Ian, 2015. *Foragers, Farmers and Fossil Fuels: How Human Values Evolve*. Princeton: Princeton University Press.

11 Adorno, Theodor W., Else Frenkel-Brunswik, Daniel J. Levinson and R. Nevitt Sanford, 1950. *The Authoritarian Personality*. New York: Harper & Row; Rokeach, Milton, 1960. *The Open and Closed Mind*. New York: Basic Books.

12 Inglehart and Welzel, 2005.

13 Inglehart, 1971.

14 Inglehart, 1977.

15 Rokeach, Milton, 1968. *Beliefs, Attitudes and Values*. San Francisco: Jossey-Bass, Inc.; Inglehart, 1977; Inglehart, 1997.

16 This hypothesis was triggered by indications of intergenerational value change that emerged during the student protest era of the late 1960s and early 1970s.

17 Böltken, Ferdinand and Wolfgang Jagodzinski, 1985. "In an Environment of Insecurity: Postmaterialism in the European Community, 1970–1980," *Comparative Political Studies* 17 (January): 453–484.

18 For detailed information on the World Values Survey and the European Values Study see their respective websites, www.worldvaluessurvey and www.europeanvaluesstudy.eu.

19 We refer to the World Bank's categorization of "low income" countries in 1990: we use income levels at this early date because there is strong evidence that one's basic values are shaped to a greater extent by the conditions experienced during one's formative years, than by current economic conditions.

20 See Inglehart and Welzel, 2005: 219–221.

21 Tversky, Amos and Daniel Kahneman, 1974. "Judgment under Uncertainty: Heuristics and Biases," *Science* 185, 4157: 1124–1131; Morewedge, Carey K. and Daniel Kahneman, 2010. "Associative Processes in Intuitive Judgment," *Trends in Cognitive Sciences* 14: 435–440; Kahneman, Daniel, 2011. *Thinking, Fast and Slow*. New York: Farrar, Strauss and Giroux.

22 Sanfey, Alan G., James K. Rilling, Jessica A. Aronson, Leigh E. Nystrom and Jonathan D. Cohen, 2003. "The Neural Basis of Economic Decision-making in the Ultimatum Game," *Science* 300, 5626: 1755–1758; De Martino, Benedetto, Dharshan Kumaran, Ben Seymour and Raymond J. Dolan, 2006. "Frames, Biases, and Rational Decision-making in the Human Brain," *Science* 313, 5787: 684–687; Soon, Chun Siong, Marcel Brass, Hans-Jochen Heinze and John-Dylan Haynes, 2008. "Unconscious Determinants of Free Decisions in the Human Brain," *Nature Neuroscience* 11, 5: 543–545.

23 Greene, Joshua and Jonathan Haidt, 2002. "How (and Where) Does Moral Judgment Work?" *Trends in Cognitive Sciences* 6, 12: 517–523; Haidt, Jonathan and Fredrik Bjorklund, 2008. "Social Intuitionists Answer Six Questions about Morality," *Moral Psychology* 2: 181–217.

24 Ridley, Matt, 1996. *The Origins of Virtue: Human Instincts and the Evolution of Cooperation.* London: Penguin Press Science.

25 Bednar, Jenna, Aaron Bramson, Andrea Jones-Rooy and Scott Page, 2010. "Emergent Cultural Signatures and Persistent Diversity," *Rationality and Society* 22, 4: 407–444.

26 Inglehart, 1971; Inglehart, 1990.

27 Inglehart, 1971; Inglehart, 1990; Inglehart, 1997.

28 Human Development Report, 2013. *The Rise of the South: Human Progress in a Diverse World.* New York: United Nations Development Programme.

29 Estes, Richard, 2010. "The World Social Situation: Development Challenges at the Outset of a New Century," *Social Indicators Research* 98, 363–402; Ridley, Matt, 2011. *The Rational Optimist: How Prosperity Evolves.* New York: Harper Perennial; Hughes, Barry B. and Evan E. Hillebrand, 2012. *Exploring and Shaping International Futures.* Boulder, CO: Paradigm Publishing.

30 Goldstein, Joshua S., 2011. *Winning the War on War: The Decline of Armed Conflict Worldwide.* New York: Plume; Pinker, Steven, 2011. *The Better Angels of Our Nature: Why Violence Has Declined.* New York: Viking Press.

31 Inglehart, Ronald, 2008. "Changing Values among Western Publics, 1970–2006: Postmaterialist Values and the Shift from Survival Values to Self Expression Values," *West European Politics* 31, 1–2: 130–146.

32 Norris, Pippa and Ronald F. Inglehart, 2009. *Cosmopolitan Communications: Cultural Diversity in a Globalized World.* New York: Cambridge University Press.

Chapter 2 The Rise of Postmaterialist Values in the West and the World

1 For fuller detail on how Materialist/Postmaterialist values are measured, and validation of the measures, see Inglehart, 1977, Chapter 1, and Inglehart, 1990, Chapter 1.

2 The samples are weighted to reflect each country's population. Since the 2006 World Values Survey did not include Belgium, we used data from the 1999 Belgian survey in the pooled analysis. This tends to reduce the amount of change observed from 1999 to 2006, but the distortion is minimal since Belgium contains only 4 percent of the six countries' population.

3 Inglehart and Welzel, 2005.

Chapter 3 Global Cultural Patterns

1 Inglehart, 1990; Inglehart and Baker, 2000; Inglehart and Welzel, 2005; Norris, Pippa and Ronald F. Inglehart, 2004, 2011. *Sacred and Secular: Religion and Politics Worldwide* (2nd edn.). New York: Cambridge University Press.
2 Inglehart and Baker, 2000.
3 GDP/capita taps only one aspect of existential security, which is also shaped by the society's social welfare institutions and its safety from crime, violence and disease. But since high-income societies tend to rank high on all of these aspects of existential security, a society's GDP/capita provides a fairly good indicator of the extent to which its people enjoy high levels of existential security.
4 Weber, Max, 1904 [1930]. *The Protestant Ethic and the Spirit of Capitalism*. London: Routledge; Bell, Daniel, 1973. *The Coming of Post-Industrial Society*. New York: Basic Books; Toffler, Alvin, 1990. *Powershift: Knowledge, Wealth, Violence in the 21st Century*. New York: Bantam.
5 Huntington, Samuel P., 1996. *The Clash of Civilizations: Remaking of the World Order*. New York: Simon & Schuster; Putnam, Robert D., 1993. *Making Democracy Work: Civic Traditions in Modern Italy*. Princeton, NJ: Princeton University Press; Fukuyama, Francis, 1995. *Trust: Social Virtues and the Creation of Prosperity*. New York: Free Press; Inglehart and Baker, 2000; Inglehart and Welzel, 2005.
6 George Orwell's classic novel *1984*, published in 1949, depicts a dystopian future where the news and the history books are regularly revised to conform to a totalitarian regime's official truth. It suddenly became a bestseller again in 2017, when a set of demonstrably untrue "alternative facts" about the number of people attending the Presidential inauguration was propounded by the newly installed Trump administration.
7 For greater detail on how these two dimensions were constructed, see Inglehart, 1997: Chapter 1.
8 Inglehart, 1997; Inglehart and Baker, 2000; Inglehart and Welzel, 2005; Inglehart, Ronald and Christian Welzel, 2010. "Changing Mass Priorities: The Link between Modernization and Democracy," *Perspectives on Politics* 8, 2: 551–567.
9 Compare the maps based on data from other waves of surveys in the appendix. The similarity of the maps, based on data from different surveys carried out at different times from 1981 to 2014, is striking.
10 His measures are explained and tested for validity in Welzel, 2013: 57–105.
11 The average standard deviation on the Traditional vs. Secular-rational dimension is smaller than the average standard deviation on the Survival vs. Self-expression dimension, which is why we show an ellipse rather than a circle.

12 Inglehart and Welzel, 2010.

13 Inglehart and Welzel, 2010.

14 Oyserman, Daphna, Heather M. Coon and Markus Kemmelmeier, 2002. "Rethinking Individualism and Collectivism: Evaluation of Theoretical Assumptions and meta-analyses," *Psychological Bulletin* 128: 3–72.

15 Hofstede, Geert, 2001. *Culture's Consequences: Comparing Values, Behaviors, Institutions and Organizations across Nations* (2nd edn.). Thousand Oaks, CA: Sage Publications.

16 Schwartz, Shalom, 2006. "A Theory of Cultural Value Orientations: Explication and Applications," *Comparative Sociology* 5, 2–3: 137–182.

17 Many others have analyzed Individualism/Collectivism, sometimes using representative national samples, but only in single countries or small numbers of countries.

18 Inglehart and Welzel, 2005.

19 Inglehart and Welzel, 2005.

20 Welzel (2013) has developed a revised and technically improved version of the Survival/Self-expression dimension, called Emancipative Values. When substituted for Survival/Self-expression values in this analysis, it also emerges as the top-loading item.

21 Gelfand et al., 2011; Thornhill and Fincher, 2009; Thornhill and Fincher, 2010.

22 Chiao, Joan Y. and Katherine D. Blizinsky, 2009. "Culture–Gene Coevolution of Individualism–Collectivism and the Serotonin Transporter Gene," *Proceedings of the Royal Society B* 277, 1681: 529–553.

23 They find a .66 correlation between Individualism and Self-expression values.

24 Acemoglu, Daron and James A. Robinson, 2006b. *Economic Origins of Dictatorship and Democracy*. New York: Cambridge University Press.

25 Shcherbak, Andrey, 2014. "Does Milk Matter? Genetic Adaptation to Environment: The Effect of Lactase Persistence on Cultural Change." Paper presented at summer workshop of Laboratory for Comparative Social Research, Higher School of Economics, St. Petersburg, Russia, June 29–July 12, 2014.

26 Meyer-Schwarzenberger, Matthias, 2014. "Individualism, Subjectivism, and Social Capital: Evidence from Language Structures." Paper presented at summer workshop of Laboratory for Comparative Social Research, Higher School of Economics, St. Petersburg, Russia, June 29–July 12, 2014.

27 Inglehart, Ronald F., Svetlana Borinskaya, Anna Cotter et al., 2014. "Genetic Factors, Cultural Predispositions, Happiness and Gender Equality," *Journal of Research in Gender Studies* 4, 1: 40–69.

28 Cavalli-Sforza, Luigi Luca, Paolo Menozzi and Alberto Piazza, 1994. *The History and Geography of Human Genes*. Princeton: Princeton University

Press; Inglehart et al., 2014. They used the forensic STR system because these data are available for many populations, including some not studied for other genes.

29 Benjamin, Daniel J., David Cesarini, Matthijs J. H. M. van der Loos et al., 2012. "The Genetic Architecture of Economic and Political Preferences," *Proceedings of the National Academy of Sciences* 109, 21: 8026–8031.

30 To avoid an unreadably complex map, this figure shows the net changes experienced by entire groups of countries using the clusters identified above, plus the changes experienced by Russia, China, India and Japan.

Chapter 4 The End of Secularization?

1   Bruce, Steve, 1992. "Pluralism and Religious Vitality," in Steve Bruce (ed.), *Religion and Modernization: Sociologists and Historians Debate the Secularization Thesis.* Oxford: Oxford University Press: 170–194; Aldridge, A., 2000. *Religion in the Contemporary World.* Cambridge: Polity Press, Chapter 3.

2   The term "fundamentalist" is used here to refer to those with an absolute conviction in the fundamental principles of their faith, to the extent that they will not accept the validity of any other beliefs.

3   Finke, Roger, 1992. "An Unsecular America," in Steve Bruce (ed.), *Religion and Modernization: Sociologists and Historians Debate the Secularization Thesis.* Oxford: Oxford University Press: 145–169.

4   Stark, Rodney and William Sims Bainbridge, 1985a. "A Supply-side Reinterpretation of the 'Secularization' of Europe," *Journal for the Scientific Study of Religion* 33, 3: 230–252; Finke, Roger and Laurence R. Iannaccone, 1993. "The Illusion of Shifting Demand: Supply-side Explanations for Trends and Change in the American Religious Market Place," *Annals of the American Association of Political and Social Science* 527: 27–39.

5   Finke, Roger and Rodney Stark, 2000. *Acts of Faith: Explaining the Human Side of Religion.* Berkeley, CA: The University of California Press: 230.

6   Finke and Stark, 2000: 237–238.

7   This theme is discussed in detail in: Mueller, John, 1989. *Retreat from Doomsday: The Obsolescence of Major War.* New York: Basic Books.

8   Norris and Inglehart, 2004: 92. Based on data from US General Social Survey, 1972–2002.

9   Norris and Inglehart, 2004: 5–6.

10 Thomas, Scott M., 2005. *The Global Resurgence of Religion and the Transformation of International Relations: The Struggle for the Soul of the Twenty-first Century.* New York: Palgrave Macmillan.

11 For reasons explained in Chapter 5, a country's level of economic security about a generation ago is a more accurate predictor of its basic cultural values today than its economic level today. The World Bank's 2014 report indicates that Russia is now classified as a high-income country – although its adult population experienced massive deprivation and declining life expectancy during their formative years.

Chapter 5 Cultural Change, Slow and Fast: The Distinctive Trajectory of Norms Governing Gender Equality and Sexual Orientation

1 Inglehart, 1990.
2 Nolan and Lenski, 2015
3 Norris and Inglehart, 2004.
4 Inglehart, 1990.
5 Lesthaeghe, Ron and Johan Surkyn, 1988. "Cultural Dynamics and Economic Theories of Fertility Change," *Population and Development Review*, 141: 1–46.
6 Van de Kaa, Dirk J., 2001. "Postmodern Family Preferences: From Changing Value Orientation to New Behavior," *Population and Development Review* 27: 290–331.
7 Broadberry, Stephen and Kevin H. O'Rourke (eds.), 2010. *The Cambridge Economic History of Modern Europe: 1700–1870*. Cambridge: Cambridge University Press.
8 Human Development Report, 2013. *The Rise of the South: Human Progress in a Diverse World*. New York: United Nations Development Programme.
9 Ridley, Matt, 2011. *The Rational Optimist: How Prosperity Evolves*. New York: Harper Perennial; Hughes, Barry B. and Evan E. Hillebrand, 2012. *Exploring and Shaping International Futures*. Boulder, CO: Paradigm Publishing.
10 Gat, Azar, 2006. *War in Human Civilization*. Oxford: Oxford University Press; Pinker, Steven, 2011. *The Better Angels of Our Nature: Why Violence Has Declined*. New York: Viking Press.
11 Prentice, Thomson, 2006. "Health, History and Hard Choices: Funding Dilemmas in a Fast-Changing World," *Nonprofit and Voluntary Sector Quarterly* 37, 1: 63S–75S.
12 Singh, Gopal K. and Peter C. van Dyck, 2010. *Infant Mortality in the United States, 1935–2007*. Rockville, Maryland: US Department of Health and Human Services.
13 This is the long-term trend, but it is subject to major fluctuations during which existential security falls.

14 Inglehart and Welzel, 2005; Andersen, Robert and Tina Fetner, 2008. "Cohort Differences in Tolerance of Homosexuality," *Public Opinion Quarterly* 72, 2: 311–330.

15 Based on the World Bank's classifications in 2000, the Low-income countries had a mean per capita income of $1,582 (PPP estimates) and a mean infant mortality rate of 54.5; these figures rise as we move through the middle-income countries and among the high-income countries the mean per capita income was $27,223 and mean infant mortality was 4.4.

16 Robinson, William, 1950. Ecological Correlations and the Behavior of Individuals. *American Sociological Review* 15, 3: 351–357.

17 These indices are factor scores generated by the analysis in Table 5.1. A similar though weaker factor structure also exists at the individual level. We use an index based on all six-items cross-sectional analyses, but we use a three-item index based on the items concerning homosexuality, divorce and abortion in time series analyses, since it provides a longer time series (the latter items were included in all surveys since 1981, but the items measuring gender equality are only available since 1995).

18 The data on GDP/capita are from the Penn World Tables; the data on life expectancy and infant mortality are from the World Health Organization.

19 Another major dimension of cross-cultural variation, Traditional vs. Secular-rational values, is uncorrelated with the Survival versus Self-expression dimension and is less central to this analysis.

20 In recent decades, West European countries have experienced large-scale immigration from low-income countries that are relatively intolerant of Individual-choice norms. Since these norms resist change, this has contributed to ethnic tensions and rising support for xenophobic parties in these countries.

21 The results shown here are based on regression analyses in which the Existential Security index for a given year was the sole independent variable. This index is based on each country's life expectancy, infant mortality and GDP/capita in a given year. Preliminary regression analyses using each of these three components separately show a similar pattern, with data from the 1960s or 1970s explaining much more of the variance in Individual-choice norms than later measures do (with the Existential Security index explaining even more variance than its components).

22 Traugott, Michael, 2001. "Trends: Assessing Poll Performance in the 2000 Campaign," *Public Opinion Quarterly* 65, 3: 389–419; Lewis-Beck, Michael S., 2005. "Election Forecasting: Principles and Practice," *British Journal of Politics and International Relations*, 7: 145–164.

23 Silver, Nate, 2015. *The Signal and the Noise*. New York: Penguin: 63.

24 Selig, James P., Kristopher J. Preacher and Todd D. Little, 2012. "Modeling Time-Dependent Association in Longitudinal Data: A Lag as Moderator Approach," *Multivariate Behavioral Research* 47, 5: 697–716.

25 Inglehart, 1971.

26 Inglehart, Ronald F., Ronald C. Inglehart and Eduard Ponarin, 2017. "Cultural Change, Slow and Fast: The Distinctive Trajectory of Norms Governing Gender Equality and Sexual Orientation," *Social Forces* (January) 1–28.

27 Inglehart, Inglehart and Ponarin, 2017: Table 5.

28 The mean score on Individual-level choice norms was calculated for each birth cohort, as measured in the earliest available survey (1981) and the latest available survey (2009). For each of the five cohorts providing data from both time periods, we then calculated the difference between its score in the earliest period and its score in the latest period. The overall within-cohort change score represents the average of these differences. The change due to population replacement is calculated by taking the difference between the overall mean scores in the earliest time period and the latest time period, and then subtracting the within-cohort effect.

29 Inglehart and Welzel, 2005.

Chapter 6 The Feminization of Society and Declining Willingness to Fight for One's Country: The Individual-Level Component of the Long Peace

1 Gat, 2006: Introduction, p. 7. This is particularly true in polygamous societies, where prosperous older men monopolize the supply of women.

2 Doyle, Michael W., 1986. "Liberalism and World Politics," *American Political Science Review* 80, 4: 1151–1169.

3 Mousseau, Michael, Håvard Hegre and John R. O'neal, 2003. "How the Wealth of Nations Conditions the Liberal Peace," *European Journal of International Relations* 9, 2: 277–314; Gartzke, Erik. 2007. "The Capitalist Peace," *American Journal of Political Science* 51, 1: 166–191; McDonald, Patrick J., 2009. *The Invisible Hand of Peace: Capitalism, the War Machine, and International Relations Theory.* New York: Cambridge University Press.

4 Rosecrance, Richard, 1986. *The Rise of the Trading State: Commerce and Conquest in the Modern World.* New York: Basic Books; Cf. Mueller, 1989.

5 Mueller, 1989.

6 Gat, 2006.

7 Pinker, 2011.

8 Angell, Norman (1933 [1909]). *The Great Illusion.* London: G.P. Putnam's Sons.

9 Oneal, John R. and Bruce M. Russet, 1997. "The Classical Liberals Were Right," *International Studies Quarterly* 41, 2: 267–293; Hegre, Håvard,

John R. Oneal and Bruce Russett, 2010. "Trade Does Promote Peace: New Simultaneous Estimates of the Reciprocal Effects of Trade and Conflict," *Journal of Peace Research* 47, 6: 763–774; Dorussen, Han and Hugh Ward, 2010. "Trade Networks and the Kantian Peace," *Journal of Peace Research* 47, 1: 29–42.

10 Gartzke, 2007; Mousseau, 2009; McDonald, 2009.

11 Dafoe, Allen, 2011. "Statistical Critiques of the Democratic Peace: Caveat Emptor," *American Journal of Political Science* 55, 2: 247–262; Dafoe, Allen and Bruce Russett, 2013. "Does Capitalism Account for the Democratic Peace? The Evidence Says No," in Gerald Schneider and Nils Petter Gleditsch (eds.), *Assessing the Capitalist Peace*. New York: Routledge:110–126.

12 Gat, Azar, 2005. "The Democratic Peace Theory Reframed: The Impact of Modernity," *World Politics* 58, 1: 73–100; Gat, 2006.

13 Pinker, 2011.

14 Goldstein, 2011.

15 Human Security Report Project, 2012. *Human Security Report 2012*. Vancouver: Human Security Press. Available at www.hsrgroup.org/human-security-reports/2012/text.aspx.

16 Chenoweth, Erica and Kathleen Gallagher Cunningham, 2013. "Understanding Nonviolent Resistance," *Journal of Peace Research* 5, 3: 271–276; Schock, Kurt, 2013. "The Practice and Study of Civil Resistance," *Journal of Peace Research* 50, 3: 277–290.

17 Ridley, 2011.

18 Human Development Report, 2013.

19 Estes, 2010.

20 Africa Progress Report, 2012. *Jobs, Justice, and Equity*. Geneva: Africa Progress Panel.

21 Welzel, 2013: 4.

22 Huntington, Samuel P., 1991. *The Third Wave: Democratization in the Late 20th Century*. Norman, OK: University of Oklahoma Press; Markoff, John and Amy White. 2009. "The Global Wave of Democratization," in Christian W. Haerpfer, Patrick Bernhagen, Ronald F. Inglehart and Christian Welzel (eds.), *Democratization*. Oxford: Oxford University Press: 55–73; Pegram, Thomas, 2010. "Diffusion across Political Systems: The Global Spread of National Human Rights Institutions," *Human Rights Quarterly* 32, 3: 729–760.

23 Møller, Jørgen and Svend-Erik Skaaning, 2013. "The Third Wave: Inside the Numbers," *Journal of Democracy* 24, 4: 97–109.

24 Pinker, 2011.

25 De Waal, Frans B. M., 1995. "Bonobo Sex and Society," *Scientific American* 272, 3: 82–88.

26 Puranen, 2008; Puranen, 2009.

27 Puranen, 2008, 2009.

28 Based on 2000 World Bank categories.

29 Iraq is not shown on this graph because data are lacking for the Individual-choice index, but it shows an exceptionally high unwillingness to fight. This reflects the ethnic conflict between Sunnis, Shiites and Kurds, who are unwilling to fight for *Iraq* – but very willing to fight each other.

30 The publics of Denmark and Iceland also show relatively high levels of willingness to fight for their country, but lack complete data on Individual-choice (6).

31 See Inglehart, Puranen and Welzel, 2015.

32 Including as an additional treatment variable the length of the time-span of each society's specific change measure does not alter the results shown here.

33 See Inglehart, Puranen and Welzel, 2015.

34 The diminishing effect of rising Individual-choice values holds controlling for ascending life opportunities and increasing democracy. But the reverse does not hold.

35 If one reverses the positions of choice values and willingness to fight in Inglehart, Puranen and Welzel's model, using falling willingness to fight predicts rising choice values, no significant effect is obtained. This suggests that the main direction of impact runs from Individual-choice values to willingness to fight rather than in the opposite direction.

Chapter 7 Development and Democracy

1 For an extensive analysis of the long-term trend in democratization, see Christian Welzel, Ronald Inglehart, Patrick Bernhagen and Christian Haerpfer. 2018. "The New Pessimism about Demoracracy," in Welzel, Bernhagen, Inglehart and Haerpfer (eds.), *Democratization* (2nd edn.). New York: Oxford University Press.

2 Lipset, Seymour Martin, 1959. "Some Social Requisites of Democracy: Economic Development and Political Legitimacy," *American Political Science Review* 53, 1: 69–105.

3 More recently, using current econometric techniques, Acemoglu and Robinson (2006b) also conclude that both economic development and democracy reflect deep-rooted institutional/cultural factors.

4 Deutsch, Karl W., 1961. "Social Mobilization and Political Development," *American Political Science Review* 55, 3: 493–514.

5 Moore, Barrington, 1966. *The Social Origins of Dictatorship and Democracy*. Boston: Beacon Press.

6 See Inglehart and Welzel (2005), Chapters 7 and 8.

7 Inglehart, Ronald, 2003. "How Solid is Mass Support for Democracy – and How Do We Measure It?" *PS: Political Science and Politics* 36, 1: 51–57.

This finding is confirmed in Inglehart and Welzel, 2005: Chapter 10; and gets further support in Welzel, Christian, 2007. "Are Levels of Democracy Affected by Mass Attitudes? Testing Attainment and Sustainment Effects on Democracy," *International Political Science Review* 28, 4: 397–424.

8 Kaufman, Kraay and Mastruzzi, 2003.

9 Welzel and Inglehart, 2004.

10 For extensive empirical evidence of this claim, see Inglehart and Welzel, 2005.

11 Inglehart and Welzel, 2005: Chapters 8 and 9.

12 See Eckstein, 1966, 1975 and Almond and Verba, 1963.

13 This reasoning applies to societal-led regime changes but not to externally imposed regime changes.

14 Since democracy and Self-expression values are measured on different scales: we transform them into comparable scales in order to calculate the difference between democracy and Self-expression values. We first normalized both variables, standardizing their scales to their empirical maximum, which was set at 1.0. We then subtracted Self-expression values from democracy, yielding an incongruence scale from −1 to +1, on which −1 represents a situation in which there is a maximum of liberal democracy and a complete absence of Self-expression values, while +1 indicates the reverse.

15 This analysis was devised by Welzel. An earlier version of Figure 7.2 appears in Inglehart and Welzel, 2005: 189.

16 Inglehart and Welzel, 2005.

17 Temporal autocorrelation is the tendency for a given variable's level at time 1 to be a strong predictor of that same variable's level at time 2. For example, a country's population in 2014 is a strong predictor of its population in 2015.

18 For insightful analysis of these changes, see: Lerner, Daniel, 1958. *The Passing of Traditional Society: Modernizing the Middle East.* New York: Free Press.

19 See Deutsch, 1961, and Deutsch, Karl W., 1966. *Nationalism and Social Communication.* Cambridge, MA: MIT Press.

20 See Almond, Gabriel A. and Sidney Verba, 1963. *The Civic Culture: Political Attitudes and Democracy in Five Nations.* Newbury Park, CA: Sage Publications; cf. Milbrath, Lester W. and Madan Lal Goel, 1977. *Political Participation: How and Why Do People Get Involved in Politics?* Boston: Rand McNally College Publishing Co.; Verba, Sidney, Norman H. Nie and Jae-on Kim, 1978. *Participation and Political Equality: A Seven-Nation Comparison.* Chicago: University of Chicago Press; Barnes, Samuel H. and Max Kaase (eds.), 1979. *Political Action: Mass Participation in Five Western Democracies.* Beverly Hills, CA: Sage Publications.

21 Inglehart,1977.

22 Inglehart,1977 makes this argument.

23 Barnes, Kaase et al., 1979 demonstrate this point, with evidence from five countries.

24 Aristotle argued 2,500 years ago that democracy is the typical regime of middle class societies. The argument was formulated anew by Dahl, 1971 and has been demonstrated in empirical analyses by Muller, Edward N., 1988. "Democracy, Economic Development, and Income Inequality," *American Sociological Review* 53: 50–68, and Vanhanen, Tatu, 2003. *Democratization: A Comparative Analysis of 170 Countries*. New York: Routledge.

25 Acemoglu and Robinson, 2006; Acemoglu, et al., 2008; Acemoglu, Daron and James A. Robinson, 2006a. "De Facto Political Power and Institutional Persistence," *American Economic Review* 96, 2: 326–330.

26 Putnam, 1993.

27 The end of the Cold War removed the most important blocking factor, but this was supplemented by such conditions as the attainment of high levels of development in Taiwan and South Korea.

28 For evidence, see Inglehart and Welzel, 2005: 118–126 and 224–227.

29 See Inglehart, Ronald, Mansoor Moaddel and Mark Tessler, 2006. "Xenophobia and In-Group Solidarity in Iraq: A Natural Experiment on the Impact of Insecurity," *Perspectives on Politics* 4, 3: 495–506.

Chapter 8 The Changing Roots of Happiness

1 See Brickman, Philip and Donald T. Campbell, 1981. "Hedonic Relativism and Planning the Good Society," in M. Appley (ed.), *Adaptation-level Theory*. New York: Academic Press, 287–305; Diener, Ed., Eunkook M. Suh, Richard E. Lucas, and Heidi L. Smith, 1999. "Subjective Well- being: Three Decades of Progress," *Psychological Bulletin* 125, 2: 276–302; Kahneman, Daniel, Alan B. Krueger, David A. Schkade, Norbert Schwarz and Arthur A. Stone, 2004. "A Survey Method for Characterizing Daily Life Experience: The Day Reconstruction Method," *Science* 306, 5702: 1776–1780.

2 Easterlin, Richard A., 1974. "Does Economic Growth Improve the Human Lot?" in P. A. David and M. Reder (eds.), *Nations, Households, and Economic Growth*. New York: Academic Press, 98–125; Kenny, Charles, 2005. "Does Development Make You Happy? Subjective Well-being and Economic Growth in Developing Countries," *Social Indicators Research* 73, 2: 199–219.

3 Ebstein, Richard P., Olga Novick, Roberto Umansky et al., 1996. "Dopamine D4 Receptor (D4DR) Exon III Polymorphism Associated with the Human Personality Trait of Novelty Seeking," *Nature Genetics* 12, 1: 78–80; Hamer, Dean H., 1996. "The Heritability of Happiness," *Nature Genetics* 14, 2: 125–126.

4 Lykken, David and Auke Tellegen, 1996. "Happiness Is a Stochastic Phenomenon," *Psychological Science* 7, 3: 186–189; Lyubomirsky, Sonja, Kennon M. Sheldon and David Schkade, 2005. "Pursuing Happiness: The Architecture of Sustainable Change," *Review of General Psychology* 9, 2: 111–131; Minkov, Michael and Michael Harris Bond, 2016. "A Genetic Component to National Differences in Happiness," *Journal of Happiness Studies*. 1–20.

5 Diener, Ed and Richard E. Lucas, 1999. "Personality and Subjective Well-being," in Daniel Kahneman, Edward Diener and Norbert Schwarz (eds.), *Well-being: The Foundations of Hedonic Psychology*. New York: Russell Sage Foundation, 213–229.

6 Headey, Bruce and Alexander Wearing, 1989. "Personality, Life Events, and Subjective Well-being: Toward a Dynamic Equilibrium Model," *Journal of Personality and Social Psychology* 57, 4: 731–739; Larsen, Randy J., 2000. "Toward a Science of Mood Regulation," *Psychological Inquiry* 11, 3: 129–141; Williams, Donald E. and J. Kevin Thompson, 1993. "Biology and Behavior: A Set-point Hypothesis of Psychological Functioning," *Behavior Modification* 17, 1: 43–57.

7 Inglehart, 1990; Diener, Edward, and Shigehiro Oishi, 2000. "Money and Happiness: Income and Subjective Well-being across Nations," in Edward Diener and Eunkook M. Suh (eds.), *Culture and Subjective Well-being*. Cambridge, MA: MIT Press: 185–218; Inglehart, Ronald and Hans-Dieter Klingemann, 2000. "Genes, Culture, Democracy, and Happiness," in Ed Diener and Eunkook M. Suh (eds.), *Culture and Subjective Well-being*. Cambridge, MA: MIT Press, 165–183; Easterlin, Richard A., 2005. "Feeding the Illusion of Growth and Happiness: A Reply to Hagerty and Veenhoven," *Social Indicators Research* 74, 3: 429–443; and Kahneman, Daniel and Alan B. Krueger, 2006. "Developments in the Measurement of Subjective Well-being," *Journal of Economic Perspectives* 20, 1: 3–24.

8 Easterlin, 1974; Easterlin, Richard A., 2003. "Explaining Happiness," *Proceedings of the National Academy of the Sciences* 100, 19: 11176–11183.

9 Diener, Ed., Richard E. Lucas and Christie N. Scollon, 2006. "Beyond the Hedonic Treadmill: Revising the Adaptation Theory of Well-being," *American Psychologist* 61, 4: 305–314; Fujita, Frank and Ed Diener, 2005. "Life Satisfaction Set Point: Stability and Change," *Journal of Personality and Social Psychology* 88, 1: 158–164. Similarly, a 15-year longitudinal study of the effects of marital transitions on life satisfaction showed that *on average*, individuals moved back toward their baseline levels of satisfaction, but that a significant numbers of individuals remained above their original baseline level, while other remained below it. Lucas, Richard E., Andrew E. Clark, Yannis Georgellis and Ed Diener, 2005. "Reexamining

Adaptation and the Set Point Model of Happiness: Reactions to Changes in Marital Status," *Journal of Personality and Social Psychology* 84, 3: 527–539.

10 Inglehart, 1990: Introduction.

11 Johnson, Wendy and Robert F. Krueger, 2006. "How Money Buys Happiness: Genetic and Environmental Processes Linking Finances and Life Satisfaction," *Journal of Personality and Social Psychology* 90, 4: 680–691.

12 Inglehart and Welzel, 2005: 140; Sen, Amartya, 2001. *Development as Freedom*. New York: Alfred Knopf.

13 Inglehart and Welzel, 2005.

14 Inglehart, 1990; Barro, Robert J., 1999. "Determinants of Democracy," *Journal of Political Economy* 107, S6: 158–183; Frey, Bruno S. and Alois Stutzer, 2000. "Happiness Prospers in Democracy," *Journal of Happiness Studies* 1, 1: 79–102; Inglehart and Klingemann, 2000.

15 Haller, Max and Markus Hadler, 2004. "Happiness as an Expression of Freedom and Self-determination: A Comparative Multilevel Analysis," in W. Glatzer, S. von Below and M. Stoffregen (eds.), *Challenges for Quality of Life in the Contemporary World*. Dordrecht, The Netherlands: Kluwer Academic Publishers, 207–229; Inglehart and Welzel, 2005; Ott, Jan, 2001. "Did the Market Depress Happiness in the US?" *Journal of Happiness Studies* 2, 4: 433–443; Veenhoven, Ruut, 2000. "Freedom and Happiness: A Comparative Study in Forty-four Nations in the Early 1990s," in Ed Diener and Eunkook M. Suh (eds.), *Culture and Subjective Well Being*. Cambridge, MA: MIT Press, 257–288; Welsch, Heinz, 2003. "Freedom and Rationality as Predictors of Cross-National Happiness Patterns: The Role of Income as a Mediating Value," *Journal of Happiness Studies* 4, 3: 295–321.

16 Inglehart and Welzel, 2005; Schyns, Peggy, 1998. "Crossnational Differences in Happiness: Economic and Cultural Factors Explored," *Social Indicators Research* 42, 1/2: 3–26.

17 Inglehart and Welzel, 2005.

18 Andrews, Frank M. and Stephen B. Withey, 1976. *Social Indicators of Well-being*. New York: Plenum.

19 Because life satisfaction is measured on a ten-point scale, and happiness on a four-point scale, and because the two questions have opposite polarity, the subjective well-being index was constructed using the following formula: subjective well-being = life satisfaction − 2.5 * happiness. If 100 percent of its people were very happy and extremely satisfied, a country would get the maximum score of 7.5. If happiness and unhappiness, and life satisfaction and dissatisfaction, were evenly balanced, the country would get a score of zero. If a majority of people were dissatisfied and unhappy, the country would get a negative score.

20 To test this, the respondents were asked to what extent they felt they had free choice and control over their lives, using a scale that ranged from 1 [*none at all*] to 10 [*a great deal*]. Respondents also indicated to what extent they felt that homosexuality can be justified, using a scale ranging from 1 [*never*] to 10 [*always*]. A number of items in these surveys tapped religiosity, but the most sensitive indicator asked: "How important is God in your life?" using a ten-point scale ranging. Respondents were also asked, "How proud are you to be [*YOUR COUNTRY'S NATIONALITY*]?"

21 Center for Systemic Peace. 2014. *Polity IV Annual Time Series, 1800–2014.* www.systemicpeace.org/polity/polity4.htm (accessed November 19, 2017).

22 See Inglehart, 1997 and Hagerty and Veenhoven, 2003.

23 Life satisfaction was assessed by asking respondents how satisfied they were with their lives as a whole, using a scale ranging from 1 [*not at all satisfied*] to 10 [*very satisfied*]. Happiness was assessed by asking respondents to indicate how happy they were, using four categories: *very happy; rather happy; not very happy; and not at all happy*. The economic data are from the World Bank.

24 One can turn this curve into a straight line by performing a log transformation of per capita GNP – but this is simply another way of acknowledging that the relationship between economic development and happiness reflects a curve of diminishing returns. The effects of economic development almost always show diminishing returns, so economists habitually use a log transformation of the economic measure. This does not change the underlying reality.

25 See Inglehart, Foa, Peterson and Welzel, 2008.

26 Norris and Inglehart, 2004.

27 Among those who said that homosexuality is never justifiable, 25 percent said they were very happy; among those who said it was always justifiable, 31 percent were very happy.

28 As one would expect, when a large number of unhappy societies suddenly shifted toward democracy around 1990, it reduced the correlation between subjective well-being and democracy.

29 This claim involves a long and somewhat technical controversy; for details, see "The Easterlin Paradox" in Appendix 1.

30 Inglehart, Foa, Peterson and Welzel, 2008 expressed this expectation before data were available to test it.

31 Information about the World database of happiness data, and the data themselves, are available at: http://worlddatabaseofhappiness.eur.nl/ (accessed October 29, 2017).

32 Sharp declines in subjective well-being do not occur often, but when they do they can have serious consequences. Though the collapse of the Soviet

Union in 1991 had additional negative effects, it was *preceded* by declining subjective well-being. Similarly, the breakup of the Belgian state in the 1980s and its reorganization into a federation based on ethnic cleavages was *preceded* by a sharp decline in subjective well-being (see Inglehart and Klingemann, 2000).

33 Cummins, Robert A. and Helen Nistico, 2002. "Maintaining Life Satisfaction: The Role of Positive Cognitive Bias," *Journal of Happiness studies* 3, 1: 37–69.

34 Ellison, Christopher G., David A. Gay and Thomas A. Glass, 1989. "Does Religious Commitment Contribute to Individual Life Satisfaction?" *Social Forces* 68, 1: 100–123; Lim, C. and Putnam, R., 2010. "Religion, Social Networks, and Life Satisfaction," *American Sociological Review* 75: 914–933.

35 In the Latin American countries, 68 percent of the public says that God is very important in their lives (choosing 10 on a ten-point scale), while in the ex-communist countries only 29 percent do so.

36 International Labor Organization, 2012. *Laborstat.* Available at http://laborsta.ilo.org/ (accessed October 28, 2017).

37 World Bank, 2012. *World Development Indicators.* Available at http://data.worldbank.org/data-catalog/world-development-indicators (accessed October 29, 2017).

38 Inglehart and Klingemann, 2000.

39 Ellison, 1989; Lim and Putnam, 2010.

40 Bahrain is the only exception that is a high-income country – but its income comes mainly from oil exports and is very unequally distributed.

41 Thomas, 2005; Thomas, 2007.

42 This figure is based on a path analysis in Inglehart, Foa, Peterson and Welzel, 2008: 280.

43 This is a smaller number than the 62 countries examined in Figures 8.4 and 8.5, since it only includes those countries for which data are available for all of the variables in Figure 8.10.

44 Easterlin, 2005.

45 See Inglehart, 1997; Inglehart and Welzel, 2005.

Chapter 9 *The Silent Revolution* in Reverse: The Rise of Trump and the Authoritarian Populist Parties

1 Inglehart, 1971; Inglehart, 1977; Inglehart, 1990.

2 As Chapter 3 demonstrated, Postmaterialist values are part of a still-broader shift from Survival values to Self-expression values. To simplify terminology, I use "Postmaterialist" in this chapter to describe this broader cultural shift.

3 Inglehart, 1971; Inglehart, 1977; Inglehart, 1990.

4 Ignazi, Piero, 1992. "The Silent Counter-revolution," *European Journal of Political Research*, 22(1), 3–34; Ignazi, Piero, 2003. *Extreme Right Parties in Western Europe*. Oxford University Press.

5 Inglehart, 1990; Inglehart, 1997.

6 Inglehart, 1990; Inglehart, 1997; Inglehart and Welzel, 2005; Norris and Inglehart, 2011.

7 The 12-item Materialist/Postmaterialist values battery includes five items that tap Postmaterialist values. Accordingly, an individual's Postmaterialism score can range from zero to five, depending on how many Postmaterialist items are given high priority.

8 Norris, 2005.

9 Kitschelt, Herbert with Anthony J. McGann, 1995. *The Radical Right in Western Europe: A Comparative Analysis*. Ann Arbor: University of Michigan Press; Betz, Hans-Georg, 1994. *Radical Right-wing Populism in Western Europe*. New York: Springer.

10 Ivarsflaten, 2008.

11 Van der Brug, Fennema and Tillie, 2005; Koopmans, R. et al., 2005.

12 With Green–Alternative–Libertarian parties at the opposite pole of a New Politics dimension. See Marks, Gary, Liesbet Hooghe, Moira Nelson and Erica Edwards, 2006. "Party Competition and European Integration in the East and West: Different Structure, Same Causality," *Comparative Political Studies* 39, 2: 155–175.

13 Kitschelt with McGann, 1995.

14 Mudde, 2007.

15 Sides and Citrin, 2007.

16 US Election, 2016.

17 Inglehart and Norris, 2016.

18 www.dw.com/en/new-poll-shows-alternative-for-germany-gaining-support/a-19569448 (accessed October 29, 2017).

19 Kitschelt, 1995; Mudde, 2007.

20 Inglehart, Moaddel and Tessler, 2006; Billiet, Meuleman and De Witte, 2014.

21 Sniderman et al., 2014.

22 Inglehart, 2015.

23 Chiao, Joan Y. and Katherine D. Blizinsky, 2009. "Culture–Gene Coevolution of Individualism–Collectivism and the Serotonin Transporter Gene," *Proceedings of the Royal Society B* 277, 1681: 529–553.

24 Most middle-income and low-income countries don't show this phenomenon; some even show significantly higher levels of xenophobia among the young than among the old.

25 Lipset, 1960.

26 Bradley et al., 2003; Iversen and Sostice, 2009.

27 Piketty, 2014.

28 World Bank, 2015.

29 Whyte, Martin K., 2014. "Soaring Income Gaps: China in Comparative Perspective," *Daedalus* 143, 2: 39–52.

30 Milanovic, Branko, 2016. *Global Inequality: A New Approach for the Age of Globalization.* Cambridge, MA: Harvard University Press.

31 www.gallup.com/poll/182918/fewer-americans-identify-middle-class-recent-years.aspx (accessed October 29, 2017).

32 Saez and Zucman, 2014.

33 Stiglitz, 2011.

34 Wolfers, 2015.

35 www.politifact.com/truth-o-meter/statements/2015/jun/15/hillary-clinton/hillary-clinton-top-hedge-fund-managers-make-more-/ (accessed October 29, 2017).

36 Case and Deaton, 2015.

37 Gilens, 2012.

38 Hacker, 2008.

39 Stiglitz, 2013.

40 Stiglitz, 2013.

41 Hacker and Pierson, 2010.

Chapter 10   The Coming of Artificial Intelligence Society

1 Stiglitz, 2011; Stiglitz, 2013.

2 Sabadish and Mishel, 2013.

3 Ford, 2015: 76.

4 National Center for Education Statistics, 2014.

5 Hicks and Devaraj, 2015.

6 Brynjolfsson, Erik and Andrew McAfee, 2014. *The Second Machine Age: Work, Progress, and prosperity in a Time of Brilliant Technologies.* New York: W. W. Norton & Company.

7 Bureau of Labor Statistics. Available at https://data.bls.gov/pdq/querytool.jsp?survey=ln (accessed October 28, 2017).

8 Eberstadt, Nicholas, 2017. "Our Miserable 21st Century," *Commentary,* February 22, 2017. Cf. Eberstadt, Nicholas, 2016. *Men Without Work: America's Invisible Crisis.* West Conshohocken, PA: Templeton Press.

9 Ford, 2015.

10 Krueger, Alan B., 2016. "Where Have All the Workers Gone?" National Bureau of Economic Research (NBER) October 4.

11 Case and Deaton, 2015.

12 Krueger, 2016.

13 "U.S. Drug Deaths Climbing Faster than Ever," *New York Times*, June 6, 2017, p. 1.

14 It fell from 78.9 years in 2014 to 78.8 years in 2015 – a small but statistically significant decline. See NCHS Data Brief No. 267 December 2016 US Department of Health and Human Services Centers for Disease Control and Prevention National Center for Health Statistics Mortality in the United States, 2015. Jiaquan Xu, M.D., Sherry L. Murphy, B.S., Kenneth D. Kochanek, M.A., and Elizabeth Arias, Ph.D.

15 Chetty et al., 2016.

16 Goos, Maarten, Alan Manning and Anna Salomons, 2014. "Explaining Job Polarization: Routine-Biased Technological Change and Offshoring," *The American Economic Review* 104, 8: 2509–2526.

17 Wiseman, 2013.

18 Higher income taxes for the very rich are only part of the solution. Even those workers who pay no income tax, pay a payroll tax covering social security and medicare. Because these are flat rate taxes on a largely capped base, they are regressive taxes that reinforce rather than offset pretax inequality – and the regressive payroll tax is more than two-thirds as large as the income tax. Making the payroll tax progressive would be a significant step toward reducing income inequality.

19 Hochschild, 2016.

20 Rothstein, Bo, 2017. "Why Has the White Working Class Abandoned the Left?" *Social Europe*, January 19. Available at www.socialeurope .eu/2017/01/white-working-class-abandoned-left/ (accessed October 29, 2017).

21 2016 Report from Federal Reserve Bank of St. Louis. Available at https://fred.stlouisfed.org/series/HNONWRQ027S (accessed October 29, 2017).

Appendix 1 The Easterlin Paradox

1 Easterlin, Richard A., 1974. "Does Economic Growth Improve the Human Lot?" in P. A. David and M. Reder (eds.), *Nations, Households, and Economic Growth*. New York: Academic Press, 98–125.

2 Inglehart, Ronald, 1990. *Cultural Shift in Advanced Industrial Society*. Princeton: Princeton University Press: 31–32.

3 Easterlin, Richard A., 2009. "Lost in Transition: Life Satisfaction on the Road to Capitalism." *Journal of Economic Behavior and Organization* 71: 130–145.

REFERENCES

Abramson, Paul and Ronald F. Inglehart, 1995. *Value Change in Global Perspective*. Ann Arbor: University of Michigan Press.

Abramson, Paul, John Aldrich, Brad Gomez and David Rohde, 2015. *Change and Continuity in the 2012 Elections*. Sage: Los Angeles.

Acemoglu, Daron and James A. Robinson, 2006a. "De Facto Political Power and Institutional Persistence," *American Economic Review* 96, 2: 326–330.

Acemoglu, Daron and James A. Robinson, 2006b. *Economic Origins of Dictatorship and Democracy*. New York: Cambridge University Press.

Acemoglu, Daron, Simon Johnson, James A. Robinson and Pierre Yared, 2008. "Income and Democracy," *American Economic Review* 98, 3: 808–842.

Adorno, Theodor W., Else Frenkel-Brunswik, Daniel J. Levinson and R. Nevitt Sanford, 1950. *The Authoritarian Personality*. New York: Harper & Row.

Africa Progress Report, 2012. *Jobs, Justice, and Equity*. Geneva: Africa Progress Panel.

Aldridge, A., 2000. *Religion in the Contemporary World*. Cambridge: Polity Press.

Almond, Gabriel A. and Sidney Verba, 1963. *The Civic Culture: Political Attitudes and Democracy in Five Nations*. Newbury Park, CA: Sage Publications.

Andersen, Robert and Tina Fetner. 2008. "Cohort Differences in Tolerance of Homosexuality," *Public Opinion Quarterly* 72, 2: 311–330.

Andrews, Edmund L., 2008. "Greenspan Concedes Error on Regulation," *New York Times*, October 23: B1.

Andrews, Frank M. and Stephen B. Withey, 1976. *Social Indicators of Well-being*. New York: Plenum.

Angell, Norman, 1933 [1909]. *The Great Illusion*. London: G.P. Putnam's Sons.

Autor, David, H. and David Dorn, 2013. "The Growth of Low-Skill Service Jobs and the Polarization of the US Labor Market," *The American Economic Review* 103, 5: 1553–1597.

Barber, Nigel. 2011. "A Cross-national Test of the Uncertainty Hypothesis of Religious Belief," *Cross-Cultural Research* 45, 3: 318–333.

Barnes, Samuel H. and Max Kaase (eds.), 1979. *Political Action: Mass Participation in Five Western Democracies.* Beverly Hills, CA: Sage Publications.

Barro, Robert J., 1999. "Determinants of Democracy," *Journal of Political Economy* 107, S6: 158–183.

Bednar, Jenna, Aaron Bramson, Andrea Jones-Rooy and Scott Page, 2010. "Emergent Cultural Signatures and Persistent Diversity," *Rationality and Society* 22, 4: 407–444.

Bell, Daniel, 1973. *The Coming of Post-Industrial Society.* New York: Basic Books.

Benjamin, Daniel J., David Cesarini, Matthijs J. H. M. van der Loos, Christopher T. Dawes, Philipp D. Koellinger, Patrik K. E. Magnusson, Christopher F. Chabris et al., 2012. "The Genetic Architecture of Economic and Political Preferences," *Proceedings of the National Academy of Sciences* 109, 21: 8026–8031.

Betz, Hans-Georg, 1994. *Radical Right-wing Populism in Western Europe.* New York: Springer.

Billiet, Jaak, Bart Meuleman and Hans De Witte, 2014. "The Relationship between Ethnic Threat and Economic Insecurity in Times of Economic Crisis: Analysis of European Social Survey Data," *Migration Studies* 2, 2: 135–161.

Boix, Carles, 2003. *Democracy and Redistribution.* New York: Cambridge University Press.

Boix, Carles and Susan C. Stokes, 2003. "Endogenous Democratization," *World Politics* 55, 4: 517–549.

Böltken, Ferdinand and Wolfgang Jagodzinski, 1985. "In an Environment of Insecurity: Postmaterialism in the European Community, 1970–1980," *Comparative Political Studies* 17 (January): 453–484.

Borre, Ole, 1984. "Critical Electoral Change in Scandinavia," in Russell J. Dalton, Scott C. Flanagan and Paul Allen Beck (eds.), *Electoral Change in Advanced Industrial Democracies.* Princeton: Princeton University Press: 330–364.

Bradley, David, Evelyne Huber, Stephanie Moller, François Nielsen and John D. Stephens, 2003. "Distribution and Redistribution in Postindustrial Democracies," *World Politics* 55, 2: 193–228.

Brickman, Philip and Donald T. Campbell, 1981. "Hedonic Relativism and Planning the Good Society," in M. Appley (ed.), *Adaptation-level Theory.* New York: Academic Press, 287–305.

British Election Survey. Available at www.britishelectionstudy.com/ (accessed October 28, 2017).

Broadberry, Stephen and Kevin H. O'Rourke (eds.), 2010. *The Cambridge Economic History of Modern Europe: 1700–1870.* Cambridge: Cambridge University Press.

Brockmann, Hilke, Jan Delhey, Christian Welzel and Hao Yuan, 2009. "The China Puzzle: Falling Happiness in a Rising Economy," *Journal of Happiness Studies* 10, 4: 387–405.

Bruce, Steve, 1992. "Pluralism and Religious Vitality," in Steve Bruce (ed.), *Religion and Modernization: Sociologists and Historians Debate the Secularization Thesis.* Oxford: Oxford University Press: 170–194.

Brynjolfsson, Erik and Andrew McAfee, 2014. *The Second Machine Age: Work, Progress, and prosperity in a Time of Brilliant Technologies.* New York: W. W. Norton & Company.

Bureau of Labor Statistics. Available at: https://data.bls.gov/pdq/querytool .jsp?survey=ln (accessed October 28, 2017).

Bureau of Labor Statistics, 1983. "Perceptions Reviewed," *Bureau of Labor Statistics Monthly Labor Review:* April: 21–24.

Burkhart, Ross E. and Michael S. Lewis-Beck, 1994. "Comparative Democracy: The Economic Development Thesis," *American Political Science Review* 88, 4: 903–910.

Case, Anne and Angus Deaton, 2015. "Rising Morbidity and Mortality in Midlife among White Non-Hispanic Americans in the 21st Century," *Proceedings of the National Academy of Sciences* 112, no. 49: 15078–15083.

Cavalli-Sforza, Luigi Luca, Paolo Menozzi and Alberto Piazza, 1994. *The History and Geography of Human Genes.* Princeton: Princeton University Press.

Center for Systemic Peace. 2014. *Polity IV Annual Time Series, 1800–2014.*

Chenoweth, Erica and Kathleen Gallagher Cunningham, 2013. "Understanding Nonviolent Resistance," *Journal of Peace Research* 5, 3: 271–276.

Chetty, Raj, David Grusky, Maximilian Hell, Nathaniel Hendren, Robert Manduca and Jimmy Narang, 2016. "The Fading American Dream: Trends in Absolute Income Mobility since 1940," *National Bureau of Economic Research* Working Paper No. 22910.

Chiao, Joan Y. and Katherine D. Blizinsky, 2009. "Culture–Gene Coevolution of Individualism–Collectivism and the Serotonin Transporter Gene," *Proceedings of the Royal Society B* 277, 1681: 529–553.

Christie, R. E. and Jahoda, M. E., 1954. *Studies in the Scope and Method of "The authoritarian personality,"* Glencoe: The Free Press.

Cingranelli, David L., David L. Richards and K. Chad Clay, 2014. "The CIRI Human Rights Dataset." Available at www.humanrightsdata.com (accessed October 28, 2017).

Cummins, Robert A. and Helen Nistico, 2002. "Maintaining Life Satisfaction: The Role of Positive Cognitive Bias," *Journal of Happiness studies* 3, 1: 37–69.

Dafoe, Allen and Bruce Russett, 2013. "Does Capitalism Account for the Democratic Peace? The Evidence Says No," in Gerald Schneider and Nils Petter Gleditsch (eds.), *Assessing the Capitalist Peace.* New York: Routledge:110–126.

Dafoe, Allen, 2011. "Statistical Critiques of the Democratic Peace: Caveat Emptor," *American Journal of Political Science* 55, 2: 247–262.

Dahl, Robert A., 1971. *Polyarchy.* New Haven: Yale University Press.

Dalton, Russell J., Scott Flanagan and Paul A. Beck (eds.), 1984. *Electoral Change in Advanced Industrial Democracies.* Princeton: Princeton University Press.

Davidson, Richard J. and Antoine Lutz, 2008. "Buddha's Brain: Neuroplasticity and Meditation," *IEEE Signal Process Magazine* 25, 1: 166–174.

De Martino, Benedetto, Dharshan Kumaran, Ben Seymour and Raymond J. Dolan, 2006. "Frames, Biases, and Rational Decision-making in the Human Brain," *Science* 313, 5787: 684–687.

De Waal, Frans B. M., 1995. "Bonobo Sex and Society," *Scientific American* 272, 3: 82–88.

Deutsch, Karl W., 1961. "Social Mobilization and Political Development," *American Political Science Review* 55, 3: 493–514.

Deutsch, Karl W., 1966. *Nationalism and Social Communication.* Cambridge, MA: MIT Press.

Diener, Ed and Richard E. Lucas, 1999. "Personality and Subjective Well-being," in Daniel Kahneman, Edward Diener and Norbert Schwarz (eds.), *Well-being: The Foundations of Hedonic Psychology.* New York: Russell Sage Foundation, 213–229.

Diener, Ed., Eunkook M. Suh, Richard E. Lucas and Heidi L. Smith, 1999. "Subjective Well- being: Three Decades of Progress," *Psychological Bulletin* 125, 2: 276–302.

Diener, Ed., Richard E. Lucas and Christie N. Scollon, 2006. "Beyond the Hedonic Treadmill: Revising the Adaptation Theory of Well-being," *American Psychologist* 61, 4: 305–314.

Diener, Edward and Shigehiro Oishi, 2000. "Money and Happiness: Income and Subjective Well-being across Nations," in Edward Diener and Eunkook M. Suh (eds.), *Culture and Subjective Well-being.* Cambridge, MA: MIT Press: 185–218.

Dorussen, Han and Hugh Ward, 2010. "Trade Networks and the Kantian Peace," *Journal of Peace Research* 47, 1: 29–42.

Doyle, Michael W., 1986. "Liberalism and World Politics," *American Political Science Review* 80, 4: 1151–1169.

Easterlin, Richard A., 1974. "Does Economic Growth Improve the Human Lot?" in P. A. David and M. Reder (eds.), *Nations, Households, and Economic Growth*. New York: Academic Press, 98–125.

Easterlin, Richard A., 2003. "Explaining Happiness," *Proceedings of the National Academy of the Sciences* 100, 19: 11176–11183.

Easterlin, Richard A., 2005. "Feeding the Illusion of Growth and Happiness: A Reply to Hagerty and Veenhoven," *Social Indicators Research* 74, 3: 429–443.

Easterlin, Richard A., 2009. "Lost in Transition: Life Satisfaction on the Road to Capitalism." *Journal of Economic Behavior and Organization* 71: 130–145.

Eberstadt, Nicholas, 2016. *Men Without Work: America's Invisible Crisis*. Conshohocken, PA: Templeton Press.

Eberstadt, Nicholas, 2017. "Our Miserable 21st Century," *Commentary*, February 22, 2017.

Ebstein, Richard P., Olga Novick, Roberto Umansky, Beatrice Priel, Yamima Osher, Darren Blaine, Estelle R. Bennett, Lubov Nemanov, Miri Katz and Robert H. Belmaker, 1996. "Dopamine D4 Receptor (D4DR) Exon III Polymorphism Associated with the Human Personality Trait of Novelty Seeking," *Nature Genetics* 12, 1: 78–80.

Eckstein, Harry, 1961. *A Theory of Stable Democracy* (No. 10). Center of International Studies, Woodrow Wilson School of Public and International Affairs, Princeton University.

Ellison, Christopher G., David A. Gay and Thomas A. Glass. 1989. "Does Religious Commitment Contribute to Individual Life Satisfaction?" *Social Forces* 68, 1: 100–123.

Estes, Richard, 2010. "The World Social Situation: Development Challenges at the Outset of a New Century," *Social Indicators Research* 98, 363–402.

Euro-Barometer Surveys. Available at http://ec.europa.eu/COMMFrontOffice/publicopinion/index.cfm (accessed October 28, 2017).

European Community Survey. Available at http://ec.europa.eu/eurostat/web/microdata/european-community-household-panel (accessed October 28, 2017).

European Value Survey. Available at www.europeanvaluesstudy.eu/ (accessed October 28, 2017).

Federal Reserve Bank of St. Louis, 2014. "Percent of Employment in Agriculture in the United States." Available at http://research.stlouisfed.org/fred2/series/USAPEMANA (accessed October 28, 2017).

Fincher, Corey L. and Randy Thornhill, 2008. "Assortative Sociality, Limited Dispersal, Infectious Disease and the Genesis of the Global Pattern of Religion Diversity," *Proceedings of the Royal Society* 275, 1651: 2587–2594.

Fincher, Corey L., Randy Thornhill, Damian R. Murray and Mark Schaller, 2008. "Pathogen Prevalence Predicts Human Cross-cultural Variability in Individualism/Collectivism," *Proceedings of the Royal Society B* 275, 1640: 1279–1285.

Finke, Roger, 1992. "An Unsecular America," in Steve Bruce (ed.), *Religion and Modernization: Sociologists and Historians Debate the Secularization Thesis*. Oxford: Oxford University Press: 145–169.

Finke, Roger and Laurence R. Iannaccone, 1993. "The Illusion of Shifting Demand: Supply-side Explanations for Trends and Change in the American Religious Market Place," *Annals of the American Association of Political and Social Science* 527: 27–39.

Finke, Roger and Rodney Stark, 2000. *Acts of Faith: Explaining the Human Side of Religion*. Berkeley, CA: The University of California Press.

Ford, Martin, 2015. *Rise of the Robots: Technology and the Threat of a Jobless Future*. New York: Basic Books.

Freedom House, 2014. *Freedom in the World*. http://freedomhouse.org/article/freedom-world-2014 (accessed October 28, 2017).

Frey, Bruno S. and Alois Stutzer, 2000. "Happiness Prospers in Democracy," *Journal of Happiness Studies* 1, 1: 79–102.

Frey, Carl Benedikt and Michael A. Osborne, 2012. *The Future of Employment: How Susceptible Are Jobs to Computerisation*. Oxford: Oxford University Programme on the Impacts of Future Technology.

Frydman, Carola and Dirk Jenter. 2010. "CEO Compensation," *Annual Review of Economics* 2, 1: 75–102.

Fujita, Frank and Ed Diener, 2005. "Life Satisfaction Set Point: Stability and Change," *Journal of Personality and Social Psychology* 88, 1: 158–164.

Fukuyama, Francis, 1995. *Trust: Social Virtues and the Creation of Prosperity*. New York: Free Press.

Gartzke, Erik, 2007. "The Capitalist Peace," *American Journal of Political Science* 51, 1: 166–191.

Gat, Azar, 2005. "The Democratic Peace Theory Reframed: The Impact of Modernity," *World Politics* 58, 1: 73–100.

Gat, Azar, 2006. *War in Human Civilization*. Oxford: Oxford University Press.

Gelfand, Michele J., Jana L. Raver, Lisa Nishii, Lisa M. Leslie, Janetta Lun, Beng Chong Lim, Lili Duan et al., 2011. "Differences between Tight and Loose Cultures: A 33-Nation Study," *Science* 332, 6033: 1100–1104.

German Election Study. Available at http://gles.eu/wordpress/ (accessed October 28, 2017).

Gilens, Martin, 2012. *Affluence and Influence*. Princeton: Princeton University Press.

Goldstein, Joshua S., 2011. *Winning the War on War: The Decline of Armed Conflict Worldwide*. New York: Plume.

Goos, Maarten, Alan Manning and Anna Salomons, 2014. "Explaining Job Polarization: Routine-Biased Technological Change and Offshoring," *The American Economic Review* 104, 8: 2509–2526.

Greene, Joshua and Jonathan Haidt, 2002. "How (and Where) Does Moral Judgment Work?" *Trends in Cognitive Sciences* 6, 12: 517–523.

Hacker, Jacob S., 2008. *The Great Risk Shift.* New York: Oxford University Press.

Hacker, Jacob S. and Paul Pierson, 2010. *Winner-Take-All Politics.* New York: Simon & Schuster.

Hadlock, Paul, Daniel Hecker and Joseph Gannon, 1991. "High Technology Employment: Another View," *Bureau of Labor Statistics Monthly Labor Review:* July: 26–30.

Hagerty, Michael R. and Ruut Veenhoven, 2003. "Wealth and Happiness Revisited – Growing National Income *Does* Go with Greater Happiness," *Social Indicators Research* 64, 1: 1–27.

Haidt, Jonathan and Fredrik Bjorklund, 2008, "Social Intuitionists Answer Six Questions about Morality," *Moral Psychology* 2: 181–217.

Haller, Max and Markus Hadler, 2004. "Happiness as an Expression of Freedom and Self-determination: A Comparative Multilevel Analysis," in W. Glatzer, S. von Below and M. Stoffregen (eds.), *Challenges for Quality of Life in the Contemporary World.* Dordrecht, The Netherlands: Kluwer Academic Publishers, 207–229.

Hamer, Dean H., 1996. "The Heritability of Happiness," *Nature Genetics* 14, 2: 125–126.

Headey, Bruce and Alexander Wearing, 1989. "Personality, Life Events, and Subjective Well-being: Toward a Dynamic Equilibrium Model," *Journal of Personality and Social Psychology* 57, 4: 731–739.

Hecker, Daniel E., 2005. "High Technology Employment: A NAICS-based Update," *Bureau of Labor Statistics Monthly Labor Review*, July: 57–72.

Hecker, Daniel, 1999. "High Technology Employment: A Broader View," *Bureau of Labor Statistics Monthly Labor Review*, June: 18–28.

Hegre, Håvard, John R. Oneal and Bruce Russett, 2010. "Trade Does Promote Peace: New Simultaneous Estimates of the Reciprocal Effects of Trade and Conflict," *Journal of Peace Research* 47, 6: 763–774.

Helliwell, John F., 1993. Empirical Linkages between Democracy and Economic Growth. *British Journal of Political Science* 24: 225–248.

Hibbs, Douglas A. 1977. "Political Parties and Macroeconomic Policy," *American Political Science Review* 71, 4: 1467–1487.

Hicks, Michael J. and Srikant Devaraj. 2015. "The Myth and the Reality of Manufacturing in America." Center for Business and Economic Research, Ball State University.

Hochschild, Arlie Russell, 2016. *Strangers in Their Own Land: Anger and Mourning on the American Right.* New York: The New Press.

Hofstede, Geert, 1980. *Culture's Consequences: International Differences in Work-Related Values*. Beverly Hills, CA: Sage Publications.

Hofstede, Geert, 2001. *Culture's Consequences: Comparing Values, Behaviors, Institutions and Organizations across Nations*. 2nd Edition, Thousand Oaks, CA: Sage Publications.

Hughes, Barry B. and Evan E. Hillebrand, 2012. *Exploring and Shaping International Futures*. Boulder, CO: Paradigm Publishing.

Human Development Report, 2013. *The Rise of the South: Human Progress in a Diverse World*. New York: United Nations Development Programme.

Human Security Report Project, 2012. *Human Security Report 2012*. Vancouver: Human Security Press.

Huntington, Samuel P., 1991. *The Third Wave: Democratization in the Late 20th Century*. Norman, OK: University of Oklahoma Press.

Huntington, Samuel P., 1996. *The Clash of Civilizations: Remaking of the World Order*. New York: Simon & Schuster.

Ignazi, Piero, 1992. "The Silent Counter-revolution," *European Journal of Political Research* 22(1), 3–34.

Ignazi, Piero, 2003. *Extreme Right Parties in Western Europe*. Oxford University Press.

Inglehart, Ronald F., 1971. "The Silent Revolution in Europe: Intergenerational Change in Post-Industrial Societies," *American Political Science Review* 65, 4: 991–1017.

Inglehart, Ronald F., 1977. *The Silent Revolution: Changing Values and Political Styles among Western Publics*. Princeton: Princeton University Press.

Inglehart, Ronald F., 1984. "The Changing Structure of Political Cleavages in Western Society," in R. J. Dalton, S. Flanagan and P. A. Beck (eds.), *Electoral Change in Advanced Industrial Democracies: Realignment or Dealignment?* Princeton: Princeton University Press.

Inglehart, Ronald F., 1990. *Cultural Shift in Advanced Industrial Society*. Princeton: Princeton University Press.

Inglehart, Ronald F., 1997. *Modernization and Postmodernization: Cultural, Economic and Political Change in 43 Societies*. Princeton: Princeton University Press.

Inglehart, Ronald F., 2003. "How Solid is Mass Support for Democracy – and How Do We Measure It?" *PS: Political Science and Politics* 36, 1: 51–57.

Inglehart, Ronald F., 2008. "Changing Values among Western Publics, 1970–2006: Postmaterialist Values and the Shift from Survival Values to Self Expression Values," *West European Politics* 31, 1–2: 130–146.

Inglehart, Ronald F., 2010. "Faith and Freedom: Traditional and Modern Ways to Happiness," in Ed Diener, Daniel Kahneman and John Helliwell (eds.), *International Differences in Well-being*. Oxford: Oxford University Press: 351–397.

Inglehart, Ronald F., 2015. "Insecurity and Xenophobia: Comment on *Paradoxes of Liberal Democracy*," *Perspectives on Politics* 13,2 (June, 2015): 468–470.

Inglehart, Ronald F., 2016 "Inequality and Modernization: Why Equality is likely to Make a Comeback," *Foreign Affairs* January–February, 95, 1: 2–10.

Inglehart, Ronald F. and Christian Welzel, 2004. "What Insights Can Multi-Country Surveys Provide about People and Societies?" APSA Comparative Politics Newsletter 15,2 (summer, 2004): 14–18.

Inglehart, Ronald F. and Christian Welzel, 2005. *Modernization, Cultural Change and Democracy: The Human Development Sequence.* New York: Cambridge University Press.

Inglehart, Ronald F. and Christian Welzel, 2009. "How Development Leads to Democracy: What We Know About Modernization," *Foreign Affairs* March/April: 33–48.

Inglehart, Ronald F. and Christian Welzel, 2010. "Changing Mass Priorities: The Link between Modernization and Democracy," *Perspectives on Politics* 8, 2: 551–567.

Inglehart, Ronald F. and Hans-Dieter Klingemann, 2000. "Genes, Culture, Democracy, and Happiness," in Ed Diener and Eunkook M. Suh (eds.), *Culture and Subjective Well-being.* Cambridge, MA: MIT Press, 165–183.

Inglehart, Ronald F. and Pippa Norris, 2004. *Rising Tide: Gender Equality in Global Perspective.* Cambridge: Cambridge University Press.

Inglehart, Ronald F. and Pippa Norris, 2016. "Trump, Brexit, and the Rise of Populism: Economic Insecurity and Cultural Backlash." Paper presented at the meeting of the American Political Science Association. Philadelphia (September).

Inglehart, Ronald F. and Pippa Norris, 2017. "Trump and the Xenophobic Populist Parties: *The Silent Revolution* in Reverse," *Perspectives on Politics* (June) 15 (2): 443–454.

Inglehart, Ronald F. and Wayne E. Baker, 2000. "Modernization and Cultural Change and the Persistence of Traditional Values," *American Sociological Review* 65, 1: 19–51.

Inglehart, Ronald F., Bi Puranen and Christian Welzel, 2015. "Declining Willingness to Fight in Wars: The Individual-level component of the Long Peace," *Journal of Peace Research* 52, 4: 418–434.

Inglehart, Ronald F., Mansoor Moaddel and Mark Tessler, 2006. "Xenophobia and In-Group Solidarity in Iraq: A Natural Experiment on the Impact of Insecurity," *Perspectives on Politics* 4, 3: 495–506.

Inglehart, Ronald F., R. Foa, Christopher Peterson and Christian Welzel, 2008. "Development, Freedom and Rising Happiness: A Global Perspective, 1981–2007," *Perspectives on Psychological Science* 3, 4: 264–285.

Inglehart, Ronald F., Ronald C. Inglehart and Eduard Ponarin, 2017. "Cultural Change, Slow and Fast," *Social Forces* (January) 1–28.

Inglehart, Ronald F., Svetlana Borinskaya, Anna Cotter, Jaanus Harro, Ronald C. Inglehart, Eduard Ponarin and Christian Welzel, 2014. "Genetic Factors, Cultural Predispositions, Happiness and Gender Equality," *Journal of Research in Gender Studies* 4, 1: 40–69.

International Labor Organization. 2012. *Laborstat*. Available at http://laborsta .ilo.org/ (accessed October 28, 2017).

Iversen, Torben and David Soskice, 2009. "Distribution and Redistribution: The Shadow of the Nineteenth Century," *World Politics* 61, 3: 438–486.

Johnson, Wendy and Robert F. Krueger, 2006. "How Money Buys Happiness: Genetic and Environmental Processes Linking Finances and Life Satisfaction," *Journal of Personality and Social Psychology* 90, 4: 680–691.

Kahneman, Daniel, Alan B. Krueger, David A. Schkade, Norbert Schwarz and Arthur A. Stone, 2004. "A Survey Method for Characterizing Daily Life Experience: The Day Reconstruction Method," *Science* 306, 5702: 1776–1780.

Kahneman, Daniel, 2011. *Thinking, Fast and Slow*. New York: Farrar, Strauss and Giroux.

Kahneman, Daniel and Alan B. Krueger, 2006. "Developments in the Measurement of Subjective Well-being," *Journal of Economic Perspectives* 20, 1: 3–24.

Kaufmann, Daniel, Aart Kraay and Massimo Mastruzzi. 2003. "Government Matters III: Governance Indicators for 1996–2002." No. 3106. The World Bank.

Kehm, Barbara M., 1999. *Higher Education in Germany: Developments, Problems Perspectives*. Bucharest: UNESCO European Centre for Higher Education.

Kenny, Charles, 2005. "Does Development Make You Happy? Subjective Well-being and Economic Growth in Developing Countries," *Social Indicators Research* 73, 2: 199–219.

Kitschelt, Herbert with Anthony J. McGann, 1995. *The Radical Right in Western Europe: A Comparative Analysis*. Ann Arbor: University of Michigan Press.

Koopmans, Ruud, Paul Statham, Marco Giugni and Florence Passy, 2005. *Contested Citizenship. Political Contention over Migration and Ethnic Relations in Western Europe*. Minneapolis: University of Minnesota Press.

Krueger, Alan B., 2016. "Where Have All the Workers Gone?" National Bureau of Economic Research (NBER) October 4.

Kutscher, Ronald E. and Jerome Mark, 1983. "The Service-producing Sector: Some Common Perceptions Reviewed," *Monthly Labor Review* 21–24.

Larsen, Randy J., 2000. "Toward a Science of Mood Regulation," *Psychological Inquiry* 11, 3: 129–141.

Lebergott, Stanley, 1966. "Labor Force and Employment, 1800–1960," in Dorothy S. Brady (ed.), *Output, Employment, and Productivity in the United States after 1800*. New York: National Bureau of Economic Research: 117–204.

Lenski, Gerhard E., 1966. *Power and Privilege: A Theory of Social Stratification*, Englewood Cliffs: McGraw-Hill.

Lerner, Daniel, 1958. *The Passing of Traditional Society: Modernizing the Middle East*. New York: Free Press.

Lesthaeghe, Ron and Johan Surkyn, 1988. "Cultural Dynamics and Economic Theories of Fertility Change," *Population and Development Review*, 141: 1–46.

Lewis-Beck, Michael S., 2005. "Election Forecasting: Principles and Practice," *British Journal of Politics and International Relations* 7: 145–164.

Lim, Chaeyoon and Robert D. Putnam, 2010. "Religion, Social Networks, and Life Satisfaction," *American Sociological Review* 75: 914–933.

Lipset, Seymour Martin, 1959. "Some Social Requisites of Democracy: Economic Development and Political Legitimacy," *American Political Science Review* 53, 1: 69–105.

Lipset, Seymour Martin, 1960. *Political Man*. Garden City, New York: Anchor Books.

Lucas, Richard E., Andrew E. Clark, Yannis Georgellis and Ed Diener, 2005. "Reexamining Adaptation and the Set Point Model of Happiness: Reactions to Changes in Marital Status," *Journal of Personality and Social Psychology* 84, 3: 527–539.

Lykken, David and Auke Tellegen, 1996. "Happiness Is a Stochastic Phenomenon," *Psychological Science* 7, 3: 186–189.

Lyubomirsky, Sonja, Kennon M. Sheldon and David Schkade, 2005. "Pursuing Happiness: The Architecture of Sustainable Change," *Review of General Psychology* 9, 2: 111–131.

Maddison, Angus, 2001. *The World Economy: A Millennial Perspective*. Paris: Development Centre Studies, OECD.

Markoff, John and Amy White. 2009. "The Global Wave of Democratization," in Christian W. Haerpfer, Patrick Bernhagen, Ronald F. Inglehart and Christian Welzel (eds.), *Democratization*. Oxford: Oxford University Press: 55–73.

Marks, Gary, Liesbet Hooghe, Moira Nelson and Erica Edwards, 2006. "Party Competition and European Integration in the East and West: Different Structure, Same Causality," *Comparative Political Studies* 39, 2: 155–175.

Marx, Karl and Friedrich Engels, 1848. *The Communist Manifesto*. London: The Communist League.

McAfee, Andrew, 2017. *A FAQ on Tech, Jobs and Wages*. https://futureoflife
.org/wp-content/uploads/2017/01/Andrew-McAfee.pdf (accessed October
29, 2017).

McDonald, Patrick J., 2009. *The Invisible Hand of Peace: Capitalism, the War
Machine, and International Relations Theory*. New York: Cambridge
University Press.

Meyer-Schwarzenberger, Matthias, 2014. "Individualism, Subjectivism, and
Social Capital: Evidence from Language Structures." Paper presented at
summer workshop of Laboratory for Comparative Social Research, Higher
School of Economics, St. Petersburg, Russia, June 29–July 12, 2014.

Milanovic, Branko, 2016. *Global Inequality: A New Approach for the Age of
Globalization*. Cambridge, MA: Harvard University Press.

Milbrath, Lester W. and Madan Lal Goel, 1977. *Political Participation: How
and Why Do People Get Involved in Politics?* Boston: Rand McNally
College Publishing Co.

Ministry of Education, Culture, Sports, Science and Technology – Japan, 2012.
"Statistics." Available at www.mext.go.jp/english/statistics/index.htm
(accessed October 29, 2017).

Minkov, Michael and Michael Harris Bond, 2016. "A Genetic Component to
National Differences in Happiness," *Journal of Happiness Studies* 1–20.

Mishel, Lawrence and Natalie Sabadish, 2013. "CEO Pay in 2012 Was
Extraordinarily High Relative to Typical Workers and Other High
Earners," *Economic Policy Institute Issue Brief #367*. Available at www
.epi.org/publication/ceo-pay-2012-extraordinarily-high/ (accessed October
29, 2017).

Møller, Jørgen and Svend-Erik Skaaning, 2013. "The Third Wave: Inside the
Numbers," *Journal of Democracy* 24, 4: 97–109.

Moore, Barrington, 1966. *The Social Origins of Dictatorship and Democracy*.
Boston: Beacon Press.

Morewedge, Carey K. and Daniel Kahneman, 2010. "Associative Processes in
Intuitive Judgment," *Trends in Cognitive Sciences* 14: 435–440.

Morris, Ian, 2015. *Foragers, Farmers and Fossil Fuels: How Human Values
Evolve*. Princeton: Princeton University Press.

Mousseau, Michael, Håvard Hegre and John R. O'neal, 2003. "How the
Wealth of Nations Conditions the Liberal Peace," *European Journal of
International Relations* 9, 2: 277–314.

Mousseau, Michael, 2009. "The Social Market Roots of Democratic Peace,"
International Security 33, 4: 52–86.

Mudde, Cas, 2007. *Populist Radical Right Parties in Europe*. New York:
Cambridge University Press, Chapter 4.

Mueller, John, 1989. *Retreat from Doomsday: The Obsolescence of Major
War*. New York: Basic Books.

Muller, Edward N., 1988. "Democracy, Economic Development, and Income Inequality," *American Sociological Review* 53: 50–68.

National Center for Education Statistics, 2014. *Integrated Postsecondary Education Data System.* Available at http://nces.ed.gov/ipeds/ (accessed October 29, 2017).

National Center of Education Statistics, 2012. *Digest of Education Statistics.*

National Science Board, 2012. *Science and Engineering Indicators 2012.* Arlington, VA: National Science Foundations (NSB 12-01).

National Science Board, 2014. *Science and Engineering Indicators 2014.* Arlington, VA: National Science Foundations (NSB 14-01).

NCHS Data Brief No. 267 December 2016. US Department of Health and Human Services Centers for Disease Control and Prevention National Center for Health Statistics Mortality in the United States, 2015. Jiaquan Xu, M.D., Sherry L. Murphy, B.S., Kenneth D. Kochanek, M.A., and Elizabeth Arias, Ph.D.

Niedermayer, Oskar, 1990. "Sozialstruktur, politische Orientierungen und die Uterstutzung extrem rechter Parteien in Westeuropa," *Zeitschrift fur Parlamentsfragen* 21, 4: 564–582.

Nolan, Patrick and Gerhard Lenski, 2015. *Human Societies: An Introduction to Macrosociology.* New York: Oxford University Press.

Norris, Pippa, 2007. *Radical Right.* New York: Cambridge University Press.

Norris, Pippa and Ronald F. Inglehart, 2011. *Sacred and Secular: Religion and Politics Worldwide* (2nd edn.). New York: Cambridge University Press.

Norris, Pippa and Ronald F. Inglehart, 2009. *Cosmopolitan Communications: Cultural Diversity in a Globalized World.* New York: Cambridge University Press.

North, Douglass C. and Barry R. Weingast, 1989. "Constitutions and Commitment: The Evolution of Institutions Governing Public Choice in Seventeenth Century England," *Journal of Economic History* 49, 4: 803–832.

OECD, 2014. *OECD Factbook Statistics.* OECD iLibrary.

Oneal, John R. and Bruce M. Russet, 1997. "The Classical Liberals Were Right," *International Studies Quarterly* 41, 2: 267–293.

Ott, Jan, 2001. "Did the Market Depress Happiness in the US?" *Journal of Happiness Studies* 2, 4: 433–443.

Oyserman, Daphna, Heather M. Coon and Markus Kemmelmeier, 2002. "Rethinking Individualism and Collectivism: Evaluation of Theoretical Assumptions and meta-analyses," *Psychological Bulletin* 128: 3–72.

Page, Benjamin I., Larry M. Bartels and Jason Seawright, 2013. "Democracy and the Policy Preferences of Wealthy Americans," *Perspectives on Politics* 11, 1: 51–73.

Pegram, Thomas, 2010. "Diffusion across Political Systems: The Global Spread of National Human Rights Institutions," *Human Rights Quarterly* 32, 3: 729–760.

Penn World Tables. http://cid.econ.ucdavis.edu/pwt.html (accessed October 29, 2017).

Piketty, Thomas, 2014. *Capital in the Twenty-First Century*. Cambridge, MA: Harvard University Press.

Pinker, Steven, 2011. *The Better Angels of Our Nature: Why Violence Has Declined*. New York: Viking Press.

Politbarometer, 2012. Available at: www.forschungsgruppe.de/Umfragen/Politbarometer/Archiv/Politbarometer_2012/ (accessed October 29, 2017).

Powell, Walter W. and Kaisa Snellman, 2004. "The Knowledge Economy," *Annual Review of Sociology* 30: 199–220.

Prentice, Thomson, 2006. "Health, History and Hard Choices: Funding Dilemmas in a Fast-Changing World," *Nonprofit and Voluntary Sector Quarterly* 37, 1: 63S–75S.

Przeworski, Adam and Fernando Limongi, 1997. "Modernization: Theories and Facts," *World Politics* 49, 2: 155–183.

Puranen, Bi, 2008. *How Values Transform Military Culture – The Swedish Example*. Stockholm: Sweden: Values Research Institute.

Puranen, Bi, 2009. "European Values on Security and Defence: An Exploration of the Correlates of Willingness to Fight for One's Country," in Y. Esmer, H. D. Klingemann and Bi Puranen (eds.), *Religion, Democratic Values and Political Conflict*. Uppsala: Uppsala University: 277–304.

Putnam, Robert D., 1993. *Making Democracy Work: Civic Traditions in Modern Italy*. Princeton, NJ: Princeton University Press.

Raleigh, Donald, 2006. *Russia's Sputnik Generation: Soviet Baby Boomers Talk about Their Lives*. Bloomington, IN: Indiana University Press.

Ridley, Matt, 1996. *The Origins of Virtue: Human Instincts and the Evolution of Cooperation*. London: Penguin Press Science.

Ridley, Matt, 2011. *The Rational Optimist: How Prosperity Evolves*. New York: Harper Perennial.

Rifkin, Jeremy, 2014. *The Zero Marginal Cost Society: The Internet of Things, the Collaborative Commons and the Eclipse of Capitalism*. New York: Palgrave, Macmillan.

Robinson, William, 1950. Ecological Correlations and the Behavior of Individuals. *American Sociological Review* 15, 3: 351–357.

Rokeach, Milton, 1960. *The Open and Closed Mind*. New York: Basic Books.

Rokeach, Milton, 1968. *Beliefs, Attitudes and Values*. San Francisco: Jossey-Bass, Inc.

Rosecrance, Richard, 1986. *The Rise of the Trading State: Commerce and Conquest in the Modern World*. New York: Basic Books.

Rothstein, Bo, 2017. "Why Has the White Working Class Abandoned the Left?" *Social Europe*, January 19. Available at www.socialeurope.eu/2017/01/white-working-class-abandoned-left/ (accessed October 29, 2017).

Saez, Emmanuel and Gabriel Zucman, 2014. "Wealth Inequality in the U.S. since 1913: Evidence from Capitalized Income Tax Data," NBER working paper No. 20625. Available at www.nber.org/papers/w20625 (accessed October 29, 2017).

Sanfey, Alan G., James K. Rilling, Jessica A. Aronson, Leigh E. Nystrom and Jonathan D. Cohen, 2003. "The Neural Basis of Economic Decision-making in the Ultimatum Game," *Science* 300, 5626: 1755–1758.

Schock, Kurt, 2013. "The Practice and Study of Civil Resistance," *Journal of Peace Research* 50, 3: 277–290.

Schwartz, Shalom, 2006. "A Theory of Cultural Value Orientations: Explication and Applications," *Comparative Sociology* 5, 2–3: 137–182.

Schwartz, Shalom, 2013. "Value Priorities and Behavior: Applying," *The Psychology of Values: The Ontario Symposium*. Vol. 8.

Schyns, Peggy, 1998. "Crossnational Differences in Happiness: Economic and Cultural Factors Explored," *Social Indicators Research* 42, 1/2: 3–26.

Selig, James P., Kristopher J. Preacher and Todd D. Little, 2012. "Modeling Time-Dependent Association in Longitudinal Data: A Lag as Moderator Approach," *Multivariate Behavioral Research* 47, 5: 697–716.

Sen, Amartya, 2001. *Development as Freedom*. New York: Alfred Knopf.

Shcherbak, Andrey, 2014. "Does Milk Matter? Genetic Adaptation to Environment: The Effect of Lactase Persistence on Cultural Change." Paper presented at summer workshop of Laboratory for Comparative Social Research, Higher School of Economics, St. Petersburg, Russia, June 29–July 12, 2014.

Sides, John and Jack Citrin, 2007. "European Opinion about Immigration: The Role of Identities, Interests and Information," *British Journal of Political Science* 37, no. 03: 477–504.

Silver, Nate, 2015. *The Signal and the Noise*. New York: Penguin.

Singh, Gopal K. and Peter C. van Dyck, 2010. *Infant Mortality in the United States, 1935–2007*. Rockville, Maryland: US Department of Health and Human Services.

Sniderman, Paul M., Michael Bang Petersen, Rune Slothuus and Rune Stubager, 2014. *Paradoxes of Liberal Democracy: Islam, Western Europe, and the Danish Cartoon Crisis*. Princeton: Princeton University Press.

Snyder, Thomas D. (ed.), 1993. *120 Years of American Education: A Statistical Portrait*. Washington, DC: US Department of Education.

Soon, Chun Siong, Marcel Brass, Hans-Jochen Heinze and John-Dylan Haynes, 2008. "Unconscious Determinants of Free Decisions in the Human Brain," *Nature Neuroscience* 11, 5: 543–545.

Stark, Rodney and William Sims Bainbridge, 1985a. "A Supply-side Reinterpretation of the 'Secularization' of Europe," *Journal for the Scientific Study of Religion* 33, 3: 230–252.

Stark, Rodney and William Sims Bainbridge, 1985b. *The Future of Religion: Secularization, Revival, and Cult Formation.* Oakland, CA: University of California Press.

Statistisches Bundesamt, 2012. "Education, Research, and Culture Statistics." Available at www.destatis.de/EN/FactsFigures/InFocus/EducationResearchCulture/VocationalTraining.html (accessed November 18, 2017).

Stenner, Karen, 2005. *The Authoritarian Dynamic.* Cambridge: Cambridge University Press.

Stiglitz, Joseph E., 2011. "Of the 1 Percent, by the 1 Percent, for the 1 Percent," *Vanity Fair,* May.

Stiglitz, Joseph E., 2013. *The Price of Inequality.* New York: Norton.

Sweet, Ken, 2014. "Median CEO Pay Crosses $10 Million in 2013," *Associated Press,* May 27, The American National Election Studies (ANES; www.electionstudies.org).

Thomas, Scott M., 2007. "Outwitting the Developed Countries? Existential Insecurity and the Global Resurgence of Religion," *Journal of International Affairs* 61, 1: 21.

Thomas, Scott M., 2005. *The Global Resurgence of Religion and the Transformation of International Relations: The Struggle for the Soul of the Twenty-first Century.* New York: Palgrave, Macmillan.

Thompson, Mark R., 2000. "The Survival of 'Asian Values' as 'Zivilisationskritik.'" *Theory and Society* 29, no. 5: 651–686.

Thornhill, Randy, Corey L. Fincher and Devaraj Aran, 2009. "Parasites, Democratization, and the Liberalization of Values across Contemporary Countries," *Biological Reviews* 84, 1: 113–131.

Thornhill, Randy, Corey L. Fincher, Damian R. Murray and Mark Schaller, 2010. "Zoonotic and Non-zoonotic Diseases in Relation to Human Personality and Societal Values," *Evolutionary Psychology* 8:151–155.

Toffler, Alvin, 1990. *Powershift: Knowledge, Wealth, Violence in the 21st Century.* New York: Bantam.

Traugott, Michael, 2001. "Trends: Assessing Poll Performance in the 2000 Campaign," *Public Opinion Quarterly* 65, 3: 389–419.

Tversky, Amos and Daniel Kahneman, 1974. "Judgment under Uncertainty: Heuristics and Biases," *Science* 185, 4157: 1124–1131.

UN Department of Economic and Social Affairs, 2012. *World Population Prospectus: The 2012 Revision.*

United Nations Department of Economic and Social Affairs, 2012. *World Population Prospectus: The 2012 Revision.* http://esa.un.org/wpp/ (accessed October 29, 2017).

United Nations Population Division – Department of Economic and Social Affairs, 2016.

United States Bureau of Labor Statistics, 2013. "International Comparisons of Annual Labor Force Statistics, 1970–2012." Available at: www.bls.gov/fls/flscomparelf.htm (accessed October 29, 2017).

United States Bureau of Labor Statistics, 2014. www.bls.gov/ (accessed October 29, 2017).

United States Bureau of the Census, 1977. *Historical Statistics of the United States: Colonial Times to 1970*. Washington, DC: US Department of Commerce.

United States Census Bureau, 2012. *Statistical Abstract of the United States*.

United States Census Bureau, 2014. "Historical Income Tables: People." Available at www.census.gov/data/tables/time-series/demo/income-poverty/historical-income-people.html (accessed October 29, 2017).

Van de Kaa, Dirk J., 2001. "Postmodern Family Preferences: From Changing Value Orientation to New Behavior," *Population and Development Review* 27: 290–331.

Van der Brug, Wouter, Meindert Fennema and Jean Tillie, 2005. "Why Some Anti-Immigrant Parties Fail and Others Succeed: A Two-Step Model of Aggregate Electoral Support," *Comparative Political Studies* 38, 537–573.

Vanhanen, Tatu, 2003. *Democratization: A Comparative Analysis of 170 Countries*. New York: Routledge.

Veenhoven, Ruut, 2014. *World Database of Happiness*, Erasmus University Rotterdam, The Netherlands. http://worlddatabaseofhappiness.eur.nl (accessed October 29, 2017).

Veenhoven, Ruut, 2000. "Freedom and Happiness: A Comparative Study in Forty-four Nations in the Early 1990s," in Ed Diener and Eunkook M. Suh (eds.), *Culture and Subjective Well Being*. Cambridge, MA: MIT Press, 257–288.

Verba, Sidney, Norman H. Nie and Jae-on Kim, 1978. *Participation and Political Equality: A Seven-Nation Comparison*. Chicago: University of Chicago Press.

Weber, Max, 1904 [1930]. *The Protestant Ethic and the Spirit of Capitalism*. London: Routledge.

Welsch, Heinz, 2003. "Freedom and Rationality as Predictors of Cross-National Happiness Patterns: The Role of Income as a Mediating Value," *Journal of Happiness Studies* 4, 3: 295–321.

Welzel, Christian, 2007. "Are Levels of Democracy Affected by Mass Attitudes? Testing Attainment and Sustainment Effects on Democracy," *International Political Science Review* 28, 4: 397–424.

Welzel, Christian, 2013. *Freedom Rising: Human Empowerment and the Quest for Emancipation.* New York: Cambridge University Press.

Welzel, Christian and Ronald F. Inglehart, 2008. "The Role of Ordinary People in Democratization," *Journal of Democracy* 19, 1: 126–140.

Whyte, Martin K., 2014. "Soaring Income Gaps: China in Comparative Perspective," *Daedalus* 143, 2: 39–52.

Williams, Donald E. and J. Kevin Thompson, 1993. "Biology and Behavior: A Set-point Hypothesis of Psychological Functioning," *Behavior Modification* 17, 1: 43–57.

Wilson, Timothy, 2002. *Strangers to Ourselves: Discovering the Adaptive Unconscious.* Cambridge, MA: Harvard University Press.

Winters, Jeffrey A., 2011.*Oligarchy.* New York, Cambridge University Press.

Winters, Jeffrey A. and Benjamin I. Page, 2009. "Oligarchy in the United States?" *Perspectives on Politics* 7, 4:731–751.

Wiseman, Paul, 2013. "Richest One Percent Earn Biggest Share since '20s,"*AP News*, September 10.

Wolfers, Justin, 2015. "All You Need to Know about Income Inequality, in One Comparison," *New York Times*, March 13.

World Bank, 2012. *World Development Indicators.* Available at http://data .worldbank.org/data-catalog/world-development-indicators (accessed October 29, 2017).

World Bank Databank, 2015. "GINI Index." Available at http://data.world bank.org/indicator/SI.POV.GINI/ (accessed October 29, 2017).

World Values Surveys, 2014. Available at www.worldvaluessurvey.org/ (accessed October 29, 2017).

www.forschungsgruppe.de/Umfragen/Politbarometer/Archiv/Politbarometer_ 2012/ (accessed October 29, 2017).

www.un.org/en/development/desa/population/migration/data/estimates2/ estimates15.shtml (accessed October 29, 2017).

www.destatis.de/EN/FactsFigures/SocietyState/SocietyState.html (accessed October 29, 2017).

Zakaria, Fareed and Lee Kuan Yew, 1994. "Culture Is Destiny: A Conversation with Lee Kuan Yew," *Foreign Affairs*: 109–126.

Zakharov, Alexei. 2016. "The Importance of Economic Issues in Politics: A Cross-Country Analysis." Paper presented at Higher School of Economics, Moscow, November 8–10.

INDEX